A Gift to America

The Story of the Gettysburg Foundation

David F. Remington

A Gift to America:
The Story of the Gettysburg Foundation

ISBN: 978-1-941066-24-9

Library of Congress Control Number: 2017916259

Originally published in hardcover
by Wordrunner Press, 2017

Cover design by
Michele Page Design Communication

Book design by Jo-Anne Rosen

Photos: Gettysburg National Military Park

Wordrunner Press
Petaluma, California

Printed in the United States of America

This book is dedicated to:

the families
of
Union soldiers who fought at
Gettysburg,

and to:

my father,
who inspired my love of
American history.

Also by David F. Remington

Ashbel P. Fitch: Champion of Old New York

List of Frequently Used Acronyms

DCP   Development Concept Plan — a project-specific plan, often for a building, that incorporates among other things the purpose of the project and the required compliance

GAO   General Accountability Office — an independent government agency that provides auditing, evaluation, and investigative services for the United States Congress

GBMA   Gettysburg Battlefield Memorial Association — founded in 1863 and disbanded in 1895 when the Gettysburg National Military Park was established

GBPA   Gettysburg Battlefield Preservation Association

GF   Gettysburg Foundation

GMP   General Management Plan and Environmental Impact Statement — the overarching long-range plan for a national park

GNBMF   Gettysburg National Battlefield Museum Foundation is antecedent to the Gettysburg Foundation.

GNMP   Gettysburg National Military Park

GNMPAC   Gettysburg National Military Park Advisory Commission

LBGA   Licensed Battlefield Guides Association

NPCA   National Parks and Conservation Association — the not-for-profit citizens' organization dedicated to protecting, preserving, and enhancing the U.S. National Park System

NPS   National Park Service

OAH   Organization of American Historians

RFP   Request for Proposals — a solicitation of a proposal, often, but not always, made through a bidding process, by an agency or company interested in procurement of a commodity, service, or valuable asset to potential suppliers

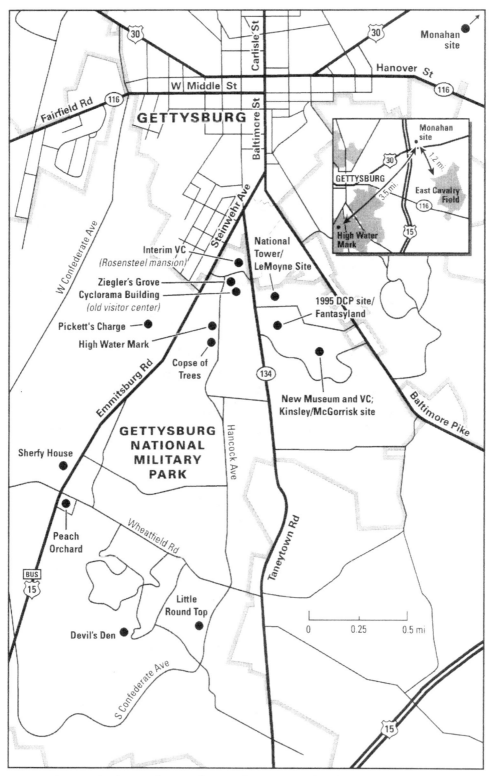

Map of Borough of Gettysburg and Gettysburg National Military Park (*south section*)

Contents

Photographs

Preface

In late June 2013 I was in Gettysburg, Pennsylvania, for the commemoration of the 150th anniversary of the Battle of Gettysburg. I'd been a member of the Board of Directors of the Gettysburg Foundation for eleven years, and Chairman of the Development Committee. I schooled myself on the Battle, its special significance in American history, and the tragedy of the American Civil War. I watched the Foundation grow and mature from next to nothing to a potent force behind the preservation and interpretation of the Gettysburg Battlefield. It was an enlightening, gratifying experience, but June 29, 2013, was my last board meeting.

Looking back on what we accomplished during those eleven years, I had only one concern, and that was how easy it all appears now. The reversal of the decline of the visitor experience at the Battlefield, the rehabilitation of the Battlefield, and the new Museum and Visitor Center, were stunning and I wondered if it all appeared to have been effortless to those who don't know better. If that were so, such an imperfect public understanding of how the Foundation began, grew, and prospered from 1998, when it was founded, to 2008, when the new Museum and Visitor Center opened, to the present day, would undoubtedly impact future partnerships, or possibly even the existing one.

So I silently decided that I would write the story of the Gettysburg Foundation. But I also supposed that my fantasy was a passing fancy that would disappear if it were ever exposed to the cold light of day, which, in fact, it was, and sooner than I expected. During those few June days at the 150th, I was riding a bus to one of the ceremonies, seated next to Bob Wilburn, retired President of the Foundation. Bob was the President and CEO of the Foundation from 2000 to 2009, and had overseen the Foundation's growth during that period.

I said, "Bob, someone should write the history of the Foundation."

"Who would write it?" he said.

"I would."

There was an audible pause. "Oh! Okay. You know, you could," he said.

There was more silence before I began back-pedaling. Every time I saw Bob over the next few days he asked me how I was coming on the book. He was relentless. Over the years, I'd come to know Bob pretty well. I knew he was persistent, but I also knew that he wouldn't waste his persistence on something that he didn't feel was important. I was still thinking about it after I returned to my home in Maine, and on July 2, I e-mailed Bob Kinsley, our Board Chairman. I told him about my conversation with Bob Wilburn, and I asked if he thought the idea was worth pursuing. The following day he "gratefully accepted my offer to write the Foundation history." A project was born.

There are several reasons why I wanted to write the Foundation's history. The first, as mentioned above, was to create a public record of the formation and the early years of the Foundation and its partnership with the National Park Service from multiple perspectives; to explore the sometimes antagonistic motivations of several of the interested parties; and to attempt to determine why the Foundation has enjoyed such success.

I also wanted to recognize the special contributions of three men who envisioned the Foundation—the architects and overseers of its early successes: Bob Kinsley; John Latschar, Park Superintendent of the Gettysburg National Military Park from 1994 to 2009, and Bob Wilburn. Each of these forceful and patriotic leaders played a prominent role in the Foundation's development and its achievements. Notwithstanding each of their considerable individual talents, I firmly believe that no one of them could have accomplished, alone, even a fraction of what they accomplished together. They were a splendid team.

And of course there is Gettysburg itself. As most readers of this history will know, 165,000 young citizens of the United States, and undoubtedly some immigrants who were not citizens, arrived from all directions at Gettysburg in July 1863. About 90,000 of them made up the Union army and the rest were rebel Confederates. Those two armies were bent on killing one another. It had happened before, at places like Shiloh, Antietam, and Fredericksburg, although not quite on such a grand scale as at Gettysburg. The carnage over the first three days in July 1863 was unheard of and unspeakable. Each side knew God was on its side, but when the Battle was over, some historians believe that a Union victory was inevitable—that it was the turning point in the Civil War. Whether it was or it wasn't, the fact that President Abraham Lincoln arrived at the Battlefield nearly five months later to address his fellow countrymen on the meaning of the Battle and why he was asking them to make such hellish sacrifices added to Gettysburg's renown.

In 1896 the United States Supreme Court, in an early eminent domain case that involved the potential commercial development of the Gettysburg Battlefield, added to the sanctity of Gettysburg by declaring that the federal government could "take possession of the field of Battle" because it was "so closely connected with the welfare of the Republic itself as to be within the powers granted Congress by the Constitution for the purpose of protecting and preserving the whole country."

The Gettysburg Foundation is a private foundation, the private half of a public/private partnership with the National Park Service. In the mid-1990s, public/private partnerships were not a new idea, and the Gettysburg partnership was not the first. It is, however, considered to be the most comprehensive one of its kind. The Foundation aims to enhance preservation and understanding of the heritage and lasting significance of Gettysburg in support of the National Park Service's goals. The Foundation though, by its mission, also becomes an integral part of the modern history of Gettysburg, another reason that I've written this history. The story covers the period from 1994, when John Latschar arrived at Gettysburg, to 2008, when the Museum and Visitor Center opened, and slightly beyond.

For well over a year, I supposed this book would be published by Penn State Press. The Commonwealth of Pennsylvania is a sizable investor in the Gettysburg Foundation and the Press's participation in this project always seemed appropriate. In late 2014 Joanne Hanley, then President of the Foundation, contacted Patrick Alexander, Director of the Penn State Press. Alexander expressed interest in this project and suggested that I contact Kathryn Yahner, acquisitions editor of the Press, which I did. In early 2016 the Press wrote me, "Enclosed is a counter-signed copy of your contract for *A Gift to America: The Story of the Gettysburg Foundation.* Please keep this copy for your records." Penn State Press had decided to publish my manuscript and here was my contract. One year later, however, in early 2017, the Press decided not to publish, citing, among other things, a "lack of balance" in the manuscript. It seems that politics has again come into play at Gettysburg, and it is now you the reader who will decide.

This book is the product of thirty-four hours of recorded interviews with twenty individuals (see Appendix I), each of whom played a prominent role in this story; extensive research in the NPS archives in Gettysburg; and a few of my own recollections. I'm especially grateful to Joanne Hanley, past President of the Gettysburg Foundation, for her encouragement and her aggressive support of this project, and to other members of her staff for their help in the late stages of the project: Dan Bringman, the Foundation's Chief Financial Officer, Tammy Becker, and Cindy Small. Katie Lawhon, NPS public affairs specialist at GNMP, assisted me in any number of ways from an important contribution to the story line of this volume to the assembling of the photographs contained herein. Greg Goodell, Director of Museum services at the GNMP, and Andrew Newman cheerfully facilitated my research in the Gettysburg archives, and I'm grateful to them both. Erin Greb, quickly and deftly created the map of the Gettysburg Battlefield. Erin was alert and especially responsive to the requisite special needs of the map I wanted. I'd also like to thank Barbara Sardella, retired Chief Counsel of the Kinsley Companies and interim President of the Gettysburg Foundation, and Dan Driver, CFO of the Kinsley Companies, for their assistance at various stages of this project. I'm also very grateful to Suzanne Cope, my freelance editor, whose commentary and encouragement throughout helped shape this work; Eric Schultz and Kitty Davis, both of whom have authored excellent books of their own and whose assistance was invaluable; my long-time attorney Adam Sonnenschein, whose advice and counsel I have treasured for years; and to all those who played a part in the story and patiently made time for me to interview them.

And I have a special appreciation and gratitude for the efforts and skills of the team of entrepreneurial self-publishers who picked me up when I was down and made this project finally come to life. My friend and fellow author Steve Bennett suggested that I contact Jo-Anne Rosen, who, as book designer, did a masterful job of coordinating the many design aspects of this book. She was also a calming voice of reason during sometimes hectic circumstances. Through Jo-Anne, I worked with copyeditors Arlene Miller and Linda Jay, both of whom worked thoroughly and quickly to improve this manuscript. My Andover classmate of sixty years ago, Eric Myrvaagnes, enlarged, sharpened, and brightened the photographs that appear herein. Thank you, Eric! Finally, Michele Page, with whom I've worked before, did her usual crisp and creative work designing the book cover. I'm grateful to them all for pitching in and quickly performing such magical work when I needed it. And, of course, I'm always grateful to my family: my children, Chelsey and Jay, and Chelsey, my wife of 56 years, who every day lend their unqualified support to my work.

Introduction

Senator Craig Thomas of Wyoming called his hearing to order to discuss issues relating to the projected Museum and Visitor Center facilities at Gettysburg National Military Park (GNMP).[1] It was February 1998. The project was funded by the privately owned Gettysburg National Battlefield Museum Foundation (GNBMF), later known as the Gettysburg Foundation (GF). Thomas seasoned his opening statement with peppery language like shortcutting, controversy, complaints, accusations, unethical kinds of action, and personal conflict. Twelve months later, Congressman James V. Hansen of Utah gaveled his hearing to order. Again, the topic was Gettysburg.[2] Hansen's language was not as pungent as Thomas's had been, but Hansen expressed forebodings about a scheme that he believed was afoot at Gettysburg. Hansen said that the situation seemed worse than it was during the Senate hearings of the previous year, that the problems were "serious and unresolved," and that they have "soured the general public's perception of the National Park Service (NPS or Park Service)."[3] Both men were struggling to grasp the intricacies of the NPS's original model of entrepreneurial philanthropy, a unique public/private partnership that it was practicing at Gettysburg.[4]

The Congressional hearings were expected to uncover sobering or even scandalous misdeeds, although very little of what Thomas or Hansen said or implied was based on facts. In spite of the colorful language that they employed, there was no evidence presented at either hearing, or accusations made, of any wrongdoing. Yet questions lingered about the project that was intended to improve conditions at Gettysburg, and people wondered why

---

1 Thomas, a Republican, was Chairman of the National Parks, Historic Preservation and Recreation Subcommittee of the Senate Committee on Energy and Natural Resources.

2 Hansen, a Republican, chaired the National Parks and Public Lands Subcommittee of the House of Representatives Committee on Resources.

3 Oversight hearing on the Gettysburg National Military Park General Management Plan and proposed Visitor Center before the Subcommittee on National Parks and Public Lands of the House Committee on Resources, Feb. 11, 1999.

4 Entrepreneurial philanthropy, as used herein, has several defining characteristics, most importantly the insertion of a third party, the not-for-profit GF, between donors and the ultimate beneficiary, the GNMP. The third party is contractually empowered to raise funds and to design, construct, and operate facilities, on behalf of the NPS over an extended period of time.

it generated such fierce opposition. There's an old saying that the way to make enemies is to try to change something, and the Park Service's project was all about change.

Conditions that led to the historic Gettysburg project had been building at the National Park for over fifty years, and the NPS in 1994 sent a new Park Superintendent to Gettysburg with instructions to fix whatever was wrong there. Four years later, at the Thomas hearing in 1998, Denis P. Galvin, Deputy Director of the NPS, explained, "In the Fall of 1994 when the current Superintendent arrived at GNMP, the NPS took the opportunity to assess the Park's resources and operations. As a result, four significant long-term goals were identified for the preservation of precious Park resources and the improvement of visitor services, battlefield interpretation, and educational capabilities. They were as follows: protect the Park's collection of objects and archives; preserve the Cyclorama painting; provide high-quality interpretation and educational opportunities for Park visitors; and restore the High Water Mark of the Battle, [that spot where Confederate forces penetrated Union defenses on July 3, 1863]." The area to be restored, known as Ziegler's Grove, is actually north of the High Water Mark, and included the modernist Cyclorama building (see map). Built in 1961, it served as the Visitor Center and home for the magnificent Cyclorama painting and would need to be removed. Galvin continued, "In January 1995, the NPS concluded that funds were not available from the service-wide construction funds and were unlikely to be appropriated by Congress any time soon to resolve deficiencies in Park facilities and to achieve the Park's goals. Consequently, the Director of the NPS approved the concept of exploring a public/private partnership to solve the problems at Gettysburg National Military Park."[5] *In other words, Galvin was forced to admit to Congress and the American people that the National Park Service needed outside help to solve the accumulated problems at Gettysburg. That determination began the process that led to the public/private partnership that Thomas and Hansen were investigating.*

John A. Latschar, the visionary and determined Park Superintendent to whom Galvin referred, arrived at Gettysburg in 1994 and began laying the groundwork for a comprehensive rehabilitation of the GNMP. The centerpiece

---

5   Hearing before the Subcommittee on National Parks, Historic Preservation and Recreation of the U.S. Senate Committee on Energy and Natural Resources to discuss the issues relating to the Museum and Visitor Center project at the Gettysburg National Military Park, February 24, 1998, 5-6.

of the enormous project was a new, privately owned and operated Museum and Visitor Center, where the Park's enormous Cyclorama painting, *The Battle of Gettysburg*, would be on display, and its priceless collection of artifacts would be stored, cared for, and exhibited. The painting, one of the largest oil paintings in the world, by French artist Paul Philippoteaux, captures the High Water Mark, a seminal moment on the afternoon of July 3, 1863, when the Confederate attack at Gettysburg reached the Union lines on Cemetery Ridge.[6]

Along the way, an inspired NPS initiative motivated a local businessman and philanthropist, Robert A. Kinsley, to volunteer to join the NPS in a partnership to rehabilitate the GNMP. Kinsley, teaming with Latschar, through his philanthropy, personal commitment, and leadership, laid the groundwork for the realization of the NPS's plans. He and his wife, Anne, established the Gettysburg National Battlefield Museum Foundation, donating millions of dollars to the project. Nearly two years after the Hansen hearings, in October 2000, Kinsley named Robert C. Wilburn first President of the Foundation. He charged Wilburn with the responsibility for operating the Foundation, hiring its first staff, and raising the necessary funds to complete the project. Together, this triumvirate—Kinsley, Latschar, and Wilburn—transformed GNMP, and indeed the Borough of Gettysburg, into a model American historic shrine—in Kinsley's words, his "gift to America."

A Gift to America: The Story of the Gettysburg Foundation is a saga of conflict, politics, and philanthropy at Gettysburg, home of the nation's premier historic national park. It recounts the story of the Gettysburg Foundation and the people who created it. The narrative revolves around Congress and the NPS, which failed in their responsibilities to the Gettysburg community for at least thirty-five years prior to 1994—the community that failed to develop the effective leadership it needed to meet that challenge—and three patriotic Americans, who arrived at Gettysburg between 1994 and 2000. They achieved, over fierce opposition, and while cutting through a thicket of tough, complex issues, what the Congress, the National Park Service, and the community had theretofore failed to accomplish. They worked through the not-for-profit Gettysburg Foundation, originally the GNBMF, in partnership with the NPS. As a result of the partnership's transformative work, Gettysburg National Military Park stands today at the pinnacle of the

---

6 Sue Boardman and Kathryn Porch, *The Battle of Gettysburg Cyclorama: A History and Guide* (Gettysburg: Thomas Publications, 2008). The painting's restoration is described in Ch. 9.

nation's historic parks. It's hard to believe that just twenty-five years ago it was among the most threatened of the nation's national parks and that its relationship with the Gettysburg community was at its nadir.

Of course, not every politician listened to Thomas, Hansen, and other Park Service opponents. Pennsylvania officials such as Republican Senator Rick Santorum and Democratic Congressman John P. "Jack" Murtha, for example, knew what was taking place at Gettysburg.[7] But some elected officials seemed more willing to give credence to rumors and innuendo. The circulating gossip that was nurtured by a toxic relationship between segments of the Gettysburg community and the Park Service made the rounds in Gettysburg and in Washington, D.C., and it was hard to overcome.

The Civil War was a monumental event, and among those many towns and villages over which armies of both sides trampled, Gettysburg stood out for the lives and property that the Battle altered forever. Looking back, the Civil War was the fulcrum of the moral, political and racial history of the United States. Before 1865 slavery was practiced legally in the United States. After the Civil War (1861–1865) and the passage of the Thirteenth Amendment to the Constitution in 1865, it was no longer legal to keep slaves. The Republican Party of Abraham Lincoln and the Civil War sent America's morality and its course of race relations in an entirely new direction. The cost of the War was enormous. There were about 31 million people in the United States at the time of the Civil War. Recent estimates of 800,000 soldier deaths in the War yield a mortality rate that if superimposed on today's population of approximately 320 million, would equate to over 8 million killed.[8] Whether or not these new estimates are accurate, it was by far the largest war ever fought on the North American continent. All of America fought in it: WASPs, Irish, Germans, Scandinavians, Jews, and Blacks, many of them immigrants; others were former slaves. Native Americans fought in it too.[9] The War's importance, therefore, its size, and its human toll, suggest that every American has a stake in the Civil War.

---

7   Rick Santorum, a Republican, served as a United States Senator representing Pennsylvania from 1995 to 2007. Murtha, a Democrat, represented Pennsylvania's twelfth Congressional district in the United States House of Representatives from 1974 until his death in 2010.

8   See James Lee McDonough, *William Tecumseh Sherman, In the Service of My Country, A Life* (New York, London, WW Norton & Company, 2016), 239-40, for a discussion of Civil War casualties.

9   Wikipedia. Retrieved from: https://en.wikipedia.org/wiki/Native_Americans_in_the_American_Civil_War

Regardless of where they live or where they were born, their lives and the lives of their descendants are affected by the Civil War.

The enormous, pivotal Battle of Gettysburg was arguably the most significant battle of this most significant war. Some historians believe that the Union victory at Gettysburg turned the tide against the South, and whether it did or not, it was a momentous victory. The Battle of Gettysburg took place near the mid-point of the Civil War on July 1–3, 1863, twenty-six months after the War began at Fort Sumter, South Carolina, and twenty-two months before it ended at Appomattox Court House, Virginia. The estimated 50,000 battle casualties, the most of any Civil War battle, came in just three days.

Because Gettysburg was the northernmost point of penetration of the Confederate Army, the spot where the Battle on Cemetery Hill culminated became known as the "High Water Mark of the Confederacy." At or about three-thirty in the afternoon of July 3, 1863, the Confederate Army, at that final moment led by General Lewis A. Armistead, battered and shot its way over a three-foot stone wall and into the midst of the defending Union Army.[10] For a few minutes, no one knew whether the Union Army would hold or shatter, but Armistead went down, mortally wounded, the Union Army held, and the Battle was over. Armistead lay dying on the ground. And the Confederate Army began its long, slow retreat from Pennsylvania south across the Potomac River and back into Virginia.

Five months later, President Abraham Lincoln visited Gettysburg to commemorate the National Cemetery in his Gettysburg Address. On November 19, 1863, he spoke the immortal words that placed the bloody, terrible Battle in its proper perspective:

> Four score and seven years ago our fathers brought forth, on this continent, a new nation, conceived in Liberty, and dedicated to the proposition that all men are created equal. Now we are engaged in a great civil war, testing whether that nation or any nation so conceived and so dedicated, can long endure. We are met on a great Battlefield of that war. We have come to dedicate a portion of that field, as a final resting place for those who here gave their lives that that nation might live. It is altogether fitting and proper that we should do this. But, in a larger sense, we cannot dedicate, we cannot consecrate, we cannot hallow this ground.

---

10 Trudeau, Noah Andre, *Gettysburg: A Testing of Courage* (New York: HarperCollins Publishers, 2002), 495-508.

The brave men, living and dead, who struggled here, have consecrated it, far above our poor power to add or detract. The world will little note, nor long remember what we say here, but it can never forget what they did here. It is for us the living, rather, to be dedicated here to the unfinished work which they who fought here have thus far so nobly advanced. It is rather for us to be here dedicated to the great task remaining before us — that from those honored dead we take increased devotion to that cause for which they gave the last full measure of devotion, that we here highly resolve that these dead shall not have died in vain -that this nation, under God, shall have a new birth of freedom and that government of the people, by the people, for the people, shall not perish from the earth.

Lincoln's words, "… the world can never forget what they did here…," are especially meaningful to Gettysburg. But the history of the Battle of Gettysburg and of the Civil War is of importance to every American who wishes to understand more about their country, especially about America's race relations. When the NPS in 1994, and the NPS/GNBMF partnership later, commenced efforts to protect priceless historic artifacts related to the Battle, to restore the Philippoteaux painting, to expand Battlefield interpretation and education for visitors, and to restore an iconic section of the Battlefield where Union troops died defending freedom that necessitated moving the GNMP Visitor Center about one mile south of its existing site, they ran into a firestorm of opposition. The resistance was rooted in insecurity, fear of the unknown, distrust, and other very understandable human tendencies. It was in the ensuing conflict over the future of the GNMP that American citizens of late twentieth and early twenty-first century came face-to-face with the ambiguity that characterized Gettysburg since Union and Confederate troops faced off there in 1863.

Today, even the very word *Gettysburg* calls up conflicting visions. Is it hallowed ground? Is it a shrine, a park, or perhaps even a classroom where one can learn about democracy? Or is it a tourist mecca, where entrepreneurs hawk their wares or fabricate their own version of history? Gettysburg is all these things, sometimes in combination, yet totally dependent on one's point of view. Heroic, glorious, but often dreadful images roll through the mind whenever the word *Gettysburg* is spoken. It's a village, a battle, a battlefield, even a movie. In the North, Gettysburg is a symbol of determination and victory; in the South of valor or perhaps bad luck—if only Stonewall Jackson were there events would have ended differently—and across America of the High Water Mark of the Confederacy.[11] Gettysburg is a paradox.

Examples of the paradox of Gettysburg recur throughout the history of the Battlefield. John Rosensteel, for example, thirteen years old in 1863, is a paradox. After the Battle, Rosensteel removed relics, which didn't belong to him, from neighboring farmland. Today he would be criticized, or even prosecuted. But 150 years after the Battle, the Rosensteel Collection at Gettysburg is the centerpiece of the largest collection of Civil War artifacts, an authentic national treasure. The collection consists of thousands of rifles, swords, sidearms, canteens, bullets, tents, equipment, clothing, shoes, bridle, and more. To some, the collection represents more than a century of ill-gotten gain. To others it's an invaluable scholarly asset that would have been lost were it not for John Rosensteel and his descendents.

In another example of the paradox of Gettysburg, Lincoln told Americans that "we cannot consecrate, we cannot hallow this ground. The brave men, living and dead…have consecrated it, far above our poor power to add or detract." Yet thirty years later, those same brave men began to re-consecrate that ground by erecting a majority of the more than 1,300 monuments that dot the 6,000-acre Battlefield today. They mark the battle lines of the troops who fought there, and they commemorate the fight. To some, the monuments leave an impression of tasteless ornamentation and mar the sanctity of the Battlefield. But to others they are somber, dramatic, and often enlightening reminders of the sacrifices soldiers made there.

A more recent example of Gettysburg's inherent ambiguity occurred in 1974 when entrepreneur Thomas Ottenstein opened a monstrous and intrusive tower that hovered over hallowed ground for twenty-six years. It was a most blatant example of the economic freedom that Union troops fought and died defending in 1863. Most people who saw the tower, although not all, resented it. Renowned historian Bruce Catton said that the tower would "break the spell of history."[12] But Ottenstein believed he had a right to open a business even though it was an obtrusion that hung over hallowed ground. He said it was free enterprise at work, and time and again the courts backed him up. Such

---

11   One of Confederate General Robert E. Lee's highest ranking subordinates, Gen. Thomas "Stonewall" Jackson, was wounded at Chancellorsville on May 2, 1863, and died eight days later, two months before the Battle of Gettysburg.

12   "Bruce Catton Tells Court Ottenstein Tower Would 'Break Spell' of History," *Gettysburg Times*, Aug. 5, 1971.

examples of contradictions, ambiguity, and conflicting interests are endemic to Gettysburg. And because Gettysburg is historic, every question is pressed, the personal and cultural stakes are high, and very few of us are willing to sweep even our smallest differences under the rug, to get over them, to move on or, to be more precise, to deal constructively with ambiguity. It's hard to imagine so many Congressional hearings for an American place other than Gettysburg.

Gettysburg's rich, shortsighted tradition may have begun soon after the Battle was over and even before the dead were buried in 1863. A Gettysburg lawyer, David McConaughy, sent his plan to preserve the Battlefield to Pennsylvania Governor Andrew Curtin. That September, McConaughy helped found the Gettysburg Battlefield Memorial Association (GBMA), but he soon realized that preserving the Battlefield would not be easy. Governor Curtin had already invited David Wills, another Gettysburg attorney and local rival of McConaughy's, to help with the proper disposition of the many Union dead. Wills, who arranged Lincoln's only visit to Gettysburg, was, like McConaughy, an ambitious man. The momentous Battle at Gettysburg had suddenly thrust the little farm town into the national limelight, and both men sought to capitalize on a once-in-a-lifetime opportunity for fame and fortune.

Several months after the GBMA's founding, Wills wrote a letter to Curtin to brief him, apparently at Curtin's request, on his (Wills') thinking regarding the GBMA's plans for Gettysburg, which he termed "visionary and impracticable." More gratuitously, Wills reported, McConaughy "is the sole projector [of the GBMA plan]. Knowing him as well as I do and probably you know his character also, I cannot fail to draw the conclusion that he originated the project and is endeavoring to carry it out for a selfish and mercenary purpose."[13] Nevertheless, the Pennsylvania legislature signed McConaughy's incorporating act into Pennsylvania law in 1864, provided the GBMA with complete control over the Battlefield, and empowered the GBMA to issue shares of stock and to create a board of directors.[14]

In its first few years, the GBMA met with only limited success. Funding was always a problem and by the mid-1870s, fewer than two hundred acres had been put aside. But tourism was growing and local businessmen continually

---

13 Barbara L. Platt, *This Is Holy Ground: A History of the Gettysburg Battlefield, 1863-2006* (Gettysburg: self-published, third revision 2006), 5.

14 Jim Weeks, *Gettysburg: Memory, Market and an American Shrine* (Princeton: Princeton University Press, 2003), 20.

devised new ways to profit from the growing tourism. The Battlefield's commercialization, epitomized by the adjacent Katalysine Springs Hotel, confirmed Gettysburg as a tourist destination. In the late 1870s, the nation's interest in the Civil War, previously muted by the terrible toll of dead and wounded only fifteen years before, was also on the rise. Membership in the Pennsylvania chapter of the Grand Army of the Republic (GAR), for example, more than tripled, and its members were impatient with the sclerotic GBMA.[15] They worried that commercial interests would soon dominate the Battlefield and they were eager to memorialize it before their time ran out. So they began buying GBMA stock and ultimately took it over, thus providing it with a new mission and new momentum under new ownership.

In the early 1880s, General Daniel E. Sickles, a nationally known murderer, soldier, politician, and hyperactive member of the GAR, reemerged as a controversial veteran of the Battle of Gettysburg. Sickles was determined to perpetuate his legacy, and by the early 1890s he was a familiar figure in Gettysburg.[16] He was no stranger to controversy. He served two terms in Congress from 1857 to 1861 and then a third term from 1892 to 1894. In 1859 he murdered Philip Barton Key, son of Francis Scott Key, in a fit of jealous rage, but he was acquitted after he pleaded temporary insanity, the first such successful plea in United States judicial history. By 1863 Sickles was a political general in the Union Army with a respectable war record despite his lack of military training. On the second day at Gettysburg, contrary to the orders of his commanding officer, General George Gordon Meade, Sickles moved his Third Corps forward from a line that would have extended south on Cemetery Ridge to Little Round Top to form a salient about a mile forward near the Sherfy Peach Orchard. Most historians regard Sickles' move as a blunder, but Sickles spent the rest of his life insisting that his forward movement disrupted Confederate General James Longstreet's attack on the Union Army's left flank later that day, and that he had saved the day for the Union. Sickles' story was enhanced by the fact that in spite of having his right leg blown off, he was carried off the Battlefield wide awake, smoking a cigar.[17]

In 1886 the New York State legislature named Sickles Chairman of the New York Monuments Commission, the ostensible job of which was to oversee

---

15   Ibid. 60.

16   Material regarding General Daniel Sickles, unless otherwise noted, is taken from: W.A. Swanberg, *Sickles the Incredible* (New York: Charles Scribner's Sons, 1956), 363-366.

17   Ibid. 217.

the placement of New York monuments at Gettysburg. But according to author Jim Weeks, the GBMA directors maintained iron-fisted control over the field; and they dictated the terms of placement of monuments, materials, and inscriptions, permitting no digressions from their vision of a formal park—for Sickles, for New York State, or for anyone else.[18] On September 24, 1891, Sickles spoke angrily at the dedication of the memorial to the 42nd Regiment (the Tammany Regiment). It was a large, ornate column surmounted by an Indian brave standing with his musket before a tepee. Although he was honored to be there, Sickles said, "I cannot fitly perform this duty without giving expression to the surprise and indignation felt by the veterans of this famous battalion when they see their monument standing in a rear line from which they advanced and repulsed the approaching enemy, whilst troops that refused to advance in obedience to the repeated orders of their brigade commander are permitted to place their monument on a line much farther to the front than they ventured to march until after the victory was won."[19]

Sickles was fighting a losing battle to preserve the Battlefield. He would continue to lose, he believed, until the federal government took it over. He was afraid of mismanagement and commercialism of the Battlefield, so, to him, a federal government takeover was the solution. Not predictable or easily deterred, Sickles launched an all-out personal effort to that end. His first move was a run for Congress in 1892, as *The New York Times* later marveled, at "an age when most men are ready to retire." He was elected for the first time since he murdered Key, thirty years before.[20] Sickles was seventy-three.

Just as Sickles gained his seat in Congress, the Gettysburg Electric Railway Company laid its tracks on the Battlefield, a pernicious example of the for-profit invasion. The Company celebrated the Battle's thirtieth anniversary by blasting rocks to prepare their railroad bed in the Devil's Den area.[21] Working tirelessly, Sickles may have had a hand in creating the federally appointed Gettysburg National Park Commission that was charged with overseeing federal expenditures for the preservation of the Battlefield

---

18 Weeks, *Gettysburg*, 60.

19 Swanberg, *Sickles the Incredible*, 365.

20 James Hessler, *Dan Sickles, The Battlefield Preservationist*. Retrieved from https://www.google.com/webhp?sourceid=chrome-instant&ion=1&espv=2&ie=UTF-8#q=James+Hessler+www.civilwar.org.)&*

21 Devil's Den, a rugged outcrop of rocks and boulders, is at the southern end of the Park, adjacent to Little Round Top (see map).

and protecting its lines.[22] The Commission moved to condemn the railroad's property. Within another year Sickles sponsored a bill that authorized the War Department to accept ownership of 522 acres of land and all other assets of the GBMA. President Grover Cleveland signed the bill into law in February 1895. Thus, Gettysburg National Military Park was born and the GBMA was disbanded.[23]

Two months later, in April 1895, the government takeover of the Gettysburg Battlefield ground to a halt. A circuit court ruled in favor of the Electric Railway Company in its protest of the Commission's condemnation. But in January 1896 the United States Supreme Court overturned the circuit court's ruling. In his majority opinion, Justice Rufus Peckham's language is worth remembering. Peckham rolled back the petty bickering and antagonisms that had engulfed Gettysburg since Lincoln spoke his immortal words at the National Cemetery. He raised the dignity of the conversation to Lincoln's loftier tone. Peckham said, "Such a use [a national park] seems so closely connected with the welfare of the Republic itself as to be within the powers granted to Congress by the Constitution for the purpose of protecting and preserving the whole country."[24] Following that ruling, control of the Battlefield moved swiftly from Gettysburg to Washington.

Looking back, from 1863 to 1895—only thirty-two years—conflicts, arguments, and rivalries dominated Gettysburg. People were either for or against monuments on the battlefield. There was even a court case to settle the placement of a monument.[25] But while the imposing monuments appeared to sprout from the ground, entrepreneurs eagerly capitalized on tourist traffic. Outside observers thought that the blooming commercialism, "images, tourist guides, and medicinal springs" near the Battlefield, was both

---

22 On May 26, 1893, Secretary of War Daniel S. Lamont appointed a three-man commission to oversee the expenditure of a Congressional appropriation of $50,000 for the preservation of the Battlefield. Edward Tabor Linenthal, *Sacred Ground: Americans and Their Battlefields* (Urbana and Chicago: University of Illinois Press, Second Edition, 1993), 104. Sickles was a Democratic Congressman, and Lamont was in the Democratic Cleveland administration.

23 Ibid.

24 Ibid, 114.

25 "In the summer of 1888 survivors of the 72nd Pennsylvania Infantry defied the GBMA, broke ground for a monument at their chosen spot at the Angle, and were arrested for trespassing. The case eventually made its way to the Pennsylvania Supreme Court, which on April 2, 1891, decided in favor of the veterans." Ibid. 109.

crass and wrong.[26] Some people, certainly Dan Sickles, believed that government control of the Battlefield was the only way to stop the commercialism. But when the government stepped in, the citizens of Gettysburg felt their Battlefield slipping away, and the "town and gown" relationship between the NPS and the town of Gettysburg began.[27] The stage was set for serious divisions between local citizens, who often favored business, tourism, and local control, and other Americans who were dismayed by the vulgar shilling for the tourist dollar and who insisted that the Battlefield was hallowed ground—an American shrine that should remain so.

The early history of dissension within the Borough of Gettysburg, especially regarding the broad themes of preservation versus commercialization or of ordinary citizens versus big government, may also have started as early as 1863. Historian and author Allen Guelzo points out that when "farmers whose properties had been trampled over, crops and orchards destroyed, and who were now staring ruin in the face [out of desperation] charged exorbitant prices for every possible service that could be rendered, soldiers and the tourists who visited the town after the battle may have resented the price gouging."[28] Thirty years later, the creation of the National Military Park laid down a template for government interest in preservation that was often at odds with the objectives of local government. Local governments everywhere were expanding and as they did, entrepreneurs gained a powerful ally. Commercialism generally meant new tax revenue and the two interests, business and local government, were often allied against historians, preservationists, and others who would protect the hallowed ground at Gettysburg without regard to economic consequences.

When the Park was founded in 1895, the federal government controlled a scant 522 acres. But the potential boundaries of the boundary-less federal footprint were considerably larger. By 1990 the Park had expanded to nearly 4,000 acres and during those ninety-five years, the number of acres of locally taxable land, permanently threatened by federal expansion, was always uncertain. When the federal government took land, local authorities, by definition, were left with less land to tax. That created upward tax pressure on the remaining privately owned property—and resentment of the federal government. In 1933 when the Military Park was transferred from the War Department to the National Park

---

26 Weeks, *Gettysburg*, 35.

27 Platt, *Holy Ground*, 25.

28 Allan C. Guelzo, *Gettysburg, The Last Invasion* (New York: Alfred A. Knopf, 2013), 470.

Service, the "town and gown" conflict that began in earnest in 1895 remained.

During the 1940s, NPS officials began dreaming of improved facilities for the Gettysburg Park which included a new home for the massive Cyclorama painting that arrived at Gettysburg in 1912 and that was declared a national historic object in 1945. Over the next decade, those dreams ultimately progressed to plans for a building to be located at Ziegler's Grove between Taneytown Road and Hancock Avenue (see map). The site had marvelous advantages, particularly the proximity that the Cyclorama painting would have to the Battlefield site that it depicted. The park historian, who rejected several other potential sites, apparently saw no contradiction in constructing a modern building on the Battlefield that the NPS was mandated to preserve.[29] Government funding of new Park Service facilities in the fifties was augmented by *Mission 66*, a celebrated, ten-year, billion dollar Eisenhower administration program, intended to build new park visitor centers and improve deteriorating facilities in the national parks. *Mission 66* enabled plans to be drawn and the building to be built: a new home for a new Visitor Center, administrative offices and the Cyclorama painting.[30]

Based on his illustrious body of modernist work, mostly in the Los Angeles area, the NPS selected West Coast architect Richard Neutra to design the new building, apparently ignoring environmental differences between California and Pennsylvania. Flat roofs, for example, worked better in California than they did in Pennsylvania. California was warmer and dryer than Pennsylvania. But in 1962, the Park Service closed its Gettysburg Visitor Center and moved it to the new, ill-fated Cyclorama building at Ziegler's Grove, adjacent to the High Water Mark. That move finally brought the conflict between the Borough of Gettysburg and the NPS out into the open.[31] One Gettysburg citizen said that the NPS's move to the Park drew

---

29 NPS, *Mission 66 Visitor Centers*, Ch. 3: *Visitor Center and Cyclorama Building.* Retrieved from https://www.nps.gov/parkhistory/online_books/allaback/vc3.htm;

30 NPS, *Mission 66* Visitor Centers, Introduction: *The Origins of Mission 66.* Retrieved from https://www.nps.gov/parkhistory/online_books/allaback/vc0.htm. The *Mission 66* program began in 1956 and ended in 1966. During those ten years, more than $1 billion was spent on infrastructure and other improvements in the parks. Gateway Arch in St. Louis was a *Mission 66* project. For more information on *Mission 66*, see NPS, *Modern Architecture in the Parks*. Retrieved from https://www.nps.gov/parkhistory/online_books/allaback/vc0b.htm

31 In 1974 the Visitor Center functions were removed to the newly acquired Rosensteel building that became an "interim" Visitor Center in 1974. Platt, *Holy Ground*, 67-71. The Visitor Center/Cyclorama building continued to be a center of controversy and in 1998 the NPS decided to remove it. After many more years of legal wrangling it was torn down in 2013.

Richard Neutra-designed Cyclorama building

visitors away from the center of town, one of the most active sites during the battle. That made the locals "mad as hornets," spawned the development of a strip of unsightly tourist spots, and led to the closing of the city's gemstone, the Gettysburg Hotel.[32]

Having infuriated townspeople by moving the Visitor Center, the NPS nevertheless recognized the new building's many inadequacies almost immediately. The building was a mistake. The entrance lobby needed to be remodeled, motorized doors never opened well due to settling of the foundation, and re-roofing the facility began as early as 1967. The building's air-handling system, which negatively affected the Cyclorama painting, was also problematic from the start.[33] But through the sixties and into the early seventies, the NPS had no other choice, and the NPS's Visitor Center operations, its Museum, and the Cyclorama painting remained at Ziegler's Grove.

32 "History, Commerce Battle at Gettysburg," *York Daily Record*, Feb. 18, 1997.

33 NPS, *Mission 66 Visitor Centers*, Ch. 3; *The Building Since 1962*. Retrieved from https://www.nps.gov/parkhistory/online_books/allaback/vc3.htm. Draft Development Concept Plan Environmental Assessment, April 1995, 8.

In 1969, seven years after the building opened, the NPS released a draft of its new Gettysburg General Management Plan and Environmental Impact Statement (GMP), the Congressionally mandated, overarching plan that defines a park's entire purpose and management direction.[34] GMPs guide and coordinate park planning and management, ideally over a fifteen- to twenty-year timeframe. GMPs are time consuming and expensive to prepare, and it often takes years for Congress to fund a new GMP. They also can have a decided impact on a community as their approval may entail a series of public meetings. Feedback, which may alter the plan and slow its completion, is invited. In this case, it slowed it considerably.

The draft GMP arrived at a time when the failures and inadequacies of the new Cyclorama building and Visitor Center had reached a point where finding a new site for a visitor center had become the single, most stubborn issue facing park planners. That, in turn, exposed the deep fissure in the community's attitude toward the Park. The Gettysburg business community was led by the Steinwehr Avenue merchants, and they relied on the new building for their store traffic. Even though the inadequacies of the Cyclorama building and Visitor Center were obvious, it became clear, as alternative sites were rejected, that those merchants, having watched the Visitor Center move from town in 1962, would fight any move of more than a few feet. They were joined by local politicians who, for tax-related reasons, often opposed land takings for new visitor center sites.

When the nearby Rosensteel mansion became available in 1971, the NPS bought it and moved their visitor center functions there in 1974. But the vintage 1921 building was not a permanent solution, or even a good solution to the visitor center predicament that was brought on by steadily increasing park visitation. As the issue was debated, both within the Park Service and the community, and facing chronic underfunding of the Park and a lack of leadership by either the NPS or the Gettysburg community, the already shaky relationship between Gettysburg and the NPS began to unravel. The 1969 Gettysburg GMP was publicly argued in Gettysburg and Washington for fourteen years before it was finally adopted in December 1982 without deciding on an alternative location for a new Visitor Center.

At about the same time that the draft GMP was first released in 1969, a group of local businessmen, also trying to capitalize on soaring visitation, were making plans to build an observation tower next to the Battlefield.

---

34 General Management Plan and Environmental Impact Statement are often referred to as "GMP/EIS." They are referred to herein as "GMPs."

Old (interim) Visitor Center (Rosensteel building)

The impending colossus temporarily refocused the local debate away from the relocation of the Visitor Center and onto the potential commercialization of the Park.[35] The group's leader, forty-one year-old developer Thomas Ottenstein of Silver Spring, Maryland, controlled newspaper distributorships at airports across the country, built apartments in Washington, and served on the board of a Bethesda, Maryland bank.[36]

In September 1970 Ottenstein applied for a permit to erect a 300-foot observation tower on the Gettysburg Battlefield.[37] This was no ordinary tower. When built, it weighed nearly two million pounds, held five miles of steel, 14,000 bolts, and was anchored in 15,000 tons of concrete. The tower was 393 feet high to the top of its flagpole. Seven- hundred-fifty visitors at a single viewing could enjoy a spectacular view of the Battlefield from 308 feet above the ground, by either climbing 508 stairs or taking one of two elevators to

35 Platt, *Holy Ground*. 63.

36 "Ottenstein's Tower Here Is 'Near Obsession' With Him; Sees its Erection His 'Duty,'" *Gettysburg Times*, Jan. 28, 1971.

37 "Application for Building Permit for Tower Filed," *Gettysburg Times*, Sept. 19, 1970.

the top.[38] There had been towers at Gettysburg before but never one as intrusive as this one. Old arguments around competing visions for the Gettysburg Battlefield that had loomed over the place for a hundred years were quickly retooled and brought out again for this latest, never-ending debate about how much and what kind of commerce should be permitted at national parks.

The Director of the NPS called the tower an "environmental insult," and several historical associations lined up alongside the NPS to fight the tower's construction. Yet within a matter of months the Department of the Interior, home of the NPS, surreptitiously reached an agreement with Ottenstein, which not only allowed him to build his tower, but also provided public access to a better site over NPS land. This was in exchange for 5 percent of the tower's net profits to be paid annually to a foundation for the benefit of the Park—profits that never materialized.[39]

Opponents were furious. No one would admit knowing the negotiations were taking place. The Interior Department's apparent duplicity was explained away as a surrender to the inevitable, the Department's good faith effort to achieve the best possible result in an unfavorable circumstance. The Department simply said that they couldn't stop the tower from being built and, instead, they provided a site that was preferable to the site Ottenstein planned to build on. However, according to the NPS, the agreement was clearly not indicative of NPS approval of Ottenstein's tower—just more ambiguity around Gettysburg. It remains a mystery, even today, as to precisely how and why negotiations began. It was reported that J. C. Herbert Bryant, Jr., special assistant to the Assistant Secretary of the Department of the Interior, orchestrated the process.[40] It strains credulity to believe that he was acting on his own. The Secretary of the Interior, after assuring the Pennsylvania governor that he intended to stop the tower, later told the governor that he was unaware of the agreement until after it was announced.[41] The Director of the NPS, who first called the tower an environmental insult and then signed off on the agreement, admitted that he had agreed to the deal over the telephone while on vacation, but he was unaware

---

38   The Gettysburg National Tower. Retrieved from http://www.gettysburgaddress.com/HTMLS/tower.html

39   John Latschar, "The Taking of the Gettysburg Tower" *The George Wright Forum*, Vol. 18, No. 1 (2001), 24-33. Retrieved from http://www.georgewright.org/181latschar.pdf

40   "New Battle of Gettysburg Rocks PA Tourism Center," *Baltimore Evening Sun*, July 22, 1971.

41   Latschar, "The Taking of the Gettysburg Tower," *The George Wright Forum*, 25.

of any right-of-way over Park Service land.[42] It appears that the agreement was a political maneuver, inspired by an unknown political motive, and it worked.

For the next three years, the question of whether Ottenstein would be permitted to build his tower was hammered out through lawsuits and appeals in the Pennsylvania courts in one action after another, where judges repeatedly concluded in similar-sounding words that "Pennsylvania failed to show clear and convincing proof that the natural, historic, scenic, and aesthetic values of the Gettysburg area will be irreparably harmed" if the tower were built.[43] In the end the tower was built and it opened on July 29, 1974. The fabric of the Gettysburg community, if not yet shredded, was badly frayed. Those who had planned to fight the tower and had counted on NPS support felt betrayed, and the arguments around the GMP and the relocation of a proposed new visitor center hung over it all. An NPS report said that it seemed that Gettysburg refused to settle down and act like a long-established Park.[44]

The tower was a daily affront to historians and preservationists, Gettysburg's most vocal visitors. A local citizen wrote, "It has been said many times but needs to be said again. We at Gettysburg are the custodians of a national shrine. We have a special responsibility."[45] But the tower had its supporters too. One person asked, "Why do those citizens who live outside of the borough limits and who do not pay any taxes in Gettysburg proper have any right to be concerned about matters in an area in which they do not contribute any tax monies."[46] Echoing these sentiments, the Gettysburg mayor said, "Attractions like that keep the town going…What about the billboards and neon signs? They're necessary and helpful, both."[47] To this, historian Garry Wills grumbled, "Gettysburg is a terrible jumble of cheap shops and souvenir museums. The fake is piled on the fake, Pelions upon Ossas of phoniness."[48] The fate of the Battlefield always hung in the balance as trust in the NPS deteriorated and hard feelings within the community became more

---

42 "*Washington Post* Detects Political Overtones in NPS Decision on Tower," *Gettysburg Times*, Oct. 29, 1973.

43 "Court Dismisses PA Petition," *Gettysburg Times*, Oct. 26, 1971.

44 National Park Service, Northeast Regional office, *Operations Evaluation*, 1973.

45 Letter to the Editor, *Gettysburg Times*, April 27, 1971.

46 Letter to the Editor, *Gettysburg Times*, Oct. 21, 1970.

47 "Mayor Favors Tower," *National Observer*, Sept. 6, 1971.

48 "Disneyland Invading Gettysburg," *Philadelphia Inquirer*, Oct. 7, 1971.

pronounced. Whereas in the distant past, community concerns about the NPS centered on land takings and their impact on the local tax base, it now appeared to local citizens that the NPS simply did what it wanted: land takings, towers, visitor centers, or anything else.[49]

One small potential land donation to the NPS in 1985 was the thirty-one acre Taney Farm that Congressman William F. Goodling initially persuaded Congress to reject. Its ultimate acceptance came only after Goodling extracted a hard freeze on further additions to the Park until a committee that included local officials studied the Park's future size and established its legal boundaries. The Park consisted of 3,622 acres of federally owned land and 243 acres of inholdings, for a total of 3,865 acres. The report, submitted in 1988, recommended adding 1,900 acres to the Park. The final bill, H.R. 3248, signed by President George H. W. Bush on August 17, 1990, added 2,050 new acres to the Park, for a total Park acreage of nearly 6,000 acres. After ninety-five years, the Gettysburg National Military Park had a legally defined boundary.[50] But wounds that had festered for years, rather than being assuaged by the new boundary definition, were about to be reopened.

Tucked away within the former H. R. 3248, later P. L. 101-337, was a small, apparently innocuous, land swap between Gettysburg College and the National Park Service. In June 1989 the *Gettysburg Times* reported that "a Gettysburg College plan to relocate campus railroad tracks cannot be finalized until an NPS boundary study is passed by Congress. Relocation will involve a complex agreement between Gettysburg College, NPS, and railroad officials."[51] In August, the newspaper said, "Gettysburg College has long wanted to move Gettysburg railroad tracks off property it wants for playing fields. [Park Superintendent] Kuehn said that an agreement may be reached that will allow a short section of the track to be relocated to NPS property at the edge of that owned by the college."[52] That much was known, at least by the *Gettysburg Times*, in 1989. But the College's intentions, clearly spelled out in the *Times* article, escaped the attention of historians and other preservationists until the College began moving the track eighteen months later.

---

49 Information in this section was derived from Platt, *Holy Ground*, 63-66.

50 Ibid. 93-98.

51 "College Must Wait to Remove Railroad Tracks," *Gettysburg Times*, June 14, 1989.

52 "Keuhn" is Park Superintendent Daniel R. Keuhn. "Superintendent Keuhn says new law may aid Park, community," *Gettysburg Times*, Aug. 25, 1989.

By the 1990 legislation, the NPS transferred seven-and-one-half acres of its land to the College and the College placed an easement on forty-seven acres of historic Battlefield land that the College owned within the Park and that the NPS wanted to remain open.[53] Five months after President Bush signed the boundary bill into law, bulldozers moved into the then college-owned seven-and-one-half acre parcel that was formerly owned and protected by the NPS and began to cut away and level the terrain to prepare the roadbed, thereafter known as the "cut," before relocating the tracks. For historians who were first on the scene, the effect of the earth-moving was stunning and painful.[54] Historic land that they assumed was protected by the National Park Service was being destroyed. To them, the NPS's responsibility is a sacred trust, and when it was violated that day, it opened a wound that never healed. From that day on, the Park Service wore a scarlet letter that its Gettysburg critics would always use to justify their dislike and distrust. As to why the "cut" happened, there were charges and counter-charges from each of the principal parties, both of whom denied any wrongdoing.

On May 9, 1994, four years later, Congressman Mike Synar, Democrat of Oklahoma, called his hearing to order.[55] Synar had assembled an impressive collection of panelists that included the Director of the National Park Service, Roger G. Kennedy. Kennedy, trained as a lawyer, arrived at the NPS from the Smithsonian after an improbably wide-ranging career that included stints as a news correspondent, television producer, radio host, and author. Synar scheduled the hearing to investigate circumstances surrounding the land exchange that had taken place four years earlier. Answering the rhetorical question, "Why now?" Synar referred to the late Supreme Court Justice Felix Frankfurter who once said, "Wisdom too often never comes, so one ought not to reject it if it comes late."[56]

Looking back to April 1990, before the boundary agreement that incorporated

---

53   Deborah Fitts, June, 1994, *Civil War News*, "Gettysburg College & Seminary Ridge"; an account of the May 9, 1994 Congressional hearing. Retrieved from http://www.gdg.org/Discussions/dtrrcut.html

54   Hearing (Synar) before the Environment, Energy and Natural Resources Subcommittee on Government Operations, House of Representatives, May 9, 1994. Excerpts taken from William Frassanito testimony, 17-22.

55   Mike Synar was Chairman of the Environment, Energy and Natural Resources Subcommittee of the House of Representatives Committee on Government Operations.

56   Synar Hearing, May 9, 1994, 6.

the land exchange became law, José A. Cisneros was appointed Gettysburg Park Superintendent. Cisneros was swept up in the aftermath of the "cut" that included the Synar hearings. By all accounts, Cisneros was affable, likable, and a competent public servant, although he appears to have been ill suited for the intense scrutiny that came with the Gettysburg Superintendent's position. In an exchange with Chairman Synar, Cisneros revealed that he had not seen the revised map prior to the execution of the land exchange in September 1990 because "I did not have an occasion to need to look at it. Everything had been done that needed to be done, and I felt no need for me to get involved."[57] When Synar asked him if he was concerned about the plans that he would have to implement, Cisneros responded, "I was under the impression that everybody before me, through superintendents, regional director, planning team, [and a] number of public meetings, had gone over all this ground in great depth ." And then:

> Mr. Synar: I want to get this straight, Mr. Cisneros. You let this land exchange go through without any review by yourself?
> Mr. Cisneros: Yes, sir.

In stark contrast to Cisneros's testimony, Director Kennedy's statement before Chairman Synar was refreshing. It was an abrupt reversal of three years of NPS denials that in this instance it had failed to preserve and protect the country's heritage at Gettysburg. Kennedy readily admitted, "… It seems to me that it is useless for the Director of the NPS to come before you to assert that this was not a mistake… I think it is also beyond debate that the [NPS's] procedures and processes then in place were inadequate."[58] Although rumors of Cisneros's departure had been circulating for months, he left Gettysburg one month after the Synar hearing, and it's hard to believe that the hearing was not connected to the timing of his departure although he denied it. Whatever were Cisneros's shortcomings, the contentious atmosphere at Gettysburg, and the often strained relations between local citizens and the Park Service, couldn't be lain at his doorstep.

There were other circumstances to blame. The turnover of Park superintendents and the lack of a consistent Park management policy, at a time when growing visitation and chronic underfunding cried out for leadership, put the Park into a downward spiral—a distressing record of poor decisions and unresolved issues. John Latschar, for example, appointed Gettysburg

---

57 Ibid. 131. Cisneros's testimony on this page is drawn from this source.
58 Ibid. 106.

Superintendent in 1994, was the fourth superintendent in ten years. The Department of the Interior and the National Park Service, after first opposing Ottenstein's tower, changed direction abruptly, not only to permit it, but to facilitate it. The drawn-out, and unsuccessful, search for a site for a new Visitor Center gave the Steinwehr Avenue business owners ample time to build an inferno of Park Service resentment from what started as a brush fire. There was a proposed two-lane paved road in the eighties that was to follow the old trolley line on the back side of Devil's Den near the southern end of the Park, about sixty-five feet below the summit of Little Round Top. The Park's historian was against it, but it was dropped only after preservationists objected loudly, and brought political pressure to bear on the NPS.[59] Several land takings left citizens feeling bullied by their government agency and contributed to official unease regarding an uncertain tax base. Even the Park's appearance suffered. A letter to the *Harrisburg Patriot-News* cited deplorable conditions at the Park. "You have to blaze a trail between monuments…[the] national shrine will become a breeding place for ticks, snakes, and other undesirable predators."[60] Years before, pictures of a junkyard opposite the Park's entrance at Baltimore Pike and overgrown weeds that covered a cannon on East Cavalry Field, graced the pages of *The Patriot-News*.[61] Commercial development and threats of more development constantly threatened the Park.[62] But of all the many problems at Gettysburg, when the time came for the Gettysburg business community to lead, they seemed afraid of change and competition, and those fears fueled opposition to the NPS's plans for a new Museum and Visitor Center.

If that chain of events is not sufficient proof of what caused turmoil at Gettysburg, there was also a short list of serious, potential problems—related to the care of the Park's priceless collections that had not yet surfaced, and a longer list of unresolved shorter-term issues—overhanging the Park. The NPS, for example, was recommending that several two-way roads through the Park be converted to one-way roads for safety reasons and to alleviate congestion. Angry citizens didn't like disruptions of their customary commuter routes. And the ubiquitous and adorable white-tailed deer were the scourge of the Park. Early in the morning, Battlefield visitors might see up to

---

59 In-person interview with Dr. Walter Powell in his office, June 20, 2014.

60 "Gettysburg in Bad Shape," *The Patriot-News*, June 12, 1990.

61 "Gettysburg Battlefield Park 'Changing Face,'" *The Patriot-News*, July 26, 1970.

62 "Battle Lines Drawn in Gettysburg over a Developer's Proposal to Build," *Philadelphia Inquirer*, June 30, 1991.

400 deer drifting across Emmitsburg Road. The estimated 1,400-head deer herd was far larger than the land could carry and far more than was healthy for deer or for oncoming traffic.[63] When the NPS explored ways to reduce the size of the herd, local animal rights activists were outraged.

Thomas Edison was supposed to have said, "Nothing that's worthwhile works by itself. You have to make the damn thing work." If Edison's observations of electrical machinery could be applied to a national park, then Gettysburg would be that park. To Americans with the strongest ties to Gettysburg—local citizens, historians, and descendents of soldiers who had fought there—the hard work of caring for the Gettysburg Battlefield was complex and contentious. Each controversy perpetuated a challenging environment at Gettysburg for its citizens, for those who cared about the Park, and for the Park Superintendent who would follow José Cisneros. Taken together, those circumstances created near chaos in Gettysburg and they cried out for leadership.

One Park Service executive, who watched the dismal conditions and the stream of bad news and negative publicity that emanated from Gettysburg during the early nineties, was Barbara J. ("BJ") Griffin, Director of the NPS's mid-Atlantic region, which included Gettysburg National Military Park. Well before the Synar hearing, Griffin prepared for the possibility of change at Gettysburg as she did with all the parks in her jurisdiction. Griffin was fortunate that Steamtown National Historic Site in Scranton, Pennsylvania, another controversial national park, was located in her region. She had her eye on the highly regarded Steamtown Superintendent, John Latschar, who had compiled a splendid record managing every aspect of Steamtown's construction as a National Historic Site.[64] Latschar was popular in Scranton and adroit at public relations. His background and his entire career record at the NPS seemed ideal for Gettysburg.

---

63 "Deer Shoot Opponents May Be Ready to Sue," *The Evening Sun*, Sept. 30, 1995.

64 "Steamtown was a very maligned Park. John was such a cheerleader for it. He made the community proud of it. He was just excellent, really, really excellent. He brought credibility to it with his history background." Telephone interview with BJ Griffin, Sept. 24, 2014; "Latschar set about the process of smoothing the political waters and developing a theme for Steamtown: a working railroad yard, roundhouse and shop where visitors can see what gritty industrial America was like early in the century, and then ride behind a steam locomotive. He appears to be making grudging progress with purist critics." "John Latschar has been the one voice of sanity in this chaos," said Jim Boyd, editor of the magazine Railfan and Railroad, who was one of the chief critics of the Park Service's plans for Steamtown." Don Phillips. "Dispute Over Costly Railroad Park, Mall in Scranton Builds Steam," *Washington Post*, Nov. 24, 1991.

A Gift to America

Chapter 1

A New Vision for Gettysburg

When it was known within the NPS that José Cisneros was leaving Gettysburg, BJ Griffin placed a telephone call to John Latschar and encouraged him to apply for the soon-to-be vacant Gettysburg Superintendent position. Griffin had followed Latschar for the two years that she headed the region. She'd heard good reports about his performance at Steamtown, and she had no doubts that Latschar was the right man for the challenging job at Gettysburg.[1] His internalized reaction to being asked to apply for the Gettysburg job was "Please, don't throw me in the briar patch."[2] When he was offered the job, he took it.

Latschar's introduction to history had come early in life. He was born in Kansas, although his family moved east to Virginia—Civil War country—when John was three.[3] His father, a career DuPont man, loved American history, and Latschar remembers that there were always short family vacations to Richmond, Williamsburg, and all of the historic sites around Virginia. In the summer, the family usually returned to Kansas to visit relatives. There were no interstate highways then, and the Latschars drove on country roads, stopping at every historic site from Virginia to Kansas and back, through Kentucky and Missouri, and across the Mississippi. After they moved to South Carolina, the tradition continued. Only the route to Kansas changed. Today, Latschar says that there isn't an historic site on those routes that he hasn't seen more than once, and that sort of exposure to history just kind of sat there and percolated. Latschar enrolled at Kansas State University in 1965. He began as a chemical engineering major, but it wasn't long before he knew he'd made a mistake. Then, in his second semester, because of an administrative error, Latschar found himself in an upper-level history course. He loved it. He became a history major, and the rest really was history.

---

1 Griffin interview, Sept. 24, 2014.

2 Latschar interview, Nov. 20, 2013.

3 Latschar's personal background data in this chapter as well as his recollections and quotations throughout this book are derived from in-person interviews at Sherfy House on Nov. 20, 2013, and Feb. 7, 2014.

Latschar graduated from Kansas State in 1969. He was in ROTC as an undergraduate, so he went into the Army after graduation both to fulfill his service obligation and for more officer training. In October 1970 he shipped out to Vietnam and was one of two officers commanding a sizeable staff that was "advising" a Vietnamese battalion in Soc Trang. Before long his partner, a captain, went on medical leave and First Lieutenant Latschar became the Acting S-2 Officer for the Intelligence Advisory team. He had two sergeants, an interpreter, and a bodyguard. His daily routine consisted of gathering intelligence reports from the field and several briefings, unless there was field duty. Field duty meant accompanying and advising a Vietnamese reconnaissance platoon. Says Latschar, "The Vietnamese battalion commander liked to use the recon platoon as [an active] blocking force. We would hike in, take sampans, or be airlifted into position. The rest of the battalion would sweep suspected Vietcong units toward our blocking position." Latschar saw plenty of action on field duty, and his unit suffered casualties. "As a consequence" he said, "the forty-eight soldiers in the recon platoon dwindled to nineteen by the time my tour was up." Latschar was one of the lucky ones.

He returned home in 1971, joined the Kansas National Guard, began working on his master's degree in history at Kansas State University, and then earned his Ph.D. at Rutgers where he transferred out of the National Guard and into the U.S. Army Reserve. When he began his job search in 1977, he realized that there were more history Ph.D.'s looking for work in academia than there were job openings. At the same time, he learned that the federal government employed more historians than all of academia combined, so he flooded government agencies with applications and received an offer from the National Park Service. After he accepted it, he was assigned to the Denver Service Center, the central planning, design, and construction management office of the NPS.

Latschar worked closely with Denis P. Galvin, who ran the Center and its six hundred employees. Galvin knew him well. Galvin was Latschar's mentor and had a lasting impact on Latschar's career.[4] Latschar began by doing mostly long-distance historic trail work, but he also did a good job for Galvin on the A-76 program, essentially putting nonessential government services out to bid to see if private contractors could perform better than the

---

4   Denis Galvin's opinions and recollections throughout this volume are taken from the author's telephone interview with Galvin on May 12, 2014.

NPS.[5] There was a human component to A-76, so coming out of that experience, Galvin was impressed with Latschar's overall competence in dealing with people. But he also noticed that Latschar was straightforward, blunt. At Gettysburg, Latschar's candor was a plus because there was so much opposition to the NPS from the town that someone who wasn't as tough as Latschar probably wouldn't have succeeded. Galvin recalled that one day Latschar said to him, "I was an officer in Vietnam. I've got management experience and if you ever see a management job that you think would suit me, keep me in mind."[6]

Latschar loved the way the Park Service approached history. His first assignment was in Death Valley where he became an instant expert on nineteenth century hard-rock mining. He next worked on a GMP for the Oregon National Historic Trail. It was practical, applied history, far different and far more interesting to Latschar than his work on Colonial America that earned him his doctorate. He also learned about construction: of the historic, and deteriorating, Crater Lake Lodge, and on a directionally drilled pipeline to bring water up to the South Rim of the Grand Canyon. Latschar was at the Denver Center for eleven years, from 1977 to 1988, either as a team member or a team captain, working on a multiplicity of Park projects across the country that had an impact on cultural resources. He saw the management and leadership styles of dozens of different Park superintendents. It was an intensive, experiential immersion in case studies of NPS management and leadership: why some superintendents succeeded and others failed.

Meanwhile, in 1983 the city of Scranton, Pennsylvania, raised $2 million to move a collection of locomotives and rail cars to Scranton from Bellows Falls, Vermont. The private developers had high hopes for their "Steamtown" amusement park, but within a few years the enterprise was nearly bankrupt. In 1985 Scranton was a typical Rust Belt city, with high unemployment and a decaying industrial base. Sensing a way to make his mark, local Congressman Joseph McDade, a long-time member of the House Appropriations Committee, came to the rescue. McDade saw the economic

---

5 In 1966 the Office of Management and Budget (OMB) issued Circular A-76, which described a methodology to compare costs of conducting commercial services in the federal government with similar services in the private sector and other agencies.

6 Galvin telephone interview, May 12, 2014.

salvation of his district in the old train collection.[7] He decided that he would make it the nucleus of a national park for Scranton, even though it was doubtful that Steamtown would gain National Park status if McDade moved it through the normal park evaluation process. Sensing that, McDade short-circuited the process that mandated evaluation of a site's worthiness and made Steamtown an NPS unit without hearings, studies, or anything else, simply by inserting a park authorization bill into an appropriations bill. In 1986 the first $8 million for Steamtown allowed the partially completed Park to open for business in 1988.

Park Service officials, Congressmen, and staff members, whose authorizing authority was circumvented, were unhappy about Steamtown and, as a result, there was a stigma in Congress and in the NPS that hung over Steamtown for years and may have followed Latschar to Gettysburg. The fact that in the eyes of railroad historians Steamtown's locomotive and railroad-car collection was not the best added to the negativity. Steamtown defenders emphasized Scranton's industrial and mining history and the railroads' role in it, rather than the quality of the collection.

Apart from the collection's worth, however, in 1988, Denis Galvin, by then Deputy Superintendent of the NPS, needed to find a superintendent for Steamtown. Galvin had visited Scranton and he knew that for the first four or five years, the new superintendent would need to prepare a management plan, decide where the interpretive emphasis would be, design the park, and, above all else, build it. Galvin needed someone who was familiar with the NPS's design and construction process as well as with the Denver Service Center. His first thought was John Latschar. Latschar had asked Galvin to keep him in mind. While Galvin and the regional director came up with a list of four candidates for the job, the regional director interviewed them all and chose Latschar.

For John Latschar, Steamtown was a dream come true. No longer a staff historian, he was now Park Superintendent, in the direct "line" of command.[8] The work suited him and he did it well, thus establishing and en-

---

7 Michael deCourcy Hinds, "Scranton Journal; Much Steaming Over 'Steamtown', " *New York Times,* Feb. 5, 1992. Information about Steamtown in the next few pages is from this newspaper article; Galvin interview was on May 12, 2014; and Latschar interview was on Nov. 20, 2013.

8 "Latschar came to Steamtown with an impressive resume. He is one of the few with a doctorate in U.S. history to work for the Park Service." Don Phillips. "Dispute Over Costly Railroad Park… *Washington Post,* Nov. 24, 1991.

hancing his reputation within the NPS. But Latschar would pay a price for his early success. The *Scranton Sunday Times* said that "Latschar's education in railroads began with his arrival in Scranton. It eventually included courses in fundraising and political infighting."[9] McDade's $8 million authorization ballooned to over $70 million before the Steamtown National Historic Site opened in 1995. In both Congress and the Park Service, funding was competitive and difficult for everyone. But Latschar, almost alone, was able to charge ahead with his Steamtown plans, uninterrupted, even though some people thought they were illegitimate. McDade provided the needed funding through direct appropriations. The same Congressional staffers who resented McDade's original end-run in 1986, were reminded of it each year as the annual appropriations piled up. Although McDade was beyond their reach, Latschar, a new Park Service Superintendent, was resented too. He learned to brief Congress directly rather than through Park Service or Congressional staff. Congressmen liked it that way, and it suited Latschar too. This was his way. It was entrepreneurial and it worked, but there were staffers who didn't like it.

While Latschar moved ahead at Steamtown, the *Gettysburg Times*, in December 1993, reported rumors that Cisneros would be leaving Gettysburg. In spite of his denials, within six months the NPS announced Cisneros's appointment as Superintendent of Big Bend National Park on the Mexican border of West Texas, while John Latschar was selected to replace him as Superintendent of GNMP.[10]

From the beginning of his Gettysburg assignment, Latschar was comfortable with Gettysburg. He was a natural leader, he was comfortable with historic preservation, and after twenty-five years of military service, he retired from the Army Reserve as a Lieutenant Colonel when he moved to Gettysburg. The military, he said, was his "ace in the hole. They are a huge user of the Park; military units from somewhere doing leadership stuff, or staff rides. I could call the Commandant of West Point if we had a problem with some of their cadets here. Before I got here the military was in the habit of showing up unannounced with convoys of high-profile visitors. I told them that if they needed extra security, or a portion of the Battlefield sealed off, we had to plan for it. If I called Carlisle and said, 'This is Lieutenant Colonel

---

9 "Steamtown Park Losing Key Man," *Scranton Sunday Times*, July 1994.

10 "Cisneros Denies Rumors He's Stepping Down," *Gettysburg Times*, Dec. 11, 1993. "Cisneros Sees June Departure," *Gettysburg Times*, May 25, 1994.

Latschar, I need to talk to the Commandant,' they'd put me through.[11] If I said, 'This is Park Superintendent Latschar calling,' they'd ask, 'what's this about?'"[12] Looking ahead, when Latschar finally turned his attention to Battlefield rehabilitation, the military would be among his strongest supporters.

The adjoining Eisenhower National Historic Site also came under Latschar's supervision and added to his sense of belonging because he felt a personal connection with the Eisenhower family. Latschar's grandfather was born and raised in Abilene, Kansas, and knew the Eisenhower family. When he died, Latschar inherited his grandfather's library that included early and rare Eisenhower books, some of which were not held by the Historic Site. He donated them all. The Eisenhowers donated the farm to the NPS in 1967, and it opened to the public in 1980.[13] It was an appropriate addition to the Park, given Eisenhower's military service, his personal history as a world leader, and the time he spent near Gettysburg as a young Army officer.[14] As a National Historic Site, the farm always operated as a separate entity with its own history, apart from the history of the Battle of Gettysburg. Latschar said, "Gettysburg was just a fit for me. Everything here made me feel like everything that happened to me in my previous career—the academic, the military, and the Park Service—was so that I could make things better here, and that's hard to say without bragging, but that's exactly how I feel."

The highly trained, well-prepared, young Superintendent was undaunted by the difficult task before him. He cheerfully embraced the challenges and the ambiguity of Gettysburg. He was aware of the competing interests and he was eager to join the fray. He rather enjoyed some aspects of the contest that would need to precede the realization of his vision. But the modern-day Battle of Gettysburg also revealed areas of conflict that may have surprised

11 Carlisle Barracks is a United States Army facility located in Carlisle, Pennsylvania. It is part of the United States Army Training and Doctrine Command and is the site of the U.S. Army War College.

12 Latschar interviews on Nov. 20, 2013 and Feb. 17, 2014.

13 The Eisenhower Farm was not included in the 1999 GMP. Since then it has become part of the GNMP and has been incorporated into the GNBMF's mission. Along with the donation of the Farm, the Eisenhowers maintained lifetime living rights. Eisenhower died in 1969 and his wife, Mamie, continued to live at the Farm until her death in 1979. Retrieved from https://www.nps.gov/nr/travel/presidents/eisenhower_nhs.html.

14 Eisenhower's first command assignment in 1918 was at Camp Colt. Camp Colt was a WW I military installation near Gettysburg, Pennsylvania that was used for Tank Corps training of recruits prior to their deployment.

Old (interim) Visitor Center lobby

him, and they became considerably more antagonistic before it was finally resolved. On his first days on the job, Latschar immersed himself in his new circumstances: his new surroundings, new people, and new problems. He had a high profile. Everything was coming at him at a fast pace, and he had very little transitional guidance.

On his first day at work, Monday, August 8, 1994, he searched for a half-hour for a parking space, and then arrived late at his second-floor office in the Rosensteel family's crumbling, ancestral home. As he looked for parking, his mind must have wandered back to that April spring day several years before when he and his family had visited Gettysburg. It was twenty minutes before they found a parking space then, and the Visitor Center was packed. Latschar recalled later that in summer, the room smelled like the stale sweat of a high school locker room, and it was difficult for the sweltering park rangers to be pleasant. But on that day, Latschar judged that it would be a half-hour before he reached the information desk and with small, impatient children in tow he left, thinking, "I pity the poor SOB who's superintendent here."

The 1920s red brick building had become the Park's interim Visitor Center in 1974. The federal government acquired it from the Rosensteel family in 1971 to escape the cramped, cold, and damp Visitor Center and Cyclorama building that was still a new building—less than ten years old.[15] Latschar carried instructions from BJ Griffin to heal the wounds within the Park staff, and between the Park and its many constituencies. She also gave him a list of specific items that she wanted him to address.[16] The rumored tradition at Gettysburg was that if a superintendent didn't "go along" he didn't last long. But Latschar was better equipped for the job than his predecessors were or than the Park's opponents may have realized. He held a Ph.D. in history, he'd spent over a year in Vietnam being shot at, and sixteen years with the Park Service, the first ten building Park Service facilities all over the country and managing the "people issues" that always come with new projects. The last six years of his Park Service tenure were in Scranton, building Steamtown out of nothing, learning about "political infighting and fundraising"; and he also was a Lieutenant Colonel in the U.S. Army Reserve. Added to these qualifications were a quiet, boyish charm, a winning smile, and a single-minded, relentless determination to fulfill his mission. When asked if he was aware of the turmoil at Gettysburg before he arrived, his quick retort was, "That's how I got here." If the Park's opponents expected Latschar to wilt under pressure, they would be disappointed.

His first move as Park Superintendent was to implement the sweeping reorganization plan that Griffin had approved the prior year that was put on hold until the new superintendent took charge. Some aspects of the plan had taken care of themselves as people retired or were transferred. Others required new positions to be filled, but Latschar needed to assess the qualities of the people he had before he brought in others from the outside.

His office was full of treasured memorabilia that he'd acquired over the years. And they carried a not-so-subtle message too. An Army advertisement taped to the front of his desk featured a dead-on look at a ferocious bald eagle as well as a chain and mace. Under the eagle were the words, "I am smiling." The sign behind his desk advised, "The beatings will stop when the complaining ends." One of his direct reports described him as "scary"

---

15   The $2.35 million transaction included 6.7 acres of land plus the Rosensteel collection of Civil War artifacts; Platt, *Holy Ground*, 67.

16   The list included one-waying of Park roads, the railroad cut, white-tailed deer management, reorganization of Park staff, the National Tower and several other items. Latschar interview, Nov. 20, 2013.

after a first meeting when he wore tinted eyeglasses that darkened in the sunlight and hid his eyes. Yet the same woman called him "smart, intelligent, and a caring, wonderful person."[17] While Latschar was wrestling with Gettysburg personnel issues, the NPS was also reorganizing: decentralizing in a move that would delegate significant new authority and responsibility to the parks, and that, too, suited Latschar perfectly.[18]

Griffin listed mostly short-term problems for Latschar's immediate attention. One of the first was the $1.4 million road-rehabilitation program that was causing a local commuter revolution and a threatened lawsuit. Cisneros had been trying to alleviate traffic congestion on certain Park roads that were too narrow to meet Federal Highway standards for two-way traffic, and, as historic roads, they couldn't be widened.[19] His controversial solution was to convert several major Park avenues to one-way traffic. Latschar's solution, after several meetings, was to convert West Confederate Avenue immediately, Reynolds Avenue no sooner than the spring of 1997, and Howard Avenue not until further notice. With that, both sides seemed satisfied. He wished that all of his controversies were resolved so easily.

But the one-way road dispute gave observers a hint of Latschar's approach to Park problems. He would be flexible with regard to issues that were not central to his mission. But how rigid would he be with regard to issues that were? The white-tailed deer herd, for example, had been a serious Park problem since the early 1980s, and in 1994 whitetails were literally destroying the Park. In 1985 the Park Service asked Penn State to study the deer's environmental impact; there were too many deer for the Park to support. The study recommended that the Park Service thin the herd. The NPS had been trying to determine how to do that, and in 1992 it published its notice of intent to prepare a draft Environmental Impact Statement (EIS) that included a range of alternatives. As part of the process, the public was invited to comment, and there were two open public meetings in Pennsylvania: one at Gettysburg and one at State College. The NPS released a draft EIS in 1994 and a final EIS in the spring of 1995. Both reports contained a range of action alternatives to avoid shooting deer. But the Record of Decision, signed in July 1995, finally determined that the NPS would control the size

---

17   Deborah Darden in-person interview at her office, May 9, 2014.

18   Superintendent's Annual Report, Fiscal Year 1995.

19   Ibid.

of the herd through a controlled harvest—shooting deer.[20]

It was hardly a rash decision. Latschar saw the size of the herd every day when he drove home from work. Penn State had studied the issue. Farmers reported staggering crop losses. Local police supported the reduction because of the number of automobile collisions with deer. The Pennsylvania Game Commission supported the reduction. Nevertheless, when Latschar walked into his first public meeting, animal rights activists were lined up on one side of the auditorium, and hunters who wanted to shoot the deer were on the other side. Of course, citizen hunters roaming a public park in the midst of automobiles, monuments, and historic structures was unacceptable. All the same, it would be a painful process because what became clear early in Latschar's tenure was that the myriad of objections to his plans for the Park were often less about opposition to his plans *per se*, and more about furthering the interests of the protesters, in this case protecting white-tailed deer. One year later, near the end of 1995, the NPS would begin thinning the herd.[21]

Three months before Latschar arrived at Gettysburg, in May 1994, Congressman Michael Synar listened, almost in disbelief, to Park Service Director Roger Kennedy admit that the NPS had made a mistake at Gettysburg regarding the "cut," the destruction of previously protected Battlefield land to construct a railroad track. Synar recounted that when he misbehaved as a child, his parents first made him admit what he had done, but oftentimes, that wasn't enough. Synar asked Kennedy what he was going to do to make amends for the "cut." Kennedy would not say, but he agreed to provide Synar with a list of mitigating options.[22] A comprehensive study carried out during the last few months of 1994 identified five possible alternatives that ranged from "landscape mitigation" (covering it up—estimated to cost $200,000–400,000) to a complete re-acquisition of the land and physical restoration of the landscape, which would cost $6 million.[23]

As the parties exchanged accusations, the issue became murkier. Director Kennedy had implied in his testimony that the land in question

---

20   United States Court of Appeals, District of Columbia Circuit.Paul Davis III, et al., Appellants, v. John Latschar, Superintendent, Gettysburg National Military Park, et al., Appellees. No. 99-5037. Decided: February 22, 2000. Background. Retrieved from http://caselaw.findlaw.com/us-dc-circuit/1177192.html

21   Latschar interview, Nov. 20, 2013.

22   Synar hearing, May 9, 1994, 139-140.

23   Superintendent's Annual Report, Fiscal Year 1995.

may not have been pristine and may have been excavated during the 1880s.[24] On the other hand, some of the aggrieved preservationists charged that Gettysburg College had rushed the transaction to complete it before the NPS realized what it had done, and that in their haste the College trustees had not done what they were required to do to make the transaction legal.[25] The argument did nothing to improve the Park's relations with the community's historians.

Latschar said that on his second day on the job, he was exploring his map rack. He pulled a set of maps from the rack labeled "Gettysburg College Land Exchange." The topographical map, date-stamped by the Park Service, showed clearly both the engineering changes the College intended to make and the "cut." Until then, Latschar had assumed the College was at fault and he was sympathetic with those who called for full restoration. But the map made it clear that although the College had fully disclosed its intentions, the Park Service had not understood them. Latschar began to back-pedal. He knew that money spent on restoration would be taken from the Park's budget. No matter how egregious the "cut," the Park Service had no money for its restoration.[26]

As the argument played out, the range of realistic alternatives narrowed. It was election season in 1994, and the federal budget deficit was front and center. Congressman Goodling announced that any request for funds to restore the railroad "cut" would be "dead on arrival" in Congress. He believed there were higher priorities. Director Kennedy asked Latschar if he would prefer to spend millions remedying the "cut" or on a park-wide sewer system. Latschar knew how much the Park needed the sewer.[27] As reality set in, and to the preservationists' dismay, dressing up the damage became the only practical alternative. College officials, seeing daylight and realizing that something needed to be done, stepped forward to underwrite the $300,000 cost of modest landscape mitigation.[28] The historians, far from mollified and still angry about the "cut," were even more distrustful of the Park and its new superintendent. Latschar knew the Park Service was wrong, and he admired Kennedy for admitting it publicly. But still, he recalled ruefully, "I can't tell

---

24 Synar hearing, May 9, 1994, 137.

25 "Congressman Synar Charges College Did NPS Land Swap Illegally" by Deborah Fitts. Retrieved by http://www.gdg.org/Discussions/dtrrcut.html

26 Latschar interview, Nov. 20, 2013.

27 Superintendent's Annual Report, Fiscal Year 1995.

28 Ibid.

you the number of public meetings I went to where someone said, 'Are you going to screw this up like you did the 'cut?'"[29]

Crises came and went daily, and as they did, Latschar came to grips with the long-term future of the Park. Beginning with his staff, many of whom were skittish, unsure, and defensive when he arrived, he rationalized assignments and altered the Park's direction. One primary example was a new Division of Resource Management that included both the former cultural resource and natural resource management specialists who, traditionally, had separate responsibilities. It was Latschar's way of saying that every natural resource issue at Gettysburg affected cultural resources and vice versa. Everything that he did was aimed at destroying internal "silos," encouraging internal communication, and encouraging the staff to work as a team. Fortunately, the concurrent NPS reorganization that delegated responsibility for personnel decisions to certain parks applied to Gettysburg, which had been recently designated as one of those parks.[30]

Latschar drove the GNMP in a distinctively new and different interpretive direction that could not have escaped the attention of either the community or his staff. Under Superintendent Cisneros, the Park was, for the first time, managed to its "Memorial Period," that is, made to appear as it did in the 1890s when it was created and when returning Civil War veterans memorialized what had taken place at Gettysburg thirty-five years before. Cisneros declared that the 1982 GMP was outdated, and his cultural resource manager, Reed Engle, coined the term "Memorial Landscape" to describe a Battlefield landscape composed of post-Battle elements superimposed upon a pre-Battle, 1863 agricultural landscape. Memorial Landscape at Gettysburg maintained the 1895 appearance of the Battlefield. Buildings that were built in the 1870s and the 1880s would be preserved. A landscape managed to 1863 would remove those buildings. Fences that were removed between 1865 and 1890 would be rebuilt if the Battlefield were managed to 1863, but not if it were managed to the Memorial Landscape.[31] There were numerous differences, but "Memorial Landscape" overall seems simpler, easier, and

---

29 Latschar interview, Nov. 20, 2013.

30 "Battlefield to Join 'Crown Jewels' of National Parks," *The Evening Sun*, Aug. 21, 1993.

31 Jennifer M. Murray, *On a Great Battlefield: The Making Management & Memory of Gettysburg National Military Park, 1933-2013* (Knoxville: University of Tennessee Press, 2014), 144.

cheaper. And it lacks authenticity to the Battle that was fought there. Battlefield rehabilitation was the first item of Latschar's new vision for the Park and, among other things, it would be impossible to carry out without removing architect Richard Neutra's Cyclorama building.

Latschar recalled a Gettysburg tradition: within a few weeks of a new superintendent's arrival, one of the senior Licensed Battlefield Guides would take him on a Park tour. A Guide's tour is shorter than an interpretive Ranger's tour; it's what most visitors get, so Latschar wanted to see and hear what visitors saw and heard. Latschar's guide, a retired Marine colonel, brought a stack of historic photographs with him and Latschar had no idea why he had them. But after a few stops, he realized that the guide couldn't give the tour without the pictures. He couldn't see, or even imagine, what soldiers saw in 1863. Forests and shrubs had replaced open fields, and whatever was visible then was hidden from view in 1994. That, too, got Latschar's attention and he knew that something had to be done about it. "That" meant not only restoring sightlines and fence posts, but it meant removal of non-historic buildings and restoration of 1863 orchards, flora, and fauna, impossible without fewer deer. Only much later did he realize the strategic consequence of his determination to remove the whitetails when he did. There could have been no Battlefield rehabilitation without removing the deer, and Battlefield rehabilitation was what most motivated John Latschar, the historian. It was the first component of his new vision for the Park.

The Memorial Period movement failed to gain traction with the public, and Latschar would have none of it. He was not interested in engaging in debates about whether it was possible to precisely restore the 1863 Battlefield, or whether monuments should be removed from the Battlefield because they weren't there during the Battle. He forbade his staff from using the term *Memorial Landscape*, and he otherwise made his intentions clear. The Park's objectives were first, to preserve the 1863 Battlefield, and second, to preserve the monuments, gun carriages, and avenues that were put in place during the memorial period.[32] Strictly speaking, it was not possible to do both, but Latschar was clearly at ease with ambiguity.

He reached out to opponents and friends alike including local governments, the GNMP Advisory Commission, the Civil War community

---

32 "Memorial Landscape" No More: Gettysburg Battlefield Staff Barred from Using Controversial Phrase," *Gettysburg Times*, Oct. 13, 1994.

in general, and the media.[33] He had ground to make up and every new relationship was not a good one. His strained relations with the Steinwehr Avenue business community, for example, began with a taped audio tour of the Battlefield. A local businessman, Saul Eric Uberman, who declined to be interviewed for this book, owned a wax museum on Steinwehr Avenue near the Visitor Center and sold a taped audio tour from his store. Uberman apparently made it clear to Latschar, and probably to Cisneros before Latschar, that he preferred the Park Service not sell a tape in competition with his. The NPS had never sold a competing tape. Competition by National Parks with local merchants was generally, and rightfully, discouraged. On the other hand, it was unusual that a visitor to a national park was unable to purchase a taped audio tour of the Park Service's own Park, at the Park Service Visitor Center. To Latschar this was unacceptable and needed to be addressed. He tried to purchase Uberman's tape for resale in the Visitor Center, but when that failed, the Park Service began selling its own taped audio tour. The Steinwehr Avenue merchants were consistent, long-standing opponents of Park Service efforts to relocate the Visitor Center because they had seen what happened to stores in Gettysburg when the Visitor Center moved out of Gettysburg in 1962. This was well before Latschar and Uberman argued over the taped audio tour. But their antagonism added fuel to the fire and tended to personalize future disputes.[34]

Latschar also had friends and partners. Eastern National Park & Monument Association (Eastern), for example, was a not-for-profit association that managed the Gettysburg bookstore as well as the Cyclorama and Electric Map programs and returned a portion of their receipts to the Park. The Friends of the National Parks at Gettysburg (Friends), with approximately 9,000 members then and growing, was founded in 1989, to support the Park with volunteer activities and donations of cash, volunteer time, and land. The Licensed Battlefield Guides Association (LBGA), founded in 1915 and made up of independent contractors, was the public face of the Park. Over the years the LBGA had gone through periods of stormy

---

33 The GNMP Advisory Commission was established by the Boundary Act of 1990 and its members represented a cross-section of the Gettysburg community, all of whom were appointed by the Secretary of the Interior. The Park Superintendent was an ex-officio member of the Commission.

34 "Gettysburg Businesses Say Tape Unfair Competition," *The Evening Sun*, Feb. 29, 1996; Latschar interview, Nov. 20, 2013.

relations with the Park, but with Latschar's arrival, those relations improved.[35] Each of these groups, and more, sought to take the measure of the new superintendent.

But the second item in Latschar's new vision of the Park's future was to provide visitors with high-quality interpretation and educational opportunities, which meant building a new Visitor Center. He had been aware of the chaotic, stifling conditions in the aging, interim Visitor Center since his first visit several years before. He knew that the old Rosensteel building needed to be replaced with a larger Visitor Center to provide many more visitors with higher quality interpretation and education opportunities. Additional parking spaces were vital. But within a month of his arrival at Gettysburg, Mike Vice, the new Curator of the Gettysburg collections, came to him with further proof of the building's inadequacy. When the NPS acquired the interim Visitor Center and the enormous collection of artifacts from the Rosensteels in 1971, it agreed to retain Angie Rosensteel Eckert's husband, Larry, as the collection's Curator for life.[36] Latschar describes Eckert, who had no formal curatorial training. as a polite, amiable, and appealing man, well-liked by everyone. He was Curator of the national collection for twenty-two years until 1993. It seems that the NPS was sufficiently eager to escape the damp, dungeon-like, Cyclorama building, even in favor of the outdated Rosensteel building, that it made an employment commitment that otherwise seemed to make no sense. Coincidentally, and seemingly indicative of the NPS's lack of purpose at the time, Eckert's hiring came at the same time that the Interior Department and the NPS made another ill-fated decision: not to oppose Ottenstein's tower.

Vice entered Latschar's office and handed him a report on the Museum's collections. It described miserable storage conditions and deteriorating artifacts, in Latschar's words, "enough to make a grown man cry." There was no temperature control in the storage areas. Temperatures ranged from 20 degrees in the winter to 90 degrees in the summer. There was no humidity control, no dust control, and no alarm system. Latschar took the report, read it and, not believing that conditions were as bad as the report indicated, called Vice. Vice invited him to the basement to see for himself. What transpired

---

35   Barbara J. Finfrock, *Twenty Years on Six Thousand Acres*, (Gettysburg: Barbara J. Finfrock, 2009), 31; Finfrock in-person interview at Sherfy House, May 22, 2014.

36   Angie Rosensteel was a direct descendent of the John Rosensteel who had initiated the Rosensteel collection 130 years before. She was the sister of Joseph Rosensteel who created the famous electric map at Gettysburg.

next would become ingrained in Park lore as Latschar's first "dismal tour." Latschar described the storage debacle to audiences as if he stopped on his way to work every day and took one shingle off the Visitor Center roof. At first, it would go unnoticed, but there would be a cumulative effect. The curatorial protection of the Park's enormous collection became the third item in Latschar's new vision for the GNMP.[37]

Looming over all of Latschar's thoughts and plans for the Park's future was a very dark financial cloud. His Superintendent's Annual Report for Fiscal 1995 finished with a paragraph entitled "Concerns for the Future" that began,

> My concerns for the future of Gettysburg National Military Park can be summarized simply—we are broke. As I often state in speeches to Civil War groups, if either GNMP or the NPS as a whole were a Fortune 500 Corporation, we would be in Chapter 11 bankruptcy protection. We are not even close to having sufficient funds to adequately care for our cultural resources or to ensure that they will be available for this and all future generations.

He described various ways and means of securing off-budget funding, which, while helpful, he admitted could never be sufficient. And then he wrote, "The only hope for the future of these parks or for the NPS as a whole is to make the American public understand how threatened their park resources are and how desperately we need adequate funding...."

One year later, the situation was not improved. The Government Accountability Office (GAO) selected Gettysburg as one of eight national parks they would study to identify internal threats to the park system. Of twenty-nine identified threats, twenty-eight were caused by insufficient funds to do the job. The report showed that the GNMP was operating at about 67 percent of what was needed to adequately preserve Park resources.[38] In his Annual Report, Latschar vowed "to talk to everyone who will listen about the abysmal status of GNMP and the National Park Service."[39] Looking back, it now seems inevitable that his outreach efforts would ultimately have led him to a private partner. Private philanthropy had played

---

37 Latschar interview, Nov. 20, 2013.

38 The Government Accountability Office is a government agency that provides auditing, evaluation, and investigative services for the United States Congress.

39 Superintendent's Annual Report, Fiscal Year 1996.

a key role in the development of the NPS since its beginning.[40] According to the NPS, "Before Congress routinely appropriated funds for Park lands, and later when land acquisition needs exceeded and continue[d] to exceed appropriations, private donations were and are responsible for substantial additions to the National Park system. Other donations have contributed significantly to park planning, development, management, and interpretation." Gettysburg was marking time, just waiting for the right private partner to appear.

---

40 NPS, *Philanthropy and the National Parks*, Retrieved from https://www.nps.gov/parkhistory/hisnps/NPSHistory/philanthropy.HTM

CHAPTER 2

The New Vision Set Back; a New Beginning

When, in November 1994, Bob Monahan, a real estate developer and local entrepreneur, approached John Latschar with an idea that he thought might solve the Park's money problems, Latschar was interested. He was having dinner with Angie (Rosensteel) and Larry Eckert and Monahan, all part of his concerted effort to develop personal relationships with influential Gettysburg citizens.[1] The Rosensteel family donated their premier Civil War collection to the NPS, and they had lived in Gettysburg for over one hundred years.

Monahan grew up in Gettysburg, attended Gettysburg College, and he'd known the Eckerts for years. His family owned a local funeral home, he was a successful real estate developer, and he was active in Republican politics. Unbeknown to Latschar, Monahan was inspired by the movie *Gettysburg* after he and his wife attended its opening in Washington the year before. When they returned home to Gettysburg that night, Monahan drove their babysitter home through the Battlefield. "It was about one in the morning on a moonlit night when I passed Round Top, Little Round Top, and the Peach Orchard, and drove through Pickett's Charge," Monahan recalled. "Having just seen the movie, all of a sudden it connected with me—what had happened there. When I was a boy, I played on the Battlefield. I went to school in Gettysburg and I never really fully understood what happened there until that night." Monahan reasoned that if the battle history of Gettysburg were a revelation to him, it might be to many others too. Suddenly, he wanted to share his inspiration by producing and showing a film about the Battle of Gettysburg to visiting audiences in Gettysburg.

At the same time, and not known to Monahan, Latschar had to solve his crowding, parking, and collection storage problems. Monahan listened to Latschar bemoan the difficulties of funding anything at Gettysburg. Congress had voted for a Civil War Museum in 1989, but never funded it.[2] Every year, the Park's budget seemed more restrictive. Monahan suggested that

---

1   Biographical information about Bob Monahan in this section and elsewhere in the chapter derives from an in-person interview with Monahan at his office, May 20, 2014.

2   Superintendent's Annual Report, Fiscal Year 1995; Draft Development Concept Plan, Environmental Assessment, April, 1995, 11.

Latschar consider a public/private venture with him, wherein he would raise money to build a Museum and an IMAX theater where he could show his movie and charge admission. Latschar, who had no other financial plan and, incidentally, no prior experience with public/private partnerships, was understandably intrigued by Monahan's proposal. Over the next several days, he and Monahan fleshed out the plan. The figure of $30 million emerged as the amount they thought they needed to build the facility, to be raised by Monahan—half of it borrowed. Monahan's suggestion that day triggered a series of events that led directly to building the Gettysburg Museum and Visitor Center fourteen years later. Denis Galvin, who by late 1994 was Deputy Director of the NPS, believes that the public/private partnership that funded the new Museum and Visitor Center wouldn't have happened without Monahan's creative idea.[3]

Public/private partnerships were not new to the NPS, but one had never been suggested for Gettysburg. Private partners generally raise private funds for public projects. If they don't work, it's usually because the partners' objectives ultimately don't mesh. Latschar describes their occasional existence in the Park Service as almost biblical. "It's like seeds thrown on the ground. A few of them sprout in the harsh environment of the Park Service. But most of them don't. Golden Gate Parks, Mount Rushmore Memorial, Independence Hall, and the Statue of Liberty are examples of successful partnerships, but they're exceptions. Most of them get choked back by weeds." More important than the isolated precedents, however, was the positive influence of Director Kennedy, who had been in his job for just over a year. Kennedy arrived at the NPS after thirteen years as Director of the Smithsonian's National Museum of American History where public/private partnerships were a way of life. He was comfortable with public/private partnerships, an original concept that another NPS director might have found alien. Kennedy was also comfortable with Latschar, whom he'd met several times both in Washington and Scranton during the construction of Steamtown.[4] So Kennedy, too, was intrigued by Monahan's proposal whereas other NPS directors might not have been. He remained a key supporter of the concept and of Latschar's vision until he retired in early 1997.[5]

As Monahan and Latschar went to work, Latschar was sidetracked when Ottenstein announced his willingness to sell the huge tower that had hovered

---

3   Galvin interview, May 12, 2014.

4   Latschar to Remington email, June 18, 2014.

5   Latschar interview, Nov. 20, 2013.

over the Battlefield for twenty years. But after a brief surge of optimism, it became clear that Ottenstein's asking price was unrealistic, unlikely to be paid by anyone, let alone the NPS. A private citizen from Baltimore then offered to lead a nationwide fundraising campaign to purchase the tower and knock it down.[6] Obviously interested in removing the tower, Latschar was suddenly weighing two very different, potential public/private partnerships—one for building a museum and the other for removing the tower. Thus burdened, he went to Washington in early January of 1995 to brief Kennedy and Galvin. Latschar thought he could pursue either the tower removal or the Museum, but that he wouldn't be able to manage both projects at the same time. The ever-wise Kennedy unhesitatingly told him to concentrate on the museum. He said, "We'll get to the tower. If you focus on that now and it comes down, then what will you do? The Museum has possibilities and the entire NPS could learn from what you do."[7] Latschar took Kennedy's advice to heart and he never forgot it. After the meeting, Galvin took Latschar aside and said, "John, you've built museums before, like Steamtown, and then you've come to me because you didn't have any dollars to operate it. Don't bring me a new Museum without the operating dollars."[8] Galvin's warning was prophetic. Shortly after that meeting, Latschar decided that the gentleman from Baltimore, who made a habit of talking to the press without first talking with Latschar, was not a likely partner, and he put the tower's removal aside.

Meanwhile, Latschar and Monahan continued to work on Monahan's proposal. They knew that strict federal regulations regarding NPS dealings with private parties would necessitate bringing in a not-for-profit group to act as an intermediary between the Park Service and the newly formed Monahan Group. Otherwise, every contract between the Park Service and Monahan would need to be put out for bid, and that would hamstring the project. The Friends appeared to be the ideal not-for-profit for the purpose and they agreed to help. The fresh proposal to the Park Service, therefore, came not directly from Monahan but from a new partnership of the Friends and the Monahan Group. It was to build the new Museum, and construct a privately owned and operated IMAX Theater at the former *Fantasyland* site, south of Hunt

---

6 Latschar, "*The Taking of the Gettysburg Tower*," 27.

7 Galvin quotation gleaned from Latschar interview, Nov. 20, 2013.

8 Ibid.

Avenue on Taneytown Road (see map).[9] And there was a new wrinkle: to remove the Cyclorama building, an important item in Latschar's new vision for Gettysburg, and relocate the historic Philippoteaux Cyclorama painting to the new facility that they would build. The new partnership would fund the design and construction of the project at no cost to the Park Service.

Latschar added the Cyclorama painting to the Monahan project after his first Cyclorama tour. There were longstanding and well-publicized problems with the modernist concrete and glass Cyclorama building that housed the painting. It functioned badly, both as a Visitor Center and as a home for the painting. Its flat roof leaked and there was never money to fix it. The leaks caused a variety of problems and, at times, the building was practically uninhabitable. But there seems to have been no connection made between the atmospheric condition inside the building and its potential for damaging the painting. Latschar asked an art conservator to provide a pro-bono, one-day assessment of the painting's condition. The conservator concluded that there were inadequate temperature and humidity controls in the building and that moisture was causing irreparable damage to the painting. In his opinion, if something weren't done within five years, paint would begin to fall off the canvas. Suddenly, the iconic painting, around which much of the Park's interpretation of the Battle was based, was known to be threatened, just as the basement archives were threatened. It seemed that the Park Service was unable to care for the nation's historic treasures at Gettysburg. Latschar knew that he had to move the painting away from the moisture and out of the Cyclorama building. And he also realized that restoration of the iconic Philippoteaux painting needed to be the fourth item of his new vision for Gettysburg.

In early 1995, with the enlarged proposal in mind, the NPS needed an experienced Park Service planner who knew the ins and outs of NPS rules and regulations, to reduce the ambitious Monahan idea to writing. NPS planning is an arcane process, filled not only with cultural and natural resource impacts, but with the requirements of Section 106 of the National Historic Preservation Act, the National Environmental Policy Act of 1969,

---

9 *Fantasyland*, a children's amusement park, opened in 1959. The site was sold to the NPS in 1974 and the Park closed in 1980. It was wooded; three ponds were created by damming Guinn Run, a stream that ran through the Park. The dams and the ponds were all part of *Fantasyland*. Mike Caverly, Emmitsburg Historical Society, "Remembering Gettysburg's Fantasyland," retrieved from http://www.emmitsburg.net/archive_list/articles/history/gb/business/fantasyland.htm

the Endangered Species Act of 1973, and on and on—an alphabet soup of Park Service acronyms. Deborah Darden arrived from Steamtown and joined the Gettysburg staff as chief planner.[10] Darden was a preeminent Park Service planner: a master of NPS protocol and the planning process.

Born and raised in Austin, Texas, Darden, an eleventh-generation Texan, earned both her bachelor's degree in American Studies and her Master's in Anthropology from the University of Texas at Austin. She first began working in college for a Texas professor and architect in a work/study program. Her employer was a believer in what she calls the (Ian) "McHarg layer-cake approach to planning." Darden says, "He was a generalist. He could look at geology and topography, and soils and cultural histories of various sites, and then do the analyses. That's what I did for ten years."

McHarg was well known and influential. He had a landscape architecture practice in Philadelphia, and he also taught architecture at the University of Pennsylvania. Darden used McHarg's book, *Design with Nature* (1969), in her work. McHarg offered a program at Penn that he called "the McHarg Year," wherein students would immerse themselves in his landscaping work. Darden had already decided that while she loved anthropology, she knew it lacked career opportunities. She also knew that McHarg was retiring, and that if there were to be a final "McHarg Year," she wanted to be part of it. So with her Master's degree in Anthropology, she applied to Penn and was admitted to the McHarg program.[11]

After Darden's year with McHarg, she went to work for the NPS in its Philadelphia regional office doing planning work for the Lackawanna Heritage Valley in Scranton. When Latschar arrived at Steamtown, he saw Darden frequently. She told him that her husband, Richard Segars, an architect, had recently left his firm. Latschar asked her if Segars would be interested in moving to Scranton as his Park architect, and within a few weeks he was there. Darden said, "Richard worked for Steamtown. Although I was in Scranton, I was still working for the NPS's Philadelphia regional office doing planning for the Heritage Valley and other projects. But I also worked a lot with John when he needed help on Steamtown." So with one stroke, Latschar had unknowingly assembled most of his Gettysburg planning team six years before he would need them there.

---

10 Biographical information about Deborah Darden in this chapter is derived from an in-person interview with Darden at her office, May 9, 2014.

11 Ibid.

With the help of Segars, and Deirdre Gibson, another experienced planner from the Philadelphia office, Darden's first Gettysburg assignment was to work on the enlarged 1995 Development Concept Plan (DCP).[12] DCPs are project-specific, NPS-initiated plans that combine a concept, generally a building, with what the building is meant to achieve and whatever compliance is required. DCPs weren't used to analyze proposals made to the NPS from the outside. "But," said Darden, the DCP "was the planning tool we had, so we used it. We modified it a little bit to try to look more at feasibility—was the project feasible—and was it in the NPS's best interest.... Part of what we're trying to do is to determine what the Park really needed. Understanding goals is a pretty basic part of concept planning." The team looked hard at Monahan's proposal to see if it was feasible, financially and otherwise, and to see if it was consistent with the Park's goals.[13]

The NPS released the draft DCP in April 1995. The finished proposal built a Civil War Museum, relocated the Cyclorama painting to a new facility, and constructed a privately owned IMAX theater, all on the *Fantasyland* site south of the interim Visitor Center on Taneytown Road (see map). It also removed the Cyclorama building and restored that landscape. The planners began by examining five alternatives and rejecting two of these out of hand: first, placing the proposed Museum/IMAX facility adjacent to the interim Visitor Center (the Rosensteel building) and second, relocating the Visitor Center function and Museum/IMAX facility (without a new Cyclorama building), to the new site. They rejected the first alternative because the Rosensteel site was not large enough to accommodate the new additions, and the second because the total project was too large and too costly. They analyzed the other three alternatives in detail. One of the three, Alternative A, was the ever-present "do nothing" alternative which, as advertised, did nothing to alleviate the dismal Visitor Center or collection storage conditions or remove the Cyclorama building. Alternative B built the Museum, a new Cyclorama building, and an IMAX theater. It maximized parking and provided expansion space for future growth. Alternative C was a smaller version of Alternative B that incorporated less parking and provided no room for expansion.[14]

The DCP cited the deteriorating conditions of the Cyclorama building, calling it "one of the most egregious encroachments" on the Battlefield,

---

12 DCPs are always supporting documents for GMPs, in this instance for the 1982 GMP.

13 Darden interview, May 9, 2014.

14 Draft Development Concept Plan, April 1995, 17-26.

and self-consciously noted that the NPS built it. Alternatives B and C both included an understated, but prescient, reminder. The DCP disclosed that "although it is less than fifty years old, the Cyclorama center may be eligible for listing on the National Register of Historic Places." If it were listed, that would preclude its removal and stand in the way of rehabilitating Ziegler's Grove.[15] When the planners wrote that, however, almost no one on Latschar's staff believed that the Cyclorama building would be eligible for the National Register, a serious miscalculation.

The public release of the DCP rumbled through Gettysburg like an earthquake and citizens "fled" in all directions. One of the Steinwehr Avenue merchants accused Monahan of trying to gain an advantage at the community's expense by creating a monopolistic business on Park Service land that would benefit him and leave others out.[16] Preservationists, still angry over the railroad "cut," the NPS's obliteration of a small section of the Battlefield five years before that was never restored, led the charge against new commercialization of the Battlefield.[17] Historian William Frassanito, comparing the construction that the NPS was endorsing in the DCP with an NPS ban on Battlefield digging, said, "If you want to get in trouble at that park, go out there with a trowel and start looking for little bullets, and they'll come down on you like the Gestapo." Some people wondered why the NPS chose Monahan instead of casting a broader net to see if there were other interested investors. The response to the 1995 DCP was unnerving for Gettysburg, revealing a fearful, leaderless community that had no plan for its future other than to fight change. For Latschar it was disappointing, but it was a first effort that held a number of important lessons for the future. The public reaction chastened him as only public rejection can. His later effort would be more careful, better researched, more nuanced, and, it would carry the day.

While the community was up in arms, the planning team was quietly harboring its own doubts about Monahan's proposal. Unspoken was any mention of how and why the Cyclorama center had been built, a cloud that hung over Park Service planning. The Cyclorama building was a *Mission 66*

---

15 Ibid. Ziegler's Grove on the Ziegler Farm was a Pickett's Charge landmark. It sheltered Union troops and artillery batteries and was splintered by shell fire during the latter two days of the Battle (see map).

16 Platt, Holy Ground, 121-122.

17 "Park Service Makes Do After Land Swap, Angering Preservationists," *Gettysburg Times*, June 1, 1995.

project (see the Introduction for more about *Mission 66*) that never met the needs of the Park Service. But *Mission 66* projects provided opportunities for architects to burnish their resumes at a time when the NPS, unsure of its direction, failed to chart its own course and was ceding project leadership to outside interests. Whereas in 1994 the Park Service was proactively restoring and protecting cultural resources, in 1962 it was not. The Cyclorama center, designed by renowned architect Richard Neutra, drew attention when it was built, but its siting in Ziegler's Grove was opposed by some Park Service historians from the outset. Even so, it was built, and the Park Service regretted the dubious quality and utility of the building immediately. The Park Service had learned its lesson. Future Park Service buildings would be built to achieve Park Service goals. No one wanted to risk building another dysfunctional building at Gettysburg.

The DCP identified several Park needs that Monahan's proposal would fill: a new Museum, expanded parking, and a new Cyclorama building. But even the most robust alternative in the DCP did nothing to provide a new Visitor Center or collections storage facility, two parts of Latschar's new vision for the Park. Beyond that, the planning team, not expert at real estate or finance, was concerned about the financial feasibility of the proposed IMAX theater. They wondered if it could carry a mortgage; and if it didn't draw sufficient audiences, would all or a portion of its cost fall back on the NPS? Whether or not Monahan got wind of the team's reservations, he certainly was surprised and disappointed by the public reaction to his proposal. In August he floated a new proposal to move the project to a county-owned tract of land at the interchange of Route 15 and Route 30 that he hoped to acquire and name "Gateway Center." It was about three-and-a- half miles, as the crow flies, northwest of the High Water Mark on Cemetery Ridge.

Monahan attributed the *Fantasyland* site's ultimate rejection almost solely to its location inside the Park, which was only one of several reasons; another was that it came out of a reactive, closed, private negotiation between Latschar and Monahan.[18] There were no other proposals nor was any effort made to open the process. In the wake of future events, it seems clear that Monahan assumed that there would be no future building allowed within the Park. But his new commitment to a site outside the Park also revealed that he, who by

---

18 "I am shocked that they would choose a plan that will put the Center on hallowed ground within the permanent boundaries of the Park. Robert Monahan, losing bidder." Quoted in "York Developer Has Winning Bid on Park Museum," *The Evening Sun*, Oct. 15, 1997.

his own admission had only recently come to understand and appreciate the rich history of Gettysburg, didn't yet understand the nuances of what it took to present Gettysburg's history to the public. The new site was too far away from the Battlefield, the High Water Mark, and the Bloody Angle.

Meanwhile, the planning team's doubts and the negative public reaction to the draft DCP were the subjects of Washington meetings of the Gettysburg, Regional NPS, and Congressional staffs. The conversations often included Deputy Director Galvin and/or Director Kennedy. All of the participants, particularly Galvin, were rankled by the reactive nature of their deliberations. Why were they accepting the limits imposed by Monahan's $30 million proposal? Why couldn't they figure out what the Park Service needed and what it would cost? And why wasn't there an inclusive, public process that began with what the NPS wanted to do?[19] These, too, were some of the lessons learned from the Cyclorama building fiasco of thirty years before.

In August 1995 at a meeting in Sandy Hook, New Jersey, a small group of NPS and Congressional personnel consisting of Galvin, Regional Director Marie Rust, Latschar, and Debbie Weatherly, Chief of Staff of the House Appropriations Subcommittee, discussed Gettysburg.[20] Galvin told them to drop the DCP. He knew that what Gettysburg needed was too far reaching to be dealt with by a DCP that was a limited format, intended by the NPS to be project specific, often even for just a single building. He knew that the current GMP didn't cover current circumstances. He said that the NPS should be the ones deciding on the location of the Visitor Center; they could work with Monahan or anyone else, but they needed a new GMP for Gettysburg.[21] Frustrated by Band-Aids, workarounds, and other temporary or less-than-ideal fixes at America's premier, historic National Park, Galvin was explicit. He was determined to start fresh with a new GMP that would provide a comprehensive new vision for Gettysburg. He could not have known then how much time would elapse before a new GMP would come to fruition.[22]

As Latschar's planning staff worked on the DCP, he was devoting more

19 Galvin interview, May 12, 2014; Latschar interview, Nov. 20, 2013; "NPS Reopens Planning Process," *The Evening Sun*, Oct. 29, 1995.

20 Park Superintendents Conference, Sandy Hook, NJ, 1995. Weatherly was Congressman McDade's assistant in Scranton. Latschar once observed, "She gave me my political education."

21 A GMP (General Management Plan) is the overarching plan that defines a Park's purpose and direction.

22 Latschar interview, Nov. 20, 2013; also Denis Galvin transcript, 59.

time to the ubiquitous white-tailed deer. The Record of Decision for the reduction plan, signed in July 1995, caused a steady drumbeat of public protest and media attention.[23] The plan was simple. Its objective was to reduce deer density in the Park—the number of deer per acre that the Park could support. Antlered deer were not to be shot. There was no money to hire a contractor, so Park rangers would do the shooting. There was a training program and a verification protocol for the rangers. Animals, once shot, always needed to be recovered. The rangers were reminded of the Park's irregular boundaries, the seventeen historic houses where Park employees lived, and monuments that were everywhere. After the Park closed at ten o'clock, volunteer rangers drove off in pickup trucks. There were three to a truck and each truck was equipped with a tripod, a rifle, and a searchlight. They drove to the woods near West Confederate Avenue that were closed to public traffic at night. The spotters shined a light on the deer and the riflemen shot them. Gettysburg citizens, looking past the Park's mission, were horrified at the shooting, and they said so.

Stepping back, objections to the NPS's Battlefield rehabilitation were often a reflection of the ambiguity that linked several protested Park Service initiatives. The Park was originally established to "preserve and protect the resources associated with the Battle of Gettysburg… and to provide understanding of the events that occurred within the context of American history."[24] That was the Park's legal *raison d'etre*. When that purpose conflicted with widely accepted societal values—wildlife protection, as in shooting whitetails; or architectural preservation as in removing an architecturally significant building; or the protection of one's right to do business as in moving a visitor center away from a business center—the Park's stated purpose trumped these competing values, and that, needless to say, frustrated protesters. But it was that simple even though it was far from easy.

No deer were shot that first night in October 1995, and only five deer were killed during the first week.[25] The Humane Society doubted that the Park Service would be able to kill several hundred deer in a year.[26] But during the first year of shooting, rangers killed 503 deer. There were no

23 "Deer Shoot Planned to Begin in October," *The Evening Sun*, July 21, 1995.

24 Preferred Alternative and Background General Management Plan and Environmental Impact Statement, Gettysburg National Military Park, Gettysburg, Pennsylvania, June 1999, 7.

25 "Oh Dear! No Deer!" *The Evening Sun*, Oct. 3, 1995.

26 "Deer Shoot Opponents May be Ready to Sue," *The Evening Sun*, Sept. 30, 1995.

reported accidents, although neighbors complained loudly and often about panicked deer stampeding through their yards, and rangers trespassing on their property. It could have been tumultuous.[27] On the positive side, NPS delivered field-dressed deer to local butchers for processing, and they, in turn, delivered 30,000 pounds of venison to local and regional food banks. By the end of the second year, during which 355 deer were taken, the deer herd was reduced to about 100 from over 1,100 before the program began.[28] Citizen complaints virtually disappeared, and the rangers had a perfect safety record. But dedicated animal rights activists never stopped protesting the program.

The early success of the deer-herd reduction plan was good news for the Park Service, which had anticipated a legal challenge and was looking for one. Years before, the NPS had tried to manage the deer herd at Cuyahoga National Park in Ohio on the basis of an Environmental Assessment (EA) that lacked scientific data to support it.[29] When they were sued and lost, they began looking for another case that could be supported by a history of creditable scientific data. Gettysburg filled the bill. So when, in February 1997, animal rights activists sued the NPS, the NPS recognized an opportunity and gave Latschar its unqualified support. That case became Davis v. Latschar and on December 31, 1998, the U.S. District Court for the District of Columbia ruled in favor of Latschar. When plaintiffs appealed, the U.S. Court of Appeals, District of Columbia Circuit, on January 26, 1999, denied the motion, again entering judgment for the defendant, Latschar.[30] The fact that Latschar was the named defendant in the case was indicative of NPS policy regarding its superintendents, who, if they were sued, were the named defendants and managed the case even though the Regional Director, the Director, and the NPS were also sued.[31]

Returning to his planning activity, Latschar wasted no time crying over

27 "Park Service Gets an Earful About Deer Kills," *Gettysburg Times*, Sept. 17, 1996.

28 A total of 858 deer were killed in two years, which, subtracted from the beginning herd of 1,148, would leave 290 head in the herd. The approximate discrepancy in the size of the herd of about 190 deer could be laid to inaccuracies in the count and/or outmigration. Superintendent's Annual Report, Fiscal Year 1997.

29 Latschar Interview, Nov. 20, 2013.

30 United States Court of Appeals, District of Columbia Circuit.Paul Davis III, et al., Appellants, v. John Latschar, Superintendent, Gettysburg National Military Park, et al., Appellees. No. 99-5037. Decided: February 22, 2000.

31 Latschar interview, Nov. 20, 2913.

the "spilt milk" of the first DCP that he dropped after the August meeting at Sandy Hook. He immediately began work on a new DCP, which if combined with a new GMP, would institutionalize his new vision for the Park. He knew Galvin had said to drop the DCP and that he (Galvin) believed that a DCP was an inadequate planning tool. He also knew that a new GMP was in the works, but he wouldn't wait for it. This was a critical decision. If, in hindsight, Latschar had waited for the GMP to be authorized before he gave his planning team the go-ahead, an eighteen-month delay might have caused the entire project to founder. Latschar's opponents recognized the danger that a DCP, or especially a new GMP, posed to them, whether it was killing deer, moving the Visitor Center, removing the Cyclorama building, or commercializing the Park; if a new GMP were approved under Superintendent Latschar, it would all be made permanent.

On October 17, 1995, Latschar released a public letter announcing NPS's deferral of its consideration of the April 1995 DCP. Instead, he said that they had taken a step back to re-engage the planning process, and that they were working with preservation groups, the Civil War community, and the public to ensure that they knew what they wanted to do before they tried to determine how they wanted to do it. Monahan's first proposal was the subject of the 1995 DCP. His new Gateway proposal was on hold, along with all other options, until the second review of facility needs was completed.[32] But Monahan's was still the only outside proposal and he remained optimistic. Whatever the NPS decided to do that required a private partner, he was determined to put together a first-class team to do it, and he was confident that his proposal would prevail.

One aspect of the NPS planning process that frustrated NPS opponents was that the Park Service controlled the design and development of the planning options it presented to the public for comment. Some opponents believed that the general public should originate planning options, or at least be on an equal footing with the NPS in that regard.[33] Otherwise, they believed the program was rigged. Or, if a segment of the public wanted more options than the NPS offered, the Park Service should consider those options, whether or not they were consistent with Park objectives. Some

32 "NPS Reopens Planning Process," *The Evening Sun*, Oct. 29, 1995; "New Planning Process in The Works tor Battlefield," *Gettysburg Times*, Oct. 19, 1995. The Friends had by this time withdrawn from the Monahan partnership.

33 See Walter Powell testimony at Hansen hearing, Feb. 11, 1999, 22-23.

citizens seemed even to believe that they could originate Park initiatives and that the Park Service should follow their lead. Reflecting this view, Congressman Hansen had said, "The NPS has narrowed the alternatives in the management plan, rendering public input meaningless."[34] But at the same hearing, NPCA's Eileen Woodford testified, "NPCA found the public planning process to be exceptional. The Park staff was willing to listen to a wide range of opinions and ideas."[35] Allowing others to design buildings was how the Cyclorama building was built in 1961. To the Park Service, surrendering their responsibility to lead the planning process was unacceptable. But the underlying tension was the price the NPS paid for previous poor decisions. Regardless of past Park Service mistakes, though, Congress mandated the Park Service, and the Park Service mandated its superintendent, to manage the Park. This did not mean that he was not interested in, did not listen to, or was not attentive to public input. He did, and he was. But originating and managing Park initiatives was the NPS's responsibility.

To initiate the public portion of the planning process for the 1996 DCP, Latschar's October 17 letter to neighbors of the Park, preservation groups, the Civil War community, and the general public formally began the "scoping" process that preceded the new DCP.[36] He outlined a set of planning assumptions that made it clear he was moving forward. He asked for public input regarding four planning questions. The Park Service, working with the GNMP Advisory Commission and the Pennsylvania Historical and Museum Commission, drafted the questions.[37] Several alternative answers were provided to each question. At the bottom of each question there was provision for suggesting other alternatives that the Park Service should consider. Latschar promised that the NPS would carefully consider all comments they

---

34 Oversight (Hansen) hearing on Gettysburg National Military Park General Management Plan and Proposed Visitor Center before the Subcommittee on National Parks and Public Lands of the House Committee on Resources, Feb. 11, 1999, 5.

35 Ibid. 21. Woodford was Northeast Regional Director for the National Parks Conservation Association.

36 Latschar to "Friend", written on United States Department of the Interior letterhead with enclosure, Oct. 17, 1995.

37 Commissioners are appointed to the Gettysburg National Military Park Advisory Commission by the Secretary of the Interior and include members of the governing bodies of the community, preservationists and representatives of the Park Service. Congress established the Commission in 1990 as part of the boundary legislation to institutionalize relations between the Park and the surrounding community. Meetings are held on a regular basis at locations and in such a manner as to ensure adequate public involvement.

received and make the necessary revisions. There was a one-month review period and then a single public meeting, after which the NPS would
move forward with the next phase. He said, "The final objectives and
criteria will be incorporated into a revised DCP to guide the search for
the most appropriate partner[s] for development of a museum or other
visitor facilities for the GNMP, whether on or off NPS land." The last
phrase was critical.

During 1995 the NPS's pursuit of the Monahan proposal forced its hand
on a new GMP to reorient the iconic Park, and Galvin finally sent it in the
right direction. Congressional funding for the GMP was not yet in hand,
but the wheels were turning. The road to the new vision of the GNMP was
temporarily blocked too, because there was still no money for that either and
there was no plan to raise it. But the core of the best idea, Monahan's public/
private partnership, lived on in the new DCP, and it was far from dead. Staff
morale was high. The drive to inventory the Park's natural and cultural resources, which was the legal and moral documentation of what is significant
at GNMP, was proceeding. The year 1995 was a good one, a strong start for
the new superintendent, but there were many challenges ahead.

As the new year began, concentrated planning work on the DCP was
the order of the day. Ordinarily it would be a period of intense, quiet staff
work. But this was Gettysburg. Instead, the staff planners were interrupt-
ed time and again by relentless and vociferous local opposition to the Park
Service. Occasionally it became personal. One staffer reported being refused
service at a local grocery store because she worked for the NPS. Beyond that,
there were a multiplicity of factors, some personal and some economic, that
represented a variety of interests, but they all shared a mutual dislike and
distrust of the Park Service. Many of the Park's opponents simply longed for
the status quo. Those folks showed little or no interest in understanding the
NPS's point of view or in helping the Park Service deal with their obvious
problems; in some instances they denied that they even existed.[38] There
were other critics, however, who read the Park Service plans as they became
public and reacted constructively. Latschar said that those critics had a decided positive impact on the result.

The planning process, in high gear in 1995, moved into higher gear after
the 1995 DCP was laid aside. The planning team devoted late 1995 and

---

38 Hansen hearing. Written statement of George J. Lower, Gettysburg citizen, re the NPS
collection – "No relic in storage is undergoing undue deterioration." 64.

the first part of 1996 to the preparation and review of a second, more comprehensive, DCP that was released in April 1996 and shared similarities,
both in style and substance, with the 1995 plan. Both had multiple alternatives that included a "do nothing" option. Both provided a new Museum
and both made provisions for moving the Cyclorama building, restoring the
Cyclorama painting, and rehabilitating Ziegler's Grove.

The differences, however, between the two documents, the second twice
as long as the first, were breathtaking. The 1996 DCP was a wide-ranging
statement of Park Service intentions for all facilities at Gettysburg.[39] The
earlier DCP responded to Monahan's single, limited proposal, and accomplished only two of the NPS's four objectives: restoration of both Ziegler's
Grove and the painting. It did nothing to improve either the Visitor Center
or the facilities to store the collection. The preferred alternative in the 1996
DCP, estimated by the planning team to cost $43 million to build, created
one comprehensive facility to satisfy all of the Park's major needs: a new
Visitor Center, a Civil War Museum, a collections storage facility, a restored
Cyclorama painting, administrative offices, and the removal of both the
Cyclorama building and the interim Visitor Center from Ziegler's Grove.
There was no IMAX theater. And there was no site specified for the complex. The *Fantasyland* site selected in the 1995 DCP became a limiting factor
then because it was inside the Park. This time the Park Service was intent
on doing away with limitations. With the simple statement, "We will need
partners," the 1996 DCP introduced an unprecedented, original process for
an NPS-sponsored, proactive, nationwide search for a partner, consistent
with Galvin's testimony before the Thomas Subcommittee that was almost
two years into the future.[40] The Park Service had decided to issue a Request
for Proposals (RFP), a widely used process that had been used before by the
NPS to select vendors, but never before to select a partner.

Prior to drafting the 1996 DCP, it was the sheer range of the Park's needs
that bedeviled the Park Service. There were simply too many. They needed
a new Visitor Center and ample parking to support it. They had wanted an
interpretive museum to tell a comprehensive story of the Civil War since
at least 1989, when it was authorized by Congress but never funded. The
enormous collection was deteriorating and badly needed better care. The

---

39 Draft Development Concept Plan Environmental Assessment; Collections Storage,
Visitor & Museum Facilities, April, 1996.

40 Ibid. 9.

Cyclorama building was a problem. The Park Service built it and they had to remove it. The Cyclorama painting needed a total restoration that would be complex and expensive. Most of all, they needed a single place to put it all. There was no suitable site available, and there was no approved process to find one. There were two approved development zones within the Park, one at *Fantasyland* on which the original Monahan facility was proposed, and the other where the interim Visitor Center and Cyclorama building stood. Both sites were inadequate, unsuitable for the new complex. Site selection, therefore, even before the size or configuration of the new facility could be determined, became a top priority, second only to finding the right partner.

Taken together it was a veritable Rubik's cube. Any move to solve one problem affected all the others. To address them one by one and have them emerge as a coherent, interpretive whole would be nearly impossible and would take years to accomplish if it could ever be accomplished. The individual projects needed to be addressed holistically, not individually. The driving force behind the 1996 DCP to combine all the Park Service's needs into one plan, rather than to address individual, piecemeal proposals, was what the Park needed. Critics, nevertheless, worried about commercialism imperiling the historic integrity of the Park; at least one critic called the process "absurd," and many area residents were skeptical.[41]

---

41 "Park Services Unveils $43 Million Controversial Plan," *The Patriot-News*, April 11, 1996; "$43 Million Project Has 90-day Deadline," *The Evening Sun,* April 19, 1996.

CHAPTER 3

Threading a Needle

The 1996 DCP, wordy and repetitious, was, without an index, nearly impenetrable. It described a multifaceted process that was both elegant and risky. At its core the plan was a cry for help—an ambitious building program that wrapped the Park's many needs into a single package and then called for an unknown partner to pay for it. It reflected Latschar's consistent, public message: "We're broke, we're not living up to our responsibilities to the American people, it's not going to change, and someone has to help us." It was elegantly bathed in the rich history of the Park. It was wrapped in an elaborate public process by which the Park promised nothing and gave very few particulars, save for its four primary objectives that were explicit: to protect the collection; to preserve the painting, which nobody opposed; to provide high-quality interpretation and education opportunities for visitors; and to rehabilitate Ziegler's Grove. To the NPS, high-quality interpretation meant facilities that would enable visitors to understand the Gettysburg Campaign in the broad context of the Civil War and American history. The rehabilitation of Ziegler's Grove meant that two intrusive buildings—the Cyclorama building (old Visitor Center) and the interim Visitor Center (old Rosensteel home)—needed to go. Both structures occupied land where on July 3, 1863, troops moved and Union soldiers fought and died.[1] Opposition to improving interpretation and education facilities, to preserving the collection, and to moving the Cyclorama building were primarily a reaction to NPS plans to move the high-traffic facilities, the Visitor Center, and the Cyclorama building away from the business district. Architects' opposition to removing the Cyclorama building hadn't yet surfaced. The scope of the DCP went well beyond the norm for a DCP. Latschar realized that, and he knew that a fresh GMP, into which the new DCP would fit nicely, was on the way, but he didn't know when, and he wouldn't wait for it. So to keep the process moving, he pursued the mammoth 1996 DCP that included an innovative and groundbreaking partner selection process.

---

1   Draft Development Concept Plan, April 1996, 8.

The DCP gave little guidance as to what type of partner the NPS was seeking, where the new complex would be built, how funds would be raised, or even how ongoing operations would be financed. These features of the plan were left open, to be determined by the proposers and the selection process. The partner selection criteria weren't particularly helpful either. The DCP was a document of belief, one way or the other. The way it was written, open, almost without limitations, with a minimum of specifics, virtually guaranteed that it would be attacked for its presumed evasiveness. Critics believed the NPS was being deceitful and that there was a secret, undisclosed plan that had already been decided.[2] For those who would never give the Park Service the benefit of the doubt, it was fresh ammunition. For those who hoped the Visitor Center would never move, it was a declaration of war. For those who were afraid that the Park would be overly commercialized, it was an open invitation to wonder how any partner could recoup his investment without intrusive commercialism in the Park—one of the few points that the critics agreed on.

But for those who believed in what the NPS was trying to accomplish after years of futility and frustration, who believed in the significance of the Gettysburg story, who believed that the Battlefield should be preserved as it was in 1863, it was a breath of fresh air. And those were the sort of people the Park Service would search for through an RFP, and they only needed one.[3] But the chances of threading that needle were close to nil. The Park Service, in an absolute sense, was risking nothing, but in a larger sense, it was risking everything. Failure to find a partner was sufficiently disastrous to the Park's already tarnished reputation as to be unthinkable. Hope is not a plan, but hope was what they had—hope for an iconic American place that was in trouble.

The timing of the new DCP's release was hardly propitious. Ottenstein's enormous observation tower hovered over the Battlefield, historians and preservationists smarted over the frustrating outcome of the "cut," Park Service rifles were just cooling down from the controversial winter harvesting of 503 white-tailed deer, and some commuters were still annoyed that the Park forced them to change their daily routine. The headline in

---

2 "$43 Million Project Has 90-Day Deadline," *The Evening Sun*, April 19, 1996; "Latschar Copes With Critics' Charges," *Civil War News*, Sept. 1999.

3 "RFP" is a Request for Proposals, a widely used process for seeking vendors, but never before used by the NPS to seek a partner.

the *Sunday Patriot-News* read, "U. S. Plan for Bigger Museum Stirs Fear – Loss of Land, Possible Profit Motive at Issue." One man said, "It's going to Las Vegas-ize Gettysburg. It's going to turn Gettysburg into a little patch of green surrounded by neon." And yet the DCP wouldn't even be issued until the following day.[4]

On April 10, Latschar unveiled the 1996 DCP at a public meeting in the Cyclorama building auditorium. There was tension in the air. Latschar was always challenged at public meetings, and he always responded when he was challenged. Neither side ever pulled a punch. Several citizens asked if the NPS considered the damage that removing the Visitor Center and Cyclorama would do to Steinwehr Avenue businesses. Latschar dismissed the question, saying that it was pointless to talk about economic impact without knowing where the new facility would be located. He admitted that in the short term, some businesses might be set back, but that others would benefit, and that over the long term, the effect on the entire community would be positive.[5] Opponents said he was stalling. Other critics feared that commercialism would imperil the historic integrity of the Battlefield.[6] A Cumberland Township official said that the Township would lose revenue if the Visitor Center moved.[7] Latschar's terse answer was that while the Township might wish the decision to be based on its interests alone, "It won't be."[8]

According to the DCP, the selection process would move quickly. The plan was released in early April, and the period for public review ended on May 24. If required, changes would be made to the draft document. Then, if a decision to proceed was made by the NPS, the RFP would be finalized. The plan said that once the RFP was released, the solicitation period, the period wherein interested partners prepare and submit proposals, would be open for at least forty-five days. Then, it was anticipated that a selection would be made within sixty days after qualified proposals were received.[9] One could easily imagine the project breaking ground by year-end. A local businessman

---

4 "U.S. Plan for Bigger Museum Stirs Fear — Loss of Land, Possible Profit Motive at Issue," *Sunday Patriot-News*, April 7, 1996.

5 "$43 Million Project Has 90-Day Deadline," *The Evening Sun*, April 19, 1996.

6 "Park Service Unveils $43 Million Controversial Plan," *The Patriot-News*, April 11, 1996.

7 The interim Visitor Center was located in Cumberland Township as is the new Museum and Visitor Center.

8 "NPS Looking For 'Partners' To Build New Complex," *The Evening Sun*, April 11, 1996.

9 Draft Development Concept Plan/Environmental Assessment, April 1996, 46-47.

called the timetable "absurd." Latschar, whistling past the graveyard, dismissed him, saying that he'd seen major proposals put together in the private sector in less than ninety days.[10]

The *Evening Sun* took Latschar's comment out of context and turned it into a headline that said, "$43 Million Project Has 90-Day Deadline." In fact, there was a deadline for volunteers to submit proposals that dated from the first release of the RFP, but there was no other deadline. On May 24, at the end of the mandated DCP review period, the Park Service would consider the comments they received from the public for as long as they felt was necessary. They needed Department of the Interior approval before they issued the RFP, and that would also take time. The RFP was, in fact, issued on December 11, 1996, approximately 210 days after *The Evening Sun*'s headline. The date set for receipt of proposals was April 11, 1997, 120 days after the RFP was issued, and it was extended to May 16 at the request of two of the proposers, roughly one year after the "90-day" headline appeared.[11] Overreaction and sensationalism generally characterized the local newspapers' coverage of the project.

In the midst of the hubbub, there was one piece of good news. In May, the Pennsylvania State Historic Preservation Officer joined the NPS in its previously announced opinion that the Cyclorama building had no historic significance, was not eligible for inclusion in the National Register of Historic Places, and could be taken down.[12] The only obstacle standing in the way of the rehabilitation of Ziegler's Grove seemed to have been removed. While future events proved this not to be true, even this miscalculation may have ultimately benefited the Park Service. If the brouhaha around the removal of the Cyclorama building that would later occur between 1998 and 2013 had begun in 1996, it, and other protests, might have derailed Latschar's plans.

The 1996 Battle of Gettysburg that began in 1995 with the release of the first DCP was unlike other contemporary Civil War battles that pitted real estate developers against Battlefield preservationists. One of those was a Disney theme park that was proposed to be built near the Manassas Battlefield in Virginia. There were those who tried to use the backlash against

10 "$43 Million Project Has 90-Day Deadline," *The Evening Sun*, April 19, 1996.

11 Request for Proposals, Visitor Center and Museum Facilities, Gettysburg National Military Park, Dec. 11, 1996, "…your proposal…must be received… on April 11, 1997…" 27; Adlerstein to Director Stanton, Oct. 13, 1997, "Six proposals were received…as of the closing date of May 16, 1997." 2; ""Deadline Extended for Visitor Center Proposals," *The Evening Sun*, April 8, 1997.

12 Draft Development Concept Plan, April 1996, 84.

Disney at Manassas against the NPS at Gettysburg.[13] But the Gettysburg battle was between the NPS, led by John Latschar, who was trying to rehabilitate GNMP but lacked the funds to do it, and a local community that opposed the changes that would occur if the rehabilitation went ahead. The loudest critics either opposed any Park Service partnership with a commercial entity, or they opposed moving the Visitor Center and the Cyclorama building to another location. Walter Powell, President of the Gettysburg Battlefield Preservation Association (GBPA), was among the former. Powell believed that land preservation was more important than building facilities, that Congress should be the sole funder of the NPS, and that any NPS partnership with a for-profit partner would ultimately degrade the Park. To buttress his arguments, he used documents he obtained through the Freedom of Information Act (FOIA).[14] Powell's arguments seemed to rest on the Park's past history of mistakes, misjudgments, and insensitivity to preservation values, particularly the "cut." Most of it was true, but it shed very little light on the 1996 DCP. In order to prevail, the GBPA would have to develop a focused argument and a realistic alternative plan.

Eric Uberman, owner of the wax museum that was within a stone's throw of the interim Visitor Center, was a leader of those who hoped the Visitor Center and the Cyclorama building would remain where they were. He had good reason. Relocation of those facilities would reduce pedestrian traffic in the immediate area and fewer customers would visit his store. He rejected the Monahan proposal in 1995, in part because he thought that Monahan was trying to take advantage of an opportunity for himself at his (Uberman's) expense and the expense of others; the Park Service was the enabler, and that was wrong. That view carried the day in 1995. But in 1996, like Powell, Uberman appeared to offer no alternative plan to achieve the Park's objectives. It seemed that he was interested in stopping the Visitor Center and the Cyclorama building from being moved anywhere.

Before the 1996 DCP was made public, *Civil War News* printed a letter from

---

13 *Disney's America* was a planned theme park that was to have been built by The Walt Disney Company near Manassas Virginia. The *New York Times*, said, "The Walt Disney Company abandoned the most irresponsible idea ever hatched in the Magic Kingdom and decided not to build a theme park near the Manassas Battlefield in Prince William County, Virginia." "Disney Retreats at Bull Run," *New York Times*, Sept. 30, 1994. Retrieved from http://www.nytimes.com/1994/09/30/opinion/disney-retreats-at-bull-run.html

14 "Need For Public/Private Venture at Issue," *The Evening Sun*, July 22, 1997; Walter Powell interview, June 20, 2014.

Uberman wherein he fabricated an elaborate forecast based on his assumptions that the new complex would over-rely on commercial development.[15] He said the complex would fail, and that NPS facilities would be stranded in an industrial park or other site distant from the Park, surrounded by a derelict amusement park. Downtown Gettysburg, Steinwehr Avenue, and Baltimore Street businesses would be devastated because traffic would be funneled to the remote NPS site and then dispersed from there to various Battlefield sites.[16]

With the considerable benefit of hindsight, Uberman's forecast was not believable: first, that the NPS could find such a site as he described; and second, convince critics in Washington and Gettysburg to build the new complex on it. Latschar responded in the next issue.[17] He pointed out what he considered to be errors in Uberman's letter, and he closed with the following: "I assure you that we will all hold the resources of the Gettysburg National Military Park in the highest regard and would never want to see those resources harmed in any way. We will use our best judgment during this entire process and will make the selection public as soon as it is proper and legal to do so." His continual reassurances found a generally sympathetic public audience, especially, but not exclusively, away from Gettysburg.

Whereas Powell's and Uberman's interests had little in common with one another, or with Monahan, or with animal rights activists, or others who had their own reasons for distrusting the Park Service and opposing the GMP, their views were legitimate. What seemed unusual were the lengths to which some of the critics were willing to go to get their way. Their letters to Congress, their frequent use of the Freedom of Information Act, and their hounding of NPS employees were excessive.[18] Nevertheless, had the critics been unified around a single alternative plan that contributed to solving NPS problems without disturbing the community, they would have fared better.

Latschar, however, was not always a sympathetic figure. Arrogant, confrontational, and "one tough SOB" were how some townies described him.[19] But Gerald Bennett, who became chairman of the Congressionally mandated

---

15 "fabricated" as in "constructed" or "built.'

16 "Gettysburg Businessman Decries Park Plan," *Civil War News*, Feb. – March, 1997.

17 "NPS Gettysburg Answers Critic," *Civil War News*, April 1997.

18 The *Washington Post* reported that Uberman was among those who peppered the office of Senator Rick Santorum with complaints. "The Second Battle Of Gettysburg," *Washington Post Magazine*, Dec. 29, 1996, 21.

19 Ibid.

GNMP Advisory Commission (GNMPAC), said, "...what Latschar's critics perceive as arrogance is not. John is honest and he tries to do what's best... "[20] Said Jim Boyd, editor of *Railfan & Railroad Magazine*, who gives Latschar credit for putting Steamtown on the right track, "As Norman Schwarzkopf said, 'When they make you boss, take command.'" Boyd added, "John does that pretty well, and he's willing to take the flak."[21] Latschar, in addition to a history of Park ineptitude, a sad lack of federal funding, and personal attacks, was contending with his own combativeness as he tried to right a ship, the *Military Park*, that was dead in the water when he arrived.

Confusion, too, enveloped the 1996 process. If Latschar were uncertain, he'd be accused of being evasive. He really couldn't know "if" or "how" his plan might work. His knowledge of the process was certain, but with unknown partners and unknown proposals, he had little or no idea about the complex that would be built, especially the "related facilities": restaurants, an IMAX theater, or retail stores that were not tied directly to the Park's four objectives.[22] His uncertainty was compounded by his critics, who wouldn't believe him, and local newspapers that often avoided their responsibility to help their readers understand complexity. The newspapers seemed to report what was easiest and what they pleased. *The Evening Sun's* "90-day deadline" was an example of what led to misunderstandings. Still, through the confusion, Latschar believed that a majority of citizens supported Park Service plans for Gettysburg. He said, "We had critics. But the majority of the critics were thoughtful, and they had good suggestions. By and large the public was with us."[23]

The May 24 deadline for public review of the DCP came and went, and the planning team turned to writing an RFP that Department of the Interior lawyers would approve. It was a major undertaking to present a totally new idea to the Interior Department's Solicitor's Office. The hope was that they would develop a document (an RFP) that would be consistent with NPS policy, avoid misunderstandings, and ensure that it wouldn't be tripped up by

---

20 "Latschar's Mission," *York Sunday News*, March 23, 1997.

21 "The Second Battle of Gettysburg," *Washington Post Magazine*, Dec 29, 1996, 21.

22 The complex to be built consisted of "Museum and Visitor Center" facilities and "Related Facilities," which were to be "fitting and appropriate to the mission and education purposes of the Park. While the NPS could have allowed no related facilities, as a practical matter, if appropriate to the NPS mission, they were needed and would enhance the visitor experience. Critics feared that related facilities would be used as a wedge that would lead to large inappropriate commercial entities, i.e., "commercialism". Request for Proposals, 8.

23 Latschar interview, Nov. 20, 2013.

an arcane illegality after it was issued. It was released on December 11, 1996, and those patriotic Americans who wanted to partner with the National Park Service went to work on their plans.

The RFP turned out to be a refined version of the DCP. For example, if the DCP was confusing about site selection, the RFP clarified it.[24] The RFP explicitly required proposers to "recommend" a building site. Descriptive passages devoted to "related facilities" left the door wide open for doubters who feared commercialization of the Battlefield. But the door was left open for philanthropy too. And while there was no mention of it in the RFP, the NPS decided that an evaluation panel (panel) would examine the proposals, select the best one, and send its recommendation to the Director of the Park Service for his approval. Latschar was determined to be part of any group that played a pivotal role in the future of "his" Park. The chairman of the panel, Michael Adlerstein, Assistant Regional Director of the Northeast Region, thought otherwise. Adlerstein told Latschar, "Whatever decision we make will be controversial. After we make it, I'm going home. But you're going to have to live with it, so you need to be able to live with a clean conscience—in other words, not be in the room when the selection is made."[25] Latschar acquiesced, and the panel did its work without him.

Proposals were to be "RECEIVED no later than April 11, 1997." The RFP stated clearly, "Late proposals will not be accepted."[26] Nevertheless, the panel granted extensions to two proposers who requested them. Two of the losing proposers, experienced real estate developers, strained credulity when they protested the extensions. For the Park Service to forgo credible proposals, regardless of what they had said and what they had intended, to enforce a self-imposed deadline would be irrational. Had they not granted the extensions, they would have been even more roundly and justifiably criticized.

On March 29, six weeks prior to the extended deadline, Director Roger

---

24   The DCP said, "depending on their proposal, potential partners may elect to choose a site for their proposal… Other potential partners may elect to suggest a site at a later date, or, in the event of a proposal for 100% donation of funds, may leave the choice of site up to NPS." Draft Development Concept Plan/Environmental Assessment, April 1996, 47. The RFP listed "site recommendation and description" as one of six items requested as part of a proposal. Request for Proposals, Visitor Center and Museum Facilities, Gettysburg National Military Park, 3. A five-page section of the RFP was devoted to "Finding an Appropriate Site."

25   Latschar interview, Nov. 20, 2013.

26   Request for Proposals, 25.

Kennedy, a strong supporter of Latschar and the RFP, retired from the Park Service.[27] Kennedy's comfort with partnerships, RFPs and Latschar, his vision, his credibility with Congress, and his instinctive understanding of the circumstances at Gettysburg provided a steady hand at the wheel. Kennedy's retirement would be devastating to Latschar's plans.

In spite of Park Service efforts to reach the broadest possible cross-section of proposers, all proposals came from real estate developers for what was, after all, a real estate project. Thus the NPS's already slim chances of finding an appropriate partner were reduced considerably. It also appeared that Park Service restrictions limited the project's profit potential for a private partner. Opponents assumed the Park Service would ultimately loosen or back away from its restrictions—open the floodgates—to get the project done. But another possibility was a philanthropic partner who would eschew profits for the sake of Battlefield preservation and good history. The Park Service provided for such a philanthropic partner, but at the same time it emphasized its willingness "to consider proposals from all possible sources."[28] As long as they left the door open to even limited commercial development, doubters feared the worst.

By its flexibility, the RFP created a catch twenty-two. While the NPS didn't know exactly what it wanted, it had a very good idea of what it didn't want. The infinitely flexible RFP encouraged as many different ideas from as many respondents as possible. To those who trusted and respected the Park Service, it was a reasonable approach. To those who distrusted Latschar, the Park Service, or even big government in general, it seemed deceptive. Those critics believed that the Park Service was hiding its true intentions. While greater specificity might have reduced suspicion, it might also have limited the number of respondents and creative ideas. The RFP listed the project's four specific objectives: protecting the collection, restoring the painting, high-quality interpretation and education for visitors, and rehabilitating Ziegler's Grove. And they required that a specific site for the project be "recommended," but beyond that, the Park Service simply asked proposers to respond with their best ideas.

Adlerstein's five-member evaluation panel received six proposals by the

---

27 NPS, "Director Roger G. Kennedy;" retrieved from https://www.nps.gov/articles/director-roger-kennedy.htm

28 Request for Proposals, 1.

May deadline.[29] The panel reviewed the proposals, prepared a short list of follow-up, clarifying questions for each candidate, and met again in July. They disqualified two of the six proposals, both submitted by qualified organizations, because they didn't provide sufficient information under the terms of the RFP. In September the panel met in Philadelphia and interviewed the principals and team members of the remaining four organizations. The estimated cost of building each of the four proposed facilities that the NPS had determined was $43 million, was between $41 and $45 million.[30]

As the evaluation panel sifted through the four proposals, the Park Service was hard at work on the new GMP for the Park. It was authorized in February 1997, eighteen months after the August 1995 Sandy Hook meeting where Galvin had told his associates that they needed a new GMP for Gettysburg. To simplify matters, the enormous 1996 DCP and the RFP were folded into the GMP, thereby streamlining the process and creating one unified planning document. But by embedding the RFP within the GMP, it may also have raised suspicions that the NPS had already identified its new partner. In July, in a now familiar format that featured a do-nothing alternative and several others, there was a public planning session to reveal and explore the various alternatives the Park Service was considering in the GMP. It was far more comprehensive than the DCPs that preceded it. Whereas the DCPs analyzed facilities, much of the GMP was devoted to Battlefield rehabilitation. Latschar emphasized that the ideas he presented were conceptual and for discussion purposes only. Nevertheless, they were as stunning as the 1996 DCP had been when that was unveiled. The most robust alternative involved returning the Battlefield as closely as possible to its 1863 condition by removing parking areas and trees, and bringing back historic lanes. That option also required restoration of orchards, fence lines, and any documented structures that were present during the conflict.[31] To those who loved and respected history and the Battlefield, and hoped to see the Battlefield's integrity reclaimed, the plan was compelling.

---

29 Other panel members included: Chuck Baerlin, Superintendent, Sandy Hook Unit, Gateway National Recreation Area; Cal Cooper, Chief of Project Management, Denver Service Center; Steve Crabtree, Assistant Regional Director, Western Region; and Rich Rambur, Superintendent, Lowell National Historical Park. Deborah Darden was one of two advisors to the panel.

30 Memorandum To: Director, National Park Service, From: Michael Adlerstein, Associate Regional Director, Chairman, Evaluation panel for Gettysburg Visitor Center and Museum Proposals, Oct. 13, 1997, 2.

31 "Battlefield May Return to Its 1863 Appearance," *The Evening Sun*, Aug. 22, 1997.

By mid-summer 1997 the panel's four surviving proposals were those from Kinsley Equities, Inc. of Seven Valleys, Pennsylvania (near York); LeMoyne, LLC of Lutherville, Maryland; the McGorrisk Group of Dallas, Texas; and the Monahan Group of Gettysburg.[32] It was hardly an overwhelming number, but they provided the panel with a variety of options. There were three separate sites, different configurations of facilities, different potential income streams, and different methods of financing the project.

Kinsley proposed an excellent site that had seen no battle action, was within walking distance of the Battlefield, and was hidden from the Battlefield behind a rise in the land.[33] The Kinsley complex would be financed through a combination of debt and donations. The related facilities in the Kinsley proposal seemed to provide a more than ample opportunity for commercialization, and that may have troubled members of the panel. The LeMoyne proposal suggested a seven-acre site that was home to Ottenstein's controversial tower. The Group appeared to rely on its hope that the panel would see the removal of the tower as an added benefit that would distinguish their proposal from the others. But it was not a plus that Ziegler's Grove, one of the NPS's four primary objectives listed in the RFP, would never be rehabilitated, and that collections storage would be located elsewhere in the Park. The project would be financed through commercial loans. The McGorrisk Group proposed the same site as Kinsley did. Their proposal was similar to Kinsley's in many respects, with the exception of an innovative use of tax-exempt bonds to fund one hundred percent of construction. Importantly, there was almost no commerce in the related facilities. The bonds would be backed by admission and parking fees. There would be a Museum bookstore at the complex and other coordinated retail activities at various other sites around Gettysburg. Monahan proposed siting all the facilities the NPS needed at the spacious Gateway Center, amidst whatever other development he planned. Gateway was more than three miles from the nucleus of Park visitation through the town center, albeit only about a mile from the nearest Park boundary. All of the funds required for construction would be donated. None of it was easy to untangle, and the panel had work to do.

From the beginning, there was nothing in the RFP's selection process that could be quantified. The panel sought the "best" proposal by filtering "best" through ten equally subjective evaluation criteria, and reasonable

---

32 Adlerstein to Director Stanton, Oct. 13, 1997, 2.

33 "Kinsley Outlines Vision For Park Complex," *Gettysburg Times*, Nov. 8, 1997.

people were bound to disagree as to which proposal was best. The Park Service needed flexibility in the selection process. They were wary of locking themselves into an unfortunate partnership, so the "selected" partner was to be selected not to build the facilities, but only "for negotiation."[34] That left the NPS an out in case negotiations failed. If the Park Service was unhappy with a selected proposer, they could terminate negotiations and move to another proposer.

One obvious fundamental attribute of the "best" proposal was the "best" partner. Webster's defines "partner" as "one who shares." The proposers may not have understood this, and it's unlikely that they would if they were captivated by their own proposals. The local newspapers by their reporting confirmed that they had only the dimmest idea of the meaning of the word "partner." *The Evening Sun* used quotation marks around it for effect, or, as the *Chicago Manual of Style* would say, "the use of quotation marks to suggest irony." The newspaper said that the NPS has decided with whom to "buddy-up" to build the facilities.[35] The stories appeared to discount the idea of a true partnership. But the NPS had created a thoughtful, careful, and deliberate selection process that bore no relationship to a dollar bid to win a project. When the selection was made, Adlerstein telephoned Latschar, not to tell him that they'd selected the best proposal, which they believed they had, but to tell him, "John, We have your man!"

The selection process that began on May 10, 1997, wrapped up in September following the Philadelphia interviews. On October 13, Chairman Adlerstein directed a letter to new Park Service Director and NPS veteran Robert G. Stanton notifying Stanton of the panel's recommendation. If Stanton agreed with the panel's work, he would sign on the dotted line and announce his decision.[36] But opponents of the NPS were making a furious goal-line stand, sending Congress, the Interior Department, and new Park Service Director Stanton angry letters, sowing the seeds of fear and apprehension. And they were as determined as ever not to lose.[37]

Two weeks before Adlerstein's letter to Stanton, a California Congressman, George Miller, the senior Democratic member of the House

---

34 Request for Proposals, 26.

35 "York Developer Has Winning Bid on Park Museum," *The Evening Sun*, Oct. 15, 1997; "NPS Awaits Signature on Bottom Line," *The Evening Sun*, Oct. 19, 1997.

36 Director, National Park Service, from Adlerstein, Oct. 13, 1997.

37 Galvin telephone interview, May 12, 2014.

Committee on Resources, wrote to Secretary of the Interior Babbitt. Miller opined that the $43 million Visitor Center would open the floodgates for unwanted commercial enterprises at Gettysburg. He promised to oppose any project that would diminish the integrity of the Gettysburg Battlefield.[38] Miller's authority seemed unclear because at the time there were no federal funds involved in the project. But Rick Healey, legislative counsel for Miller's committee, said that if the Park Service wanted to build something outside of the Park boundary, they would need Congressional approval. Healey was one of several staffers who, years before, had watched Steamtown emerge from outside his committee's jurisdiction.[39]

Responding to Healey's comments, Galvin was quoted in *USA Today* to the effect that he was aware that there was skepticism in Congress about the Gettysburg plan, and that the NPS was going to have to prove that the project would be done with the dignity that befits Gettysburg. Galvin insisted that the development must be "tasteful." He also pointed (Healy) to a 1935 law that allowed the Park Service to build the complex outside the Park. But at the same time he said he planned to brief Miller. In a typically conciliatory tone, with a distinctive nod to Congressional authority that he would always have to deal with on other matters, he said, "Certainly if we don't satisfy Congressman Miller and other members of the committee… they can block it."[40]

The evaluation panel had worked for five months without any hint of a security breach. Yet on October 15, two days after Adlerstein's letter reached Stanton's Park Service office, the panel's work was prematurely thrust into the open. Unknown to anyone at Gettysburg, *USA Today* reporter Edward Pound had been working the Gettysburg story, and he obviously had good sources within the NPS. Pound wrote that the NPS had selected a plan submitted by Kinsley Equities and Kinsley Construction Company of the York, Pennsylvania, area.[41] His article contained details about Kinsley's proposal that could only have come from someone who had seen it, notably that "Kinsley would be allowed to construct profit-making commercial facilities," and that the complex "would be built by Kinsley on a site within the

38 "Battlefield Project — California Congressman Voices Doubts About Visitor Center Complex," *Gettysburg Times*, Sept. 30, 1997.

39 Ibid.

40 "Park Service Alert to Skepticism about Gettysburg Center," *USA Today*, Sept. 30, 1997; Galvin telephone interview, May 12, 2014.

41 "Developer Selected for Gettysburg Center," *USA Today*, Oct. 15, 1997.

Park." To its credit, the newspaper also reported that "the Park Service will begin negotiations with the developer on a final plan, and if they can't reach an agreement, the plan would be scrapped."

The NPS, without denying Pound's story, denied that a decision had been made. Monahan, with the 1995 debacle and the negatives that were raised at that time regarding a site within the Park probably in his mind, said he was "shocked that they would select a site within the Park boundaries."[42] After all, he'd invested considerable sums in his recommended site because, based on his first-hand experience, he seemed sure that a site within the Park wouldn't be selected. In succeeding days, local newspapers had a field day. *The Evening Sun* said that "NPS chose… Kinsley to act as their 'partner' …."[43] Monahan, defending his site, said, "Preservationists and historians will demand a facility outside the Park."[44] Yet Walter Powell, surprisingly, said that the site chosen by Kinsley "might not be so bad after all."[45] Harper, of the McGorrisk Group, said, "We planned no commercial development," the implication being that Kinsley did, and for that reason he, Harper, should have been chosen.[46] When a spokesperson for the LeMoyne Group failed to protest, simply congratulating the winner, Kinsley was the only one of the four eligible proposers who had not been heard from.

As days passed and there was no announcement from the Park Service, attention turned to the leak and how it occurred. The agency continued denying that a decision had been made. Stanton was reportedly briefed by Adlerstein, with twelve to fifteen members of Stanton's staff, a large group for a highly confidential matter. He was reported to be holding his decision until after he met with Congressman Miller.[47] Latschar went to Washington to expedite the decision but he got nowhere.[48] As the days dragged on, unsubstantiated stories multiplied. *USA Today* reported that the NPS was rethinking its plan. The newspaper said that top Park Service officials were

---

42 Ibid.

43 "York Developer has Winning Bid on Park Museum," *The Evening Sun*, Oct. 15, 1997.

44 "NPS Announcement — To Be or Not To Be?" *The Evening Sun*, Oct. 28, 1997.

45 "York Developer has Winning Bid on Park Museum," *The Evening Sun*, Oct. 15, 1997.

46 Ibid.

47 "NPS Awaits Signature on 'Bottom Line,'" *The Evening Sun*, Oct. 19, 1997; "Gettysburg Center Battle Continues," *York Sunday News*, Oct. 19, 1997.

48 "Park Service Chief Heads To Washington To Try To Untangle Visitor Center Imbroglio," *Gettysburg, Times*, Oct. 20, 1997.

considering backing away from the plan because there was widespread opposition in the Civil War community and questions from members of Congress. An open letter to 3,000 Civil War buffs from Jerry Russell, head of the Civil War Round Table Associates, described Latschar's plan as "a rape of the Battlefield."[49] The stories fed the critics' hopes to defeat the plan.

Stanton let Latschar and Kinsley twist in the wind for nearly a month. Opponents of the plan, which now included two losing proposers, Harper and Monahan, each with their own agendas, railed against a plan about which they knew very little. One is left with the impression that Stanton, new to his job, was in over his head. The more experienced Kennedy would have signed the panel's recommendation at once, thereby denying Park Service opponents a multi-week opportunity to build public sentiment against it. Supporters were obliged to remain silent as they awaited Stanton's decision.

On November 7, 1997, twenty-five days after Adlerstein's letter, Stanton approved the panel's recommendation. When Kinsley originally announced his plan, he referred to Gettysburg as "an opportunity [for him] to give back because we have been so fortunate." He added, "This is a gift to the country."[50] Answering Kinsley's expression of philanthropy and patriotism, *The Evening Sun* pronounced "Kinsley offers 'gift' to America," with *gift* in quotes and reported that he was "handed" the "plum" contract by the NPS. In fact, he had been given an opportunity to negotiate with the NPS, and there was no contract. There wouldn't be one for more than two-and-a-half years.

Don Troiani, one of the country's premier Civil War artists and collectors said, "It's war. I'm against it. If we can stop Disney World, the Park Service shouldn't be much of a problem." Russell again urged his membership to bring pressure to bear on Congress. Harper said he planned to file a formal protest with the Park Service and the Department of the Interior over the bidding process. If he was quoted accurately, it was an indication that he too mistook what was a partner selection process for a "bidding" process. There was no bidding. "This is not over," Harper said. Kinsley was about to encounter new challenges that surprised and disappointed him and that would test his mettle. But the NPS's new vision for Gettysburg was one step closer to reality.[51]

---

49 "Gettysburg Plan Gets A Second Look – Foes' Counter Attack Puts Pressure on Park Service," *USA Today*, Oct. 28, 1997.

50 "York's Kinsley Gets Plum Contract," *The York Dispatch*, Nov. 7, 1997.

51 "Kinsley Offers 'Gift' to America," *The Evening Sun*, Nov. 7, 1997; Kinsley Offers 'gift' to America," *The Evening Sun*, Nov. 7, 1997.

Meanwhile, Senator Santorum submitted a letter to the Senate Appropriations Subcommittee requesting full funding for the National Park Service for 1998. Of Gettysburg, Santorum wrote, "I have visited the Park on many occasions, always reminded of both its beauty and its rich history. Each visit, though, brings with it painful notice of our nation's failure to live up to its obligations with respect to Gettysburg." Continuing, he wrote, "Proper maintenance is essential to protect the many monuments and cultural and historical artifacts from irreparable damage, and to prevent an irretrievable loss for future generations."[52] In early July he attended a small Battlefield ceremony to celebrate the Friends' donation to the Park Service of a 135-acre easement on East Cavalry Field. Santorum loved the Park. He was invited there whenever possible and always kept apprised of Park Service issues. In mid-July, the Park received word that the Senate Appropriations Subcommittee, due to Santorum's initiative, and helped along considerably by Committee Chairman Slade Gorton of Washington, included a "base operating increase" for Gettysburg of $1,052,000, the exact amount of Park Service estimates of what it would cost to restore the Park's artifacts, cannon carriages, buildings, and monuments.[53] The hidden significance of a base operating increase is that it's absorbed into the annual budget. It becomes part of the base on which future budget increases are calculated so it effectively remains in place and continues to grow year after year. This was Santorum's first on-the-record assistance to the Gettysburg National Military Park, and it was a shot in the arm, improving the Park's appearance and its long- term financial outlook, as well as boosting morale. He would do much more.

52 "Santorum Asks For More Park Funds," *Gettysburg Times*, June 18, 1997. The new budget funds, while unusual, were part of the normal appropriations process and as such were not part of the Museum and Visitor Center project.

53 "Santorum Successful in Battle for Gettysburg Funds," *Sunday Patriot-News*, July 20, 1997.

CHAPTER 4

The Needle Threaded

One month before Adlerstein's letter to Stanton, on October 10, 1997, Bob Kinsley was on his horse in the Colorado Rockies surveying the majestic landscape around him when he heard his cell phone. It was Dan Driver, his chief financial officer, calling from York. Driver told Kinsley that the Park Service was on the line. Kinsley said, "Put 'em through." A Park Service representative wanted to tell Kinsley that there had been a "leak." The word was out, through *USA Today* reporter Ed Pound, that the NPS had selected Kinsley's proposal and would Kinsley please not speak to anybody about it. Kinsley told him not to worry, that he was away in the mountains. After the brief conversation, Kinsley called Driver and asked him to look into hiring public relations counsel. His life was about to change.

Bob Kinsley is a true American success story.[1] He was born in Philadelphia. His family moved to York when he was five. Kinsley was the middle child of five, with two older sisters, and two younger. His mother, Molly, an artist, arrived in New York from London in 1929 with her mother and her sister, and gravitated to Wrightsville, Pennsylvania, just east of York. Kinsley's father, also Robert, attended Penn and then sold hardware for a New York distributor. Kinsley remembers handing out literature at trade shows to help his father. After several years of marriage, Bob and Molly Kinsley managed to buy a small farm south of York. But the elder Kinsley was a troubled man, and he and Kinsley's mother were divorced after Kinsley graduated from high school.

After her divorce, Molly Kinsley hung onto their farm, and that's where she raised her children. She's a transcendent figure in Bob Kinsley's life. Kinsley has two indelible childhood memories that directly connect him to Gettysburg. The first is his mother's advice to "stick to it until it's finished." That attitude would define him although it would be tested by events at Gettysburg. Kinsley also remembers school and Boy Scout visits

---

1   From an in-person interview with Kinsley in his office on Nov. 21, 2013 and many other conversations; an in-person interview with Anne Kinsley at the Kinsley offices on Feb. 17, 2014; an in-person interview with Rob Kinsley at his office on May 21, 2014; and "Kinsley's Charge," *York Daily Record*, Dec. 4, 1998.

to Gettysburg, playing on the Battlefield, climbing over the rocks at Devil's Den, and once riding a horse on a trail ride over the Battlefield. Bob Kinsley did well in school in history and geography; he learned the meaning of Gettysburg long ago when he was a little boy, and he carried it with him for the rest of his life.

Money was tight in the Kinsley household, and Kinsley began earning his way at an early age, picking produce and doing other farm chores for a local farmer. After high school graduation in 1958, he operated excavation equipment for a small contractor. The following summer he bought a truck and a tractor and started a lawn grading and seeding business that ultimately grew into Kinsley Construction, Inc., and he attended classes at York Junior College. He met Anne Whelan in 1959 at a friend's wedding, and two years later, in January 1961, he and Anne were married. Kinsley then transferred to the local Penn State campus to continue his formal education in business, but he stopped going to class when he had to choose between school and the financial responsibilities of a growing family. He added concrete construction to the trades he offered and re-lettered his trucks to read "Robert A. Kinsley – Contractor." Needing more space for both business and family, Kinsley returned to his roots by acquiring the thirteen-acre farm where he was raised.

By 1980, Kinsley-company revenues passed $8 million from next to nothing fewer than twenty years before. Today revenues exceed $1 billion, and his companies employ about 2,600 people. They own and operate six construction companies; three steel fabrications plants; a materials division that supplies York County with transit mix concrete, and aggregate and asphalt paving materials; and they have real estate holdings in Pennsylvania, Maryland, New Jersey, and West Virginia. It's among the largest enterprises in Pennsylvania, a testament to the will and enterprise of Bob Kinsley. He and Anne also have five sons, all of whom play important roles in the company business. Kinsley is a founding member of the Farm and National Lands Trust of York County, and he's placed his now 1,750-acre farm under a conservation easement. He and Anne are well known for their generosity to local charities.

Personally, Kinsley is private, competitive, tenacious, ethical, understated, unpretentious, and more. But when you boil it down, you're left with hard work and honesty. He's not as much of a "planner" as he is a "doer." He says his management style is "walking around," but those who've tried to stay with him know that it's hard to keep up. At five feet seven inches, it's not his long stride that accounts for his fast pace. One of Kinsley's sons says that his father "allows you to learn from your mistakes, but he doesn't allow you to make them over and over." Kinsley good-humoredly credits Anne with "raising the kids and I raised the business." It's a good line, but Anne worked in the business for years, and it's hard to imagine Kinsley not involved with his sons. Bob and Anne Kinsley do things together.

Kinsley says that history was one of his favorite subjects in school; he's an amateur historian. And he also considers himself both a builder and an environmentalist. So when the NPS's opponents began publicly castigating him in 1997 for profiteering at Gettysburg's expense, the German philosopher Goethe's observation comes to mind: "No one would talk much in society if he knew how often he misunderstands others."[2]

Kinsley's new relationship with Gettysburg developed almost accidentally and in stages.[3] Recollections are hazy, but it seems that he first met John Latschar in the summer of 1996, between the release of the 1996 DCP and the release of the RFP. A friend of Kinsley's asked him to visit the Cumberland Township offices. The Township collected $77,000 annually from an admission tax on the interim Gettysburg Visitor Center. Town officials wanted to talk with an independent real estate developer about ways to keep the Visitor Center within the Township. Kinsley says Latschar was there, but Latschar doesn't remember the meeting. Kinsley was "sniffing out" a potential construction job. He recalls that Latschar and a few of the town supervisors talked about the project, "but of course I knew nothing about it and [at that time] had little interest in it."[4]

That fall Monahan asked Kinsley if he'd be interested in joining his investment group to answer the soon-to-be-released RFP. Kinsley knew Monahan through a variety of business activities. He remembers having a breakfast meeting with Monahan to talk about the Gettysburg project and whether or not Kinsley would like to participate. Kinsley recalls thinking that Monahan's proposal would locate the Museum and Visitor Center too far away from the Battlefield, in a mall-type venue that he believed was less than ideal for teaching Battlefield history to children. He decided to pass.

---

2   *Elective Affinities*, by Johann Wolfgang von Goethe, translated by James Anthony Froude, (1808) bk. 1, Ch. 4.

3   Latschar interview, Nov. 20, 2013; Anne Kinsley interview, Feb. 17, 2014; Bob Kinsley interview, Nov. 21, 2013; Monahan interview, May 20, 2014.

4   Kinsley interview, Nov. 21, 2013.

But whether he realized it or not, Kinsley was slowly being drawn toward the Gettysburg vortex. He was a well-known, successful real estate developer with an abiding interest in Gettysburg history. His reputation in Gettysburg was as the developer who had converted the Hotel Gettysburg from a burned out, vacant shell of a building to a showpiece attraction that added to the tax rolls.[5] He was seen in the Cumberland Township offices with Latschar; he was seen at breakfast with Monahan; and those who saw him had to have wondered why he was there. And like a honey pot attracts bees, Kinsley began to receive telephone calls. And day after day he was learning about the 1995 DCP, the 1996 DCP, the forthcoming RFP, and Latschar's plans to rehabilitate the Battlefield to its 1863 appearance, which he thought "was about the neatest thing I ever saw."[6] As he mulled it over, he finally realized that there was going to be an important NPS project built in Gettysburg whether he was part of it or not. And he cared about Gettysburg. It was part of him, and it had been with him all of his life.

After his breakfast meeting with Monahan, Kinsley fielded another call from an acquaintance who invited him to dinner and tried to interest him in land he had for sale on Route 15 that he thought would be ideal for a new Museum and Visitor Center. Obviously, word of Kinsley's interest was out. Driving home from dinner that night, he called Anne and told her that he thought the Gettysburg project was interesting and that maybe they should look at it more closely. He was hooked. Years later he would tell audiences that Anne said he was crazy and that they were not doing this. After she heard him say it more than once, she asked him to stop. She didn't say it and she didn't think it.[7]

In the autumn of 1996, it was still unclear to Kinsley whether the Gettysburg project could be a moneymaker. But if the profit potential was unclear, it was crystal clear to him, as he recalled his boyhood explorations of the Battlefield that he didn't want his grandchildren to learn the history of the Battlefield, away from the Battlefield, in a shopping mall at the corner of Route 30 and Route 15, or at any other mall on Route 15. He made up his mind then that if he truly believed in what he thought, he should submit a plan of his own. His mind must have been swimming in the enormity of what he was considering. In the world of real estate development, it may not

---

5 "Palatable Plan," *The Evening Sun*, July 23, 1998.

6 Kinsley interview, Nov. 21, 2013.

7 Anne Kinsley interview Feb. 17, 2014.

be good etiquette for Kinsley to compete for a project against another developer who had previously offered him the opportunity to participate in the project. If, on the other hand, the project is philanthropic, not economic, and there is no profit at stake, the only competition is for how and where to teach history to children; more alternatives are better and conventional business niceties are beside the point.

Another of the several bees buzzing around the Kinsley honey pot was an architect named Greg Powell, who alerted Kinsley to the imminent release of the RFP. Powell and an associate, John Adams, a grant writer, pursued a business relationship with Kinsley.[8] While not openly soliciting an assignment, they appear to have hoped to do sufficient work on Kinsley's proposal that Kinsley would want to retain them. Kinsley, for his part, not knowing where the proposal would lead, accepted their help, but he didn't ask for it, and he made no promises. There are only obligations if there are profits. Kinsley donated his time and fortune to Gettysburg, and he hoped that others were doing the same.

Kinsley's response to the RFP was cobbled together by Greg Powell with input from Driver and others from December 1996, when the RFP was released, through the first months of 1997. Driver worked on it just as he worked on other conventional real estate proposals, estimating likely expenses, revenues, and investment returns. Kinsley recalls, though, that it wasn't long before he realized that it had to be a not-for-profit. He called it "kitchen table economics." "I kind of looked at it—how do you amortize $40 million? There aren't enough visitors paying the two dollars and seventy-five cents that they were paying."[9]

As Powell and Driver prepared the proposal, Kinsley concentrated on finding the right site for his proposed complex. His first inclination was that the Museum and Visitor Center belonged within the town of Gettysburg, along with the railroad station, where Lincoln arrived and departed on November 18 and 19, 1863, and the Wills House, where Lincoln slept the night he arrived. His first thought was Tom Metz, owner of Gettysburg Tours, which operated Battlefield bus tours; Metz, who also owned land in Gettysburg, actively followed Latschar's plans for the Park. Kinsley met with

---

8   Bob Kinsley interview, Nov. 21, 2013; Dan Driver in-person interview at his office on Feb. 7, 2014; Adams to Kinsley letter, July 17, 2001; Kinsley to Adams letter, Aug. 13, 2001.

9   The Park Service charged $2.75 to view the electric map and $2.75 to view the Cyclorama painting.

Metz, some of whose land bordered the railroad, to see if Metz would be willing to sell it. Without hesitating, Metz told Kinsley that he'd be willing to sell Kinsley his land, but it wasn't located where a new Museum and Visitor Center should be built. He offered to take Kinsley for a ride, as Kinsley recalls, to a forty-seven-acre site owned by the LeVan family, long-time Gettysburg residents. Kinsley said, "Metz had given the site a lot of thought. He'd been in the tour business for a long time. He knew that Gettysburg was not the right place for a large Park Service Museum and Visitor Center. He knew a lot about history and Battlefield action. The land he showed me bordered on the Battlefield, and it was a pretty clean piece of ground."[10] Kinsley agreed with Metz's assessment of the land, so Metz made an appointment for them both to meet with David LeVan, Chairman of Conrail, in Philadelphia.[11]

LeVan listened to Kinsley, and then suggested Kinsley speak with his mother, Mildred, whose home was on land that bordered the land being discussed. Kinsley thought Mrs. LeVan was delightful, and she reminded him of his own mother.[12] They had a cordial conversation, and as Kinsley was leaving, Mrs. LeVan asked if she would be able to see the Museum and Visitor Center from her kitchen window. Kinsley said she would. She recalled how much her late husband loved the land and after Kinsley left her, he wasn't sure he still wanted to buy it. But he reported the conversation to David LeVan, who asked if Kinsley would give him some time to talk with his mother and other members of his family. A week later, LeVan called Kinsley and told him that it was time for the family to sell. But he wouldn't set a price for his land.

Bob and Anne Kinsley spent weekend hours touring the Battlefield, as work on the proposal continued. They were with or without guides, and they evaluated the Visitor Center and bookstore, observed the sales staff, listened to comments, and watched visitors move in and out of the Visitor Center, toward Gettysburg or the Battlefield. They took the pulse and learned the logistics of the Battlefield, and they did some of the due diligence that a sizable investment required. Kinsley recalls meeting with Latschar "several times [while they were] putting their proposal together. But" he says, "you have to be careful... He has to be careful in answering my questions. With a government RFP, once you ask questions, they become public, so that information has to be

---

10　Details of the Metz meeting are drawn from the Kinsley interview, Nov. 21, 2013.

11　Ibid.

12　Information regarding David LeVan in this section is drawn from a telephone interview with LeVan on Jan. 5, 2016; Kinsley interview, Nov. 21, 2013.

disseminated to all of the people who are answering the RFP." Each proposer needed to have the same information that every other proposer had.[13]

By mid-April 1997 the proposal was coming together, but Kinsley was increasingly apprehensive, not only about how to acquire LeVan's land, but about how to raise the $30 million or so that he thought he'd need to build the complex. He was well known in York, Pennsylvania, but not outside of York. He was concerned that if he were selected to partner with the NPS, the funds he'd need would mean that he'd have to lead a national fundraising campaign. He thought he'd need a nationally recognized partner to help lead the campaign and for that he contacted National Geographic's Destination Cinema, Inc. They were receptive, but only if the complex included an IMAX theater, so Kinsley agreed to it. He also invited Metz to join his team because he liked him, he knew Gettysburg, and Metz could be helpful.

Kinsley's pursuit of the LeVan parcel was difficult because LeVan steadfastly refused to set a price on his land. But unknown to Kinsley, the LeVan family had decided before Kinsley met with David LeVan to try to sell their forty-seven-acre parcel to the winning proposer. For LeVan, that meant that the more proposers who recommended his site, the greater the probability that his site would be sold. LeVan had given the McGorrisk Group permission to use his land in their proposal, and he said he tried unsuccessfully to persuade Monahan to use it. In retrospect, the purpose of Kinsley's visit to LeVan's mother was not to get her approval, as Kinsley believed, to sell; but to get her approval to sell to Kinsley. According to LeVan, Kinsley "passed the mom test," and so two of the final four bidders, Kinsley and McGorrisk Group, recommended the LeVan parcel in their proposals.[14]

According to Kinsley, he insisted that he needed to know the price for the land. But LeVan deferred, and instead told Kinsley to name the price. Kinsley had bought and sold land in the York area for years. So he said that he made an offer to LeVan. LeVan, again according to Kinsley, said that Kinsley's price "sounded about right," and he asked Kinsley to send him a confirmation letter that Kinsley expected LeVan would sign, although he never did. For his part, LeVan says he has no recollection of price discussions with Kinsley, although he does remember telling Kinsley that he could use the LeVan land in his response to the RFP. Kinsley remembers that he missed the Park Service deadline for submitting his proposal because he waited too

---

13 Kinsley interview, Nov. 21, 2013.
14 LeVan interview, Jan. 5, 2016.

long for LeVan to sign and return the letter to him. When the letter didn't appear, Kinsley asked the Park Service for an extension, which they granted even though they were criticized for doing so. But it was LeVan's verbal authorization to use his land in Kinsley's proposal that satisfied the "agreement" that was specified in the RFP.[15]

Kinsley, as principal of Kinsley Equities and Kinsley Construction Company, submitted his final proposal in May. At the last minute, Powell included an architectural drawing with the proposal that Kinsley disliked. To him it was modern, sleek, and pretentious, not right for Gettysburg. But it was too late to change it, so he reluctantly included it with the rest of the proposal. His team consisted of National Geographic Television; Destination Cinema, Inc., a unit of National Geographic; Gettysburg Tours, Metz's company; and John L. Adams and Company, grant writers. Kinsley's proposal accomplished each of the NPS' four objectives and he recommended an excellent site for the new complex.

On June 6, 1997, the evaluation panel, after reviewing each of the proposals they received, in order to clarify the proposals, asked each proposer eight questions relating primarily to finances and site specifications. One question about donations to the project elicited Kinsley's first mention of what would become the Gettysburg National Battlefield Museum Foundation. He said he would create "a new not-for-profit 501 (c) (3) corporation that will hold a key position in the development process."[16] He answered each of the panel's questions by June 30 and then heard nothing from the NPS for nearly two months. The panel used the time to evaluate the proposals, and it may have made inquiries into the business reputations, character, and personalities of each of their prospective partners—routine business practice for anyone looking for a partner. Kinsley, hearing nothing from the panel, assumed that he was out of contention, but at the end of August the panel invited Kinsley and the other three proposers, to the Belvedere Hotel in Philadelphia for a September interview. He was accompanied by Tom Metz, Greg Powell, the architect, and Dan Driver, his CFO.

---

15   The RFP, under "Site Recommendations," says, "All proposals must include a specific recommended site for the Complex so that adequacy of the site and site control may be assessed as part of the evaluation process." Further, under "Site Control" it says the site must be NPS-owned or subject to an agreement or contract that insures the sites availability and compatibility with Park purposes and visitor services. There is no requirement for a written contract or agreement.

16   Kinsley to evaluation panel members, June 30, 1997.

The interview was vintage Kinsley. One of the oldest tricks in a salesman's book is to assume the sale; begin working with a client as if you've already won the business. Figuratively, Kinsley moved to the Park Service's side of the table and began working the problem. When he entered the room he took off his jacket, rolled up his sleeves, and directed his attention, not toward his proposal, but toward what the NPS wanted to achieve. The Kinsley team was there to work. He apologized to the panel for the architectural drawing that he didn't like, and told them he would change it. Darden recalls, "His integrity came across. You could believe in him and you could believe that he was going to do what he said."[17] In his June response to the panel's questions, he'd said, "We believe that you will find our team extremely flexible and easy to work with," and he set out to prove it that day in Philadelphia.[18] When a panel member, in an attempt to gauge the importance of profit to Kinsley, asked how much he would pay for the opportunity to be selected, Kinsley bristled. Regardless of his proposal, it was a labor of love for him and "if they wanted Disney, they would have to look elsewhere."[19] It was a virtuoso performance, and the panel was smitten. His proposal achieved the NPS's four objectives: protect the collection; preserve the painting; offer high-quality interpretation and education to visitors; and rehabilitate Ziegler's Grove. And Kinsley had selected a site for the Museum and Visitor Center that seemed perfect. He convinced the panel that far from being mesmerized by his own proposal, he was happy to work with the NPS toward achieving their goals. As a result, Kinsley was the partner they wanted. The Kinsley interview was the first of four for the panel that day, but his performance preempted his competitors, and they wouldn't recover. Entering the meeting, the panel was unsure, and probably divided, as to their preferential partner.[20] At the end of Kinsley's presentation, the panel was unanimous that he was the one. As Adlerstein told Latschar later in the day, "John, we have your man!"[21]

Adlerstein's October 13 letter to Stanton described the results of the panel's deliberations and its recommendation. "Other proposals were as good

17 Darden interview, May 9, 2014.

18 Kinsley to the evaluation panel members, June 30, 1997.

19 Kinsley interview, Nov. 21, 2013.

20 Recounting of the Philadelphia interview was drawn from the Darden interview, May 9, 2014; Driver interview, Feb. 27, 2014; and Kinsley interview, Nov. 21, 2013.

21 Latschar interview, Feb. 17, 2014. The quotation is Latschar's recollection of Adlerstein's remark.

as the Kinsley proposal in certain respects. Overall, however, the evaluation panel believes the Kinsley proposal provides the best opportunity for the Gettysburg National Military Park to achieve its principal objective of cooperative development and management of a new Museum and Visitor Center for the benefit of the Park and its visitors."[22] He went on, "However, the evaluation panel points out that neither the Kinsley proposal nor any of the others fully achieve all of what NPS would like to achieve under the terms of the RFP. Although we consider it the best proposal received, there are several aspects of the Kinsley proposal as it now stands that would need to be negotiated in order to achieve an acceptable co-operative agreement."[23] In other words, the Kinsley proposal was not acceptable as it stood. There was an IMAX theater and too many retail stores. But the panel was searching for the best partner—"one who shares"—and that was Kinsley.

For his part, Kinsley knew what was in his proposal. He knew that the economics of a conventional real estate deal were not there, and that he and Anne, if selected, would start a charitable foundation to receive his gifts and those of others. It would become his largest philanthropy. The commercial outlets he planned for the complex were upscale, tasteful, and consistent with the NPS mission; his profit would go to the Foundation, not to him. He told the press, "There are no motels, no convention centers, no strip malls."[24] Adlerstein wrote Stanton that "in general, the limited facilities suggested [by Kinsley] would appear to be acceptable under the terms of the RFP," a careful approval, yet well short of a ringing endorsement.[25]

Kinsley's motivation to answer the RFP originated with his desire to see Gettysburg history taught appropriately to children. But several citizens of Gettysburg, spurred on by the local newspapers, refused to believe it. To those folks, Kinsley was a rich, remote, self-interested developer. They believed that he saw the RFP as an opportunity to make money out of building the Museum and Visitor Center, and in spite of his assertions and actions to the contrary, they would not be moved. Kinsley surely failed to anticipate the intense public opposition to his proposal he encountered. But he didn't have time to worry about it. Instead, he had to figure out how he was going to raise $30 million.

---

22 To: Director, National Park Service, From: Michael Adlerstein, Oct. 13, 1997, 8.

23 Ibid.

24 "Kinsley Offers 'Gift' to America," *The Evening Sun*, Nov. 7, 1997.

25 Adlerstein to Director Stanton, Oct. 13, 1997.

On November 7, 1997, the day that Stanton, in Washington, announced Kinsley's selection, the spotlight was on Kinsley in Gettysburg. He was clearly out of his comfort zone, standing in the Gettysburg Hotel ballroom crowded with reporters, flanked by easels with NPS maps and other material, and staring at a battery of microphones. Kinsley was an awkward public speaker. His forte was one-on-one or small groups, where he had already demonstrated extraordinary proficiency to the evaluation panel. In front of an audience, he read from a draft of his remarks that was printed in large bold type. His syntax could be disjointed and his speech halting. But on this day, his self-consciousness at the podium served him well. Anyone hearing Kinsley for the first time would know instinctively, and immediately, that he was no promoter. He looked to be just what he was—an honest, small-town, self-made man who could be believed.

Latschar recalled the event. [26] He had been forbidden to talk to Kinsley before Stanton's written approval, so, as he recalled it, the first time they spoke was a half-hour or so before the public press conference. Latschar's part of the conference was to get the facts straight. Kinsley's part was to introduce himself. There was hope and fear in Kinsley's first performance. Although he was not an impressive public speaker, in his emotions he was. He stood there and bared his soul. He said that the Museum and Visitor Center was going to be his gift to America, and that made Latschar feel good. Kinsley said, "We expect to make very little money… It is a labor of love, an opportunity to give back because we have been so fortunate." He added, "There are no motels, no convention center, no strip malls. This is a gift to the country." [27]

The *Gettysburg Times* reported that Kinsley vowed to take no profit from the venture. But when he was asked about the profit for his construction companies, he hedged on specifics that only reflected his inexperience in the public arena. He said, "I guess what I'll have to say to you is that in our *pro forma* at this point, there are no developers' fees. The only profit is the normal overhead and profit that a contractor would have on a job. But I would speculate that because of my enthusiasm for this project my heart may get ahead of my head," [28] In other words, at that point there may have been a normal construction profit in the *pro forma*, but he was speculating that he would probably end up waiving it.

---

26 Latschar interview, Nov. 20, 2013.

27 "Kinsley Offers 'Gift' to America," *The Evening Sun*, Nov. 7, 1997.

28 "Kinsley Outlines Vision for Park Complex," *Gettysburg Times*, Nov. 8, 1997.

Newspaper headlines included, "It's war," and "Kinsley offers 'gift' to America," the ironic notation of what they seemed to assume was a Kinsley deception.[29] The newspaper reminded its readers that the Friends were still undecided about the plan. It pointed out that Congressman Miller had voiced reservations, and that Monahan and Harper were crying foul because of an extension in the deadline for submissions. It claimed that Kinsley didn't have a signed agreement to buy the proposed site, which the RFP did not require him to have and which Harper did not have.[30] After the article reported that Kinsley "has vowed to take no profit from the venture," the paper, in a nasty aside, wrote "one developer who asked not to be named, said contractors often include the cost of airplanes, personal cars, country club fees, and other entertainment in construction estimates."[31] All in all it was a cynical reaction to a well-intentioned Kinsley proposal.

A few newspapers brought a more constructive perspective to the story. The York Daily Record, while acknowledging threats to the Battlefield, wrote, "While those interested in maintaining the legacy of Gettysburg have just cause for vigilance, they should find comfort in knowing the project is in the command of someone who respects Gettysburg and what it means to the national character."[32] And from historic Boston, The Boston Globe reviewed the NPS's uneven record at Gettysburg and concluded, nevertheless, "Civil War enthusiasts should hold their fire until the design is unveiled late next year."[33]

But as time passed, the critics showed no signs of letting up. At a public meeting, Walter Powell of the GBPA asked Kinsley, "How do you expect to excite anyone to donate money when you are profiting off the project?" in spite of Kinsley's assertions to the contrary.[34] Dick Peterson of Gettysburg, in a letter to the editor, railed against "giving up part of our greatest national treasure to private enterprise," even though the Park Service was doing no such thing.[35] Powell added, "It's like building a McDonald's in the middle

29 "York's Kinsley Gets Plum Contract," York Dispatch, Nov. 7, 1997.

30 E-mail Remington to LeVan and LeVan to Remington, April 17, 2017.

31 "Kinsley Outlines Vision for Park Complex," Gettysburg Times, Nov. 8, 1997.

32 "Kinsley has Power to Add or Detract," York Daily Record, Nov. 13, 1997.

33 "The Future at Gettysburg," The Boston Globe, Nov. 17, 1997.

34 "Public Gets First Shots at Battlefield Proposal," The Evening Sun, Nov. 26, 1997.

35 "Don't Hand Treasures to Free Enterprise," Gettysburg Times, Nov. 26, 1997.

of a cemetery," which it wasn't.[36] Two Congressional staffers complained that Director Stanton had not briefed them and that the NPS process was deceptive.[37] Another matter that attracted their attention was Kinsley's insistence that personal financial information that he had shared with the evaluation panel with the understanding that it not be disclosed, in fact, should not be disclosed.

Randy Harper, a principal of the McGorrisk Group, and Monahan lodged formal protests against the NPS's decision. Harper objected to Kinsley's lack of "full control" of his proposed site, notwithstanding the fact that he (Harper) had no more control of his site than Kinsley did. He objected to the extension the NPS granted to the submission date of Kinsley's proposal and misrepresentations of his own proposal.[38]

Both protests seem misguided. It was clearly in the NPS's best interest to grant an extension to any eligible and qualified proposer, and it would have been foolhardy to deny it. The deadline notwithstanding, the NPS needed as many potential partners as possible. To refuse to allow a qualified potential partner to participate because their proposals arrived late would have worked against the NPS's interests. In fact, in a November 17, 1997, letter to Stanton protesting the NPS's decision to select Kinsley, Monahan's attorneys do not appear to have mentioned it.[39]

Monahan had every reason to be disappointed as his proposal was, no doubt, excellent. But his criticism of the Kinsley site failed to pass a "common sense" test. Kinsley's site was well within the "Area of Consideration" as defined in the RFP on page 12. The RFP cautioned proposers, as Monahan noted, that sites within the Park were unlikely to be desirable, but it also added on page 2 that "Sites both inside and outside the Park's boundary will be considered…" The other proposers understood that. Kinsley, McGorrisk, and LeMoyne all recommended sites within the Park. And the distinct advantage of the Kinsley site does not appear to have been a secret. LeVan promoted it. Metz knew it and he told Kinsley. Latschar probably knew it. Harper knew it

---

36 "Gettysburg Goes Commercial; History at What Price?" Lynchburg, Virginia *News & Advance*, Dec. 14, 1997.

37 Todd Hull and P. Daniel Smith. "Politics & Legal Threats Warm-Up NPS Meeting," *The Evening Sun*, Dec. 18, 1997.

38 "Contender Files Protest, Asks Independent Review," *Civil War News*, Dec. 1997.

39 Scott Heimberg/Patrick J. Christmas of Akin, Gump representing Monahan to Stanton, Nov. 17, 1997.

and he proposed it. But irrespective of Monahan's criticism of the Kinsley site, and in spite of his enthusiasm and passion for his own site, he seemed to be almost alone in thinking that his site was a good one. The consensus was that the new Museum and Visitor Center didn't belong there: it was too far away and it might be overshadowed by other commercial development at Gateway.

Harper's proposal was also surely excellent and contained all the positive features that he said it did, especially the same excellent site that Kinsley proposed; and they proposed no related facilities and no commercialism, on their site. He complained though that Kinsley said he had "full control" of his site when, according to LeVan, Harper and Kinsley both had LeVan's permission to use his land in their proposal, no more and no less, and that was what the Park Service required. Monahan could have used the site too. LeVan encouraged him to use it. Harper also said that the panel omitted from NPS evaluation documents that his proposal had no commercial component. But Adlerstein's October 13, 1997, letter to Stanton said of the McGorrisk proposal, "It proposes no 'related facilities' on-site. The panel considers it strong with respect to the RFP's goal II, compatible related facilities."[40]

So of the four final proposals, why was Kinsley's chosen? On the surface, it appears that the LeMoyne proposal fell short because, by its site selection, it foreclosed the possibility of rehabilitating Ziegler's Grove. Monahan's proposal probably failed because his site, several miles distant from the High Water Mark, the first day's Battle, and Little Round Top, was limited in its potential for high-quality interpretation and education. The two remaining proposers, Kinsley and McGorrisk, made proposals that achieved the NPS's four objectives: protection of the collection; restoration of the painting; high-quality interpretation and education for visitors; and rehabilitation of Ziegler's Grove. Each was on the same site as the other, and each proposal had its drawbacks. How could the panel choose?

From the beginning, the NPS was determined to find a real partner. The RFP listed ten evaluation criteria ranging from 1) "Consistency with the NPS goals" to 10) "Financial benefits to the NPS." Four was stated simply "Site." Five, interestingly, was "Organizational and management approach …, the degree to which the co-operators management approach will assist in achieving the NPS's goals." Kinsley should have scored well on each of these, particularly the latter, his management approach. The RFP stated further:

---

40   To: Director, National Park Service, From: Michael Adlerstein, Oct. 13, 1997, 6.

The Evaluation Criteria will be used to assess the quality of proposals. They may be utilized by NPS by means of numerical weighting and scoring or by means of a narrative assessment of each proposal under the Evaluation Criteria. Under either method, the objective is to select the best overall proposal determined upon application of the Evaluation Criteria.[41]

Stated another way, the RFP said that the panel may rank each proposal by some weighted scoring method or, alternatively, they may just talk about it: "a narrative assessment." Either way was acceptable. This was the subjective selection process that the NPS wanted, needed, and described in the RFP. It was the same sort of process that every contractor or developer goes through whenever they compete for business. Unless it's a low bid, no one ever really knows just why they won or lost. The RFP described a step-by-step process that was built on a broad platform of useful and relevant considerations. It provided the panel with more then enough flexibility to select whomever they wanted. It protected them from having to select a partner they didn't want because of a self-imposed metric. In comparing McGorrisk to Kinsley, for example, perhaps the panel knew Kinsley by reputation, or were bowled over by his presentation. Maybe they believed that Kinsley would be more amenable to modifying his proposal than would McGorrisk. Perhaps the panel saw virtue in Kinsley's living in the local Congressman's district, rather than in Dallas. Or maybe they liked him. It may never be known exactly why the five members of the panel unanimously chose Kinsley over all the others. But there were no dissenters. It wasn't a close call. They followed the process that they said they would follow, and with hindsight their judgment was inspired.

As a result of the protests and the hullabaloo that followed Kinsley's selection, and Harper's, Monahan's, and Uberman's efforts to stop the project, on February 8, 1998, the Senate Subcommittee, chaired by Senator Craig Thomas, scheduled an oversight hearing for February 24. The hearing was apparently requested by Senator Dale Bumpers of Arkansas, the ranking Democrat on the Committee, who may have been moved by complaining letters that he received from Gettysburg. Bumpers had been in the Senate for twenty years. It was reported that he was especially concerned with the details of the Park concession contracts, but there were no contracts at the

---

41   Request for Proposals, Visitor Center and Museum Facilities, Gettysburg National Military Park, 24.

time. It was also reported that Bumpers simply wanted a better understanding of how it was all working.[42] Monahan seemed to have had higher hopes for the hearing. The *Gettysburg Times* said that he expected the public would hear a lot of details that have not been presented by Park Service officials at public discussions about the Kinsley proposal.[43]

Thomas led off the hearing by recounting the history of poor NPS decisions at Gettysburg.[44] He honed in on the NPS planning process and the numbers of calls and complaints that his subcommittee had received that involved accusations of unethical activity. At the same time he said that his staff had found no unethical activity at Gettysburg. Thomas welcomed the senior NPS spokesman, Denis Galvin, to the witness stand, and Galvin summarized the history of the Gettysburg project as recounted in the Introduction to this volume. Thomas questioned Galvin about the mechanics of the Kinsley proposition. Galvin told Thomas that they were in negotiations. Thomas asked if there was a contractual agreement with Kinsley, and Galvin said there wasn't. "You do not have anything with Kinsley?" asked Thomas, an indication that he may not have been briefed.[45] He then yielded the floor to Bumpers, who directed his questions toward how Kinsley was possibly going to make money from the project. When Galvin told him (Bumpers) he didn't intend to, Bumpers allowed that Kinsley was "a good Samaritan indeed," to which Galvin quite seriously responded, "We believe he is, actually."[46]

Santorum followed Galvin to the stand. He outlined the need for new facilities at Gettysburg, and he strongly endorsed the Park Service. Said he, with appropriate political correctness, "with proper oversight from this committee," we are trying to dramatically improve the circumstances at Gettysburg.[47] The Park Service believed in Latschar and Kinsley. Santorum

---

42 "Congress Wants to Hear the Gettysburg Battle Call," *York Sunday News*, Feb. 8, 1998.

43 "Monahan to Push for Congressional Hearings on Visitor Center," *Gettysburg Times*, Feb. 10, 1998.

44 Testimony in the succeeding three pages is drawn from the transcript of the (Thomas) hearing before the Subcommittee on National Parks, Historic Preservation, and Recreation of the U.S. Senate Committee on Energy and Natural Resources to discuss the issues relating to the Visitor Center and Museum facilities project at the Gettysburg National Military Park, Feb. 24, 1998.

45 Thomas hearing, Feb. 24, 1998, 11.

46 Ibid. 15.

47 Ibid. 20.

believed in Latschar and Kinsley. But Thomas and Bumpers were skeptical. They doubted Kinsley's capacity to raise the necessary funds to complete the enormous project, and they were afraid that the government would be left holding the bag. After the hearing, Bumpers asked Secretary Babbitt to "stop the process until we have answers," but Babbitt had no reason to stop the process.[48] With no contract in place and no federal money promised, it was risky political business without very good reason, for a senator or a congressman to step in the way of a program that the Park Service wanted and that appeared to have broad national support, notwithstanding the critics in Gettysburg.

Two additional aspects of the testimony before the Thomas Subcommittee are noteworthy. First, Galvin, who often appeared before Congress, and rarely came close to revealing his own feelings in his testimony, or worse, showing annoyance at a line of questioning from an elected official, nevertheless did so with Bumpers. This was the same Galvin who had once warned Latschar to "remember, no matter how stupid the questions are, they're members of Congress, and they have the right to ask stupid questions. So don't let on by your face, your posture, your demeanor, or your answer, how stupid you think their questions are."[49]

In this instance, it wasn't a matter of stupidity, but respect. Bumpers told Galvin, "You realize that one of the most vigorous arguments against doing this is the commercialization of the Park?"

Galvin replied, "I realize that." Something in Galvin's answer betrayed his feelings, betrayed his annoyance. Bumpers, alert, said, "Does that bother you?"

Galvin answered, "We spend a lot of time in the NPS worrying about the control of commercialization in parks. I've been in the design and construction business in parks for fifteen or twenty years, and for the most part I'd line up the good taste, good architecture, and good landscape architecture in Parks against any landscape in this country. I don't think we intend to do anything to denigrate that reputation at Gettysburg." In light of the NPS's poor track record at Gettysburg, its doubters and critics refused to take their expertise seriously. Yet, there was mounting evidence that Galvin's confidence in the NPS was justified.[50]

---

48 Ibid. 8.

49 Galvin quotation from Latschar interview, Nov. 20, 2013. When asked to confirm the quotation, Galvin responded that he certainly might have said it.

50 Thomas hearing. Feb. 24, 1998, 16.

Another witness, Ralph W. Tarr, Counsel to McGorrisk Group, in detailed testimony, described his frustration with the NPS, which revealed his misunderstanding of the evaluation process. Tarr said, "It's like punching a pillow. If the chairman asked a question, the proposal changes to meet the chairman's concerns." Tarr complained that there were no rules. He bemoaned the lack of "careful economic analysis," when on the face of it, the process was openly and purposefully designed with a minimum of rules and no economic analysis.[51] The selection process was subjective and infinitely flexible, purposely created to help the NPS find a partner to work with. Tarr called the NPS's handling of the process "amateurish and inept." And he was frustrated by his inability to go over Latschar's head to Secretary Babbitt or Director Stanton.[52]

Tarr misunderstood the purpose of the openly subjective process. He also failed to recognize the Park Service's decentralization; the extent to which it relied on the superintendents of their large parks. Kinsley's proposal that carried the day was flexible; he was unconditionally willing to adapt it to the needs of the NPS, and he was totally committed to carrying out the NPS's objectives for the complex, not his own. Latschar once said, "This is the Park Service, and most of what we do and who we are is abstract rather than tangible."[53] Tarr's complaints amounted to congratulatory praise for the proficiency that marked the RFP process from start to finish. The NPS, beginning with the RFP, set out to find a partner, and against all odds, they winnowed out the proposers that would not have made as good a partner as the one they found.

---

51 Ibid. 38-39.
52 Ibid. 43.
53 Latschar interview, Nov. 20, 2013.

CHAPTER 5

Struggle, 1998

When Stanton announced Kinsley's selection in November 1997, it marked the beginning of NPS's contract negotiations with the Kinsley team to build and operate a new Museum and Visitor Center complex. By this time it was clear that Latschar's vision—the four Park objectives written in the GMP and the RFP—were dictating the course of events at Gettysburg.[1] He'd articulated the vision for the Park and without funds he'd nevertheless initiated an original process for raising the money that was needed to accomplish the four objectives. While no money had been raised, negotiations with Kinsley were the first step toward monetizing the process that Latschar had set in motion.

At the same time, day-to-day GMP planning that was once held up awaiting the panel's and then Stanton's, decision, resumed. Both outcomes, a contractual agreement with Kinsley and final GMP approval, had important ramifications both for Kinsley and for local opponents of the project. A GMP sets a Park's management direction for the succeeding fifteen or twenty years. The RFP, by which Kinsley was selected, was "folded into," or made an intrinsic part of, the GMP earlier in the year so any contract that the NPS made with Kinsley to build the Museum and Visitor Center would endow that project with the same permanence as the GMP. When Kinsley began raising funds for the project, the opponents' hopes for frustrating the NPS's vision would be over. So, beginning in 1998 with the Thomas hearings, they re-doubled their efforts. They spent most of the succeeding two-and-a-half years trying to delay the project, throwing up roadblocks, writing letters to Congress, spreading false rumors, and encouraging local officials to withhold their support. This was their time.

---

1 "Despite repeated efforts, the GBC (Gettysburg Battlefield Coalition) has failed to engage the Secretary of the Interior or the Director of the NPS to carefully reconsider what Superintendent Latschar is proposing to do at Gettysburg. Secretary Babbitt has completely refused to respond to our entreaties and Director Stanton has only sporadically, and always belatedly, responded. Our impression, therefore, is that headquarters is simply backing up the Superintendent and has never become directly involved in or knowledgeable about the Superintendent's decisions." Testimony of Ralph W. Tarr on behalf of the Gettysburg Battlefield Coalition, Thomas hearing, Feb. 24, 1998, 43.

The NPS's and Kinsley's negotiations were relaxed and amicable from the start, "more a process of mutual education—some of it was easy and some of it was difficult."[2] The NPS team, primarily Latschar, Darden, and Lars Hanslin from the Department of the Interior's Solicitor's office, met regularly with Kinsley; sometimes with Driver or other Kinsley staff members; Steve Schrum, the project manager; or Barbara Sardella, his new legal counsel. Latschar remembers that at a weekly meeting at Kinsley's Seven Valleys' office, Kinsley stretched his arms over his head, sighed, and said, in exasperation, "What I really need is a lawyer who understands the Park Service."[3] Darden and Latschar exchanged knowing smiles. Sardella had impressed them at Steamtown. She was moving to Gettysburg, and before she did she contacted them looking for job opportunities. They gave Kinsley Sardella's phone number, and within a month Kinsley had hired her.

Kinsley intended, first, to establish a 501 (c) (3), and then negotiate a Letter of Intent (to sign a contract) between his new not-for-profit and the NPS, to build a new Museum and Visitor Center. His objective was a self-financing project that would sustain itself over the long-term with revenues generated from visitation, rents, and other services. Kinsley tried his best, sometimes with difficulty, to show the NPS what he meant by "break-even," the revenue that was needed to cover all costs, fixed and variable. The Park Service gently insisted that Kinsley remove from his proposal the commercial space that aggravated some preservationists but would also have provided more revenue. Latschar said that Kinsley volunteered to remove it. Either way, Kinsley was amenable, but only after trying to satisfy himself that there would be sufficient revenue to cover costs. He was never sure if the NPS really understood "break-even."

But the Park Service knew a thing or two about their business too. Kinsley included a "white tablecloth" restaurant in his proposal, because he thought it would be nice and might generate revenue. Latschar thought it was inappropriate. He explained that the Park Service specialized in "catastrophic feeding," a term that Kinsley found amusing. As Latschar explained it, "We don't get white tablecloth people. We get a family of four from Nebraska. It may be the one time in their life that they'll take their only vacation to the East Coast. They've been down to Washington for a few days, and they're stopping at Gettysburg for one day on the way back. We've got them for only

2   Quotations in this paragraph were taken from the Latschar interview, Nov. 20, 2013.

3   Ibid.

half a day, or a day, at the most. The kids get hungry and you've got to feed them. If you don't feed them, if they have to go out of the Park, they never come back." Kinsley understood. The upscale restaurant was out. But the size of the cafeteria that replaced it became a target of the Steinwehr Avenue business owners. To the Gettysburg business community, every meal served at the Visitor Center was a meal not served in Gettysburg.

The open give-and-take between Kinsley and Latschar during the first six months of 1998 provided a placid backdrop to a heated battle that was being waged between Kinsley and Latschar on one side and their local opponents on the other. These opponents included historians and preservationists, still smarting from the NPS's bungling of the "cut" in 1990, and unhappy about potential commercialization of the Battlefield; animal rights activists, who were still in court trying to prevent Latschar from thinning the deer herd; disgruntled commuters; and local business owners who would do almost anything to prevent the removal of the Visitor Center from within a stone's throw of their doorways.

It was an awkward time for Kinsley and Latschar because they were just beginning to know one another. Latschar was delighted with his new partner, who appeared to be all that Adlerstein's panel had hoped he would be. The project's opponents could see the new Foundation launch in another six months, a preliminary Letter of Intent, the first step toward a final contract that was also in the offing, and a new draft GMP that would be released within months. Taken together, Latschar's project must have seemed unstoppable. As that realization set in, the critics grew more desperate to stop the project and the changes to the Park and the Borough that it promised, particularly removing the Visitor Center and Richard Neutra's modernist Cyclorama building. They campaigned vigorously in the press and in the halls of Congress to have the partnership shut down. Latschar worried that Kinsley, who could not have anticipated the resistance, would decide that the entire affair was repugnant, and pull out. One witness to the events said that people treated Kinsley badly and even began heckling Anne Kinsley at public meetings, so Kinsley stopped bringing her.[4]

In light of the attacks, Kinsley, who had thought he had volunteered to help solve a problem, was taken aback. Latschar's inclination was to support the Kinsley proposal, warts and all, notwithstanding that the evaluation panel had said that it did not achieve everything the NPS wanted to achieve.

4 Gerald Bennett in-person interview at Sherfey House, May 19, 2014.

The panel's primary concern was with the potential commercialization of a sacred historic Battlefield: an IMAX, a "mall," retail stores, and a high-end restaurant. It was hard for Latschar when his staff and friends told him, "John, you've got to back off; Kinsley's proposal is not okay, people are right to say it, and we have to listen."[5] He may have been apprehensive about losing Kinsley, whom he'd come to like, and he instinctively saw a need to protect him. And, of course, if he lost Kinsley, he'd also lose the source of funds that the panel had selected to secure his vision for the Park. But he knew that Kinsley's proposal could be improved, and as he digested the good advice he received and saw first-hand Kinsley's flexibility, optimism, and determination, to his credit, he adapted.

Kinsley, for his part, admitted to having thoughts of giving it up. He confided in Anne, who had similar thoughts, but she says he was never ready to give up. He knew it was up to him, and that the only way out was straight ahead. By any standard, Kinsley was a wealthy man, and as his enthusiasm and his ideas for Gettysburg expanded, fortunately his resources and his willingness to commit them were growing too. As he had predicted on the day his selection was announced, when it came to Gettysburg, his heart was ahead of his head. And while he may have been surprised by all the negativity, within a few months, he and Latschar were true partners, and he was warming to the task at hand. The eight months prior to the signing of the Letter of Intent in July 1998 and the release of the draft GMP in August 1998—the first eight months of 1998—was a pitched battle.

From the beginning, Latschar's training and instincts told him that project delay could be fatal. If his adversaries found ways to delay the project, they could kill it, and they wouldn't let up. They did everything in their power to slow it down. Kinsley and Latschar were defending and attacking on multiple fronts, but their discipline was to remain on schedule. They resisted calls for delay because partnerships are rare and fragile, and one learns in the transaction business to strike while the iron is hot.

To Latschar, even the National Tower, hovering over the tormented Battlefield, was a potential delay. He was ever mindful of Director Kennedy's admonition to concentrate on the Museum. The tower was a single project, and Kennedy knew they'd get to it some day. The Museum was different. Kennedy thought that the entire NPS might learn from it. Dennis Frye, President of the Association for the Preservation of Civil War sites, and

5 Darden interview, May 9, 2014.

a Harper associate, testifying before the Thomas Subcommittee in opposition to the GMP, stated with irrefutable logic, "A 300-foot, space-age tower hovers over the entire field, with the Visitor Center beneath its shadow. Removing a Visitor Center to restore an un-restorable landscape is ridiculous and a waste of money."[6] Others echoed Frye's sentiment. But leaving aside for the moment the idea that the tower might not be there forever and that whatever money would be wasted was not Mr. Frye's or the government's, Latschar was very much aware of the tower. He always knew he would ultimately get to it. But to him, at that moment, removing the tower was a distraction, a superficially appealing undertaking that had the potential of derailing the Museum and Visitor Center project. He ignored it. When the question was raised, "Can taking down the National Tower be part of this deal?" he responded with a terse, "Theoretically it could. Right now it's not."[7] When the question was raised again in a late 1998 interview, he said there was no connection between the GMP and the tower, and he didn't regret not linking them because "it would have been too much." He realized that tower demolition would be politically attractive, but Ottenstein's price "would make it unfeasible."[8]

Latschar pressed on with efforts to promote his program. He offered special "dismal tours" to show off the preservation problems he faced in the interim Visitor Center and to build public confidence in the NPS's judgment regarding the condition of the collection. Rare treasures in the Park's collection helped spur attendance. About 140 people came to a January event, a second two-day session sold out for February, and the Park Service was considering a third event in March.[9] The tours were part of an extraordinary public outreach program during fiscal year 1998 that ran from October 1997 through September 1998,

> Five newsletters were released to the park's mailing list (which had grown to 3,800 by the time the draft GMP was released), seventeen public meetings were held, and three open houses were conducted to allow the public a first-hand view of the abysmal collection storage conditions, and a "behind the scenes" view of the Cyclorama painting. The Park provided briefings to fifty-nine Congressional members and staff, and the Superintendent

6   Thomas hearing, Feb. 24, 1998, 34.

7   "Dr. John A. Latschar: Park Superintendent Discusses the Furor over a New Museum, Family, Shooting More Deer, and Standing in the Line of Fire," *Gettysburg Times*, March 10, 1998.

8   "The Gettysburg Plan," *York Daily Record*, Oct. 11, 1998.

9   "A Look Behind Closed Doors," *The Evening Sun*, Feb. 1, 1998.

presented twenty-three speeches to Civil War groups and civic organizations from Pennsylvania to North Carolina and from Washington, D.C. to California. The public response was overwhelmingly positive. During this public involvement effort, the NPS received over 3,700 written comments, which assisted considerably in both the revisions to the Visitor Center/Museum proposal and the GMP itself. Approximately 85% of the comments received indicated strong support for restoration of the Park historic landscapes and for implementation of the proposed partnership with the Gettysburg National Battlefield Museum Foundation.[10]

Latschar commissioned an economic research study to ascertain the economic impact of his proposal and to try to convince the Steinwehr Avenue merchants that there would be a business life after the new Museum and Visitor Center was built. The thick report, begun in February, was delivered in August 1998.[11]

In March, the NPS sent Kinsley a letter expressing its concern, based on public reaction and the opinion of an economic consultant, with the size and suitability of an IMAX theater for the proposed complex. He was requested to eliminate it from his proposal.[12] He promptly removed it in favor of a conventional theater. The formal request arrived as the two sides were negotiating the amount of commercial retail space downward. The large-format theater had found its way into Kinsley's proposal at National Geographic's insistence. National Geographic was only willing to invest in a for-profit development. As Kinsley became increasingly aware of the economic limitations of the project, and of NPS sensitivities around commercialization, National Geographic's and Kinsley's interests grew apart. The elimination of the IMAX was the last straw and the two parted ways.

At a public meeting, Kinsley said, "The comments, suggestions, objections, and advice have been extremely valuable. We have been listening."[13] The direction the negotiations were taking was clear. There would

10 Superintendent's Annual Report, Fiscal Year 1998.

11 The Office of Thomas J. Martin, Economic Research and Management Consultants, Economic Impact Evaluation, Gettysburg National Military Park, General Management Plan Alternatives; Prepared for the National Park Service, Aug. 1998.

12 Unknown individual at NPS to Kinsley, RE: Large Format Theater Proposed for GNBMF, March 2, 1998.

13 "Developer, Park Service May Scale Down Visitor Complex," Gettysburg Times, March 3, 1998.

be significantly less commercialism in the new facility than he originally proposed. Some critics expected Kinsley to refuse to go along, and when he went along, it was disarming. Later in the week, *The Evening Sun* reported details that Kinsley plans "to reduce some aspects of the project between 45 and 50 percent," to "not utilize the IMAX format," to "cut the size of the National Geographic store, [and] eliminate the art gallery and gift shop," and to "decrease the size of the food service by half." Latschar said, "Public opinion overwhelmingly supports this project…"[14]

Congressman Goodling was not helpful. During the period leading up to Kinsley's selection, he was quiet. *The Evening Sun* admonished him for his silence. The paper, in an editorial, said that Goodling shouldn't shy away from his leadership role because he feels he has to choose between Monahan and Kinsley. It should be a matter of doing what's best for the Gettysburg National Military Park and his constituents.[15] Goodling was Kinsley's Congressman and Seven Valleys neighbor. Kinsley supported his election but Monahan did too. It was the NPS's good fortune, and possibly its foresight, that the man with whom they chose to negotiate was a Goodling constituent. Goodling might have criticized or even opposed every element of the project if the preferred partner hailed from Texas, or some other far-off locale, and if both contenders from his district, his constituents, had been rejected.

Two weeks after the selection, Goodling cautiously waded back into the fray, possibly smarting from *The Evening Sun's* rebuke. Responding to Harper's protest to Babbitt, he said that he never received a full briefing and was, therefore, not in a position to comment. But then he did manage to add, "Some of the issues Mr. Harper raises, if true, are troubling".[16] Four months later, after learning that there was less space devoted to private commerce than originally planned, Goodling gratuitously opined that he wouldn't start selling tickets for the groundbreaking. He said that reduced commercial activity in the proposed facility could affect the income potential of the project. In other words, without the unpopular "commercialism," there would be no project because there would be no way to pay for it. Goodling said

---

14 "85% Respond Positively to Visitor Center Plan," *The Evening Sun*, March 7, 1998. The store had already been removed from the project but the newspaper wasn't aware of it.

15 "Let's Hear From the Congressman," *The Evening Sun*, Oct. 29, 1997.

16 "Goodling Concerned About Troubling Aspects of Park Service Visitor Center," *Gettysburg Times*, Nov. 18, 1997.

that Kinsley couldn't make it work the way he originally intended unless he wanted to lose his shirt, which he would be crazy to do.[17]

A Licensed Battlefield Guide, Frederick Hawthorne, informed the readers of his blog on December 8, 1997, that while he did not know Kinsley personally, he could certainly assure his readers that he (Kinsley) has no intention of sinking a lot of money into this process until such time as the GMP is signed, sealed, and delivered; and they do not have that assurance yet. He then shared a list of items that needed to be taken care of before construction could start: architectural drawings, site elevations, building footprints, parking lot details, traffic surveys, access routes, vegetation screening, archaeological surveys, and environmental impact studies. Hawthorne's to-do list was a good start.[18] Kinsley, using his own funds, was working on it well before he contracted with the NPS to build the Museum and Visitor Center. Throughout the project Kinsley's critics consistently underestimated him. Congressman Goodling and LBG Hawthorne, both with knowledge of Kinsley at least on a par with Adlerstein's evaluation panel, arrived at sharply differing appraisals of Kinsley than did the panel.

On May 15, 1998, Anne and Bob Kinsley established the Gettysburg National Battlefield Museum Foundation that Kinsley had envisioned in his June 17, 1997, letter to the evaluation panel. At the time, it was a prosaic legal filing, probably not celebrated because it was a fundraising vehicle that had no fundraising capability. That would come later. But in retrospect, the Foundation constructively altered the future of Gettysburg National Military Park in ways that have been obvious since its founding, and in other ways that are still playing out at this writing.

Foundation opponents countered their every move. Anxious to slow the project down, John Eline, Gettysburg Council President, announced that he was sure the Council would unanimously oppose a new Visitor Center. Eline's major issues, according to the *Gettysburg Times,* were (a) unfair commercial competition between the proposed Visitor Center and the downtown Gettysburg merchants; (b) the necessity for a significant NPS presence in the Borough such as a Museum and Research Center; and (c) a substantial reduction of food service at the Visitor Center. Joyce Jackson, President of the seventy-member Gettysburg

17 "Goodling "Not Optimistic" About Museum Proposal," *Gettysburg Times,* April 20, 1998.

18 Frederick Hawthorne blog, Dec. 8, 1997; retrieved from http://www.gdg.org/Research/Other%20Documents/cease.html

Retail Merchants Association, said that she was in total agreement with the Council and she was very happy they came forward with their concerns.[19]

The business community's fear of commercial competition from the new Park complex was being undercut by Kinsley's willingness to remove commercial entities from his initial proposal. The idea of a new NPS facility in Gettysburg, such as John Eline suggested, was not realistic, if for no other reason, because none of the four final proposals received by the NPS suggested such a site.[20] But there was Battle history in Gettysburg, and there were ways in which the Park Service could, and would, be constructive, which left only the Borough's last major issue—a substantial reduction of food service at the Visitor Center that the Borough viewed as being competitive with local merchants.

As was often the case at Gettysburg, there was a rich history of Borough-NPS relations behind the Borough's opposition to the GMP. Latschar, like his predecessors, was inclined to act as if his responsibilities as Park Superintendent ended at the Park's edge. Strictly speaking he was correct, and the multiplicity of government entities—the Borough of Gettysburg, Cumberland Township, and Adams County—created conflicting interests that discouraged Park Superintendents from ever thinking too far outside the Park. That said, the Borough of Gettysburg, the scene of important action during the first day's Battle, had been isolated from the Park since 1961 when the NPS moved its Visitor Center out of the Gettysburg Post Office and into the new Cyclorama building. The Borough's economic fortunes went into decline thereafter, and whether the NPS's exit was to blame or not, many people thought it was.

In mid-April 1998, a potentially influential new voice was heard. Gerald Bennett, Chairman of the GNMP Advisory Commission and moderator of the many public meetings, had remained silent throughout the fractious debates about the GMP. Bennett grew up in Baltimore, not Gettysburg.[21] But he remembers driving through Gettysburg in the family car when he was a boy and seeing all the cannons up on the hill. He too was an amateur historian, and when he retired from the Bell System in 1990, he moved to his Gettysburg farm. He joined the Advisory Commission in 1992 for

---

19 "Gettysburg to Oppose Kinsley Plan," *The Evening Sun*, May 4, 1998.

20 The McGorrisk Group proposed "coordinated retail activities at various sites in the Borough of Gettysburg" but not a Museum or Research Center. Adlerstein to Stanton, Oct. 13, 1997.

21 Personal and other data regarding Gerald Bennett on the next several pages is taken from an in-person Bennett interview at Sherfy House, May 19, 2014.

what turned out to be twenty years of community service, fifteen as the Commission's Chairman. While Gettysburg smoldered, Bennett was a consistent, often lonely, public voice of moderation and conciliation.

Bennett was also active in Main Street Gettysburg, a not-for-profit organization devoted to preserving and revitalizing downtown Gettysburg. In 1990 there was an initiative to link the Visitor Center with the town of Gettysburg through a historic pathway, "waysides" that were interpretive signs lining the historic route of the Battle action in 1863. The first of nine waysides, which would grow to over forty, was dedicated at the Gettysburg Hotel, and installed in the spring of 1994.[22] Waysides connected the Battle events of July 1 that occurred north and west of Gettysburg, with the events of July 2 and 3 that took place south and southeast of Gettysburg. They tracked the movements of both armies through the town that first night as Confederate soldiers chased the Union Army through the streets of Gettysburg and on to Cemetery Hill. Before the waysides, there was an interpretive hole in the Gettysburg story that the Park Service told, and local citizens resented it.

Bennett paid a call on Latschar in 1994, shortly after Latschar's arrival at Gettysburg, to introduce the Advisory Commission and, hopefully, receive some guidance from the new Superintendent. Bennett, an admirer of Latschar's today, called it a "most frustrating and unpleasant interview." According to Bennett, he did all the talking, and when he was through, Latschar thanked him for coming, and the meeting was over. Latschar was a tough nut to crack. He wouldn't be distracted, and the Borough was another distraction. But Bennett kept at it, and before long he was arguing earnestly with Latschar. "I kept saying, John, you have to find a way to help, to be involved with the town; politically you need that."

Latschar said, "I can't be responsible for that." The town was equally obstinate. They said the NPS left the Borough in 1961 when their offices were in Gettysburg. "After that you were no longer concerned with our problems."[23] It was a thirty-five-year problem that Latschar didn't create and that he was reluctant to acknowledge. But as he fought to launch his new vision for the Park, an unprecedented, historic, interpretive, and rehabilitation program at GNMP, he couldn't avoid the reality of the first day; his program couldn't be complete without the dramatic story of troop movements, civilian horror, heroism, and chaos in the Borough of Gettysburg that night of July 1, 1863.

22 "First Historic Pathway Marker Unveiled," *Gettysburg Times*, Nov. 18, 1993.

23 Bennett interview, May 19, 2014.

In late 1997 Bennett visited Latschar's office to wish him a Merry Christmas. Latschar invited him in. Latschar showed him the first draft of his letter to Borough Council President John Eline. It was a declaration and an outline of a formal and permanent partnership between the Borough and the Park Service, and it specified what the Park was willing to do to help connect the Park and the Borough. Bennett had fought Latschar, and in that letter Latschar was saying that he'd changed his mind and Bennett was right.

Finally, in April 1998 Bennett ended his long silence. At a public meeting he said that the town would "surely perish if the 'status quo' is maintained and the Visitor Center is not updated. Gettysburg," he said, "could no longer sit back and expect tourist visitation to grow automatically. The community, Borough, Township, County, retail merchants, and the NPS needed to take action collectively." It was a call for the entire community to work together to devise a way to positively manage change and to ensure their market competitiveness in the future, and he concluded by pointing out that it was the NPS, through a new GMP, that was taking the first step.[24] Bennett hoped his words would lay the groundwork for reconciliation. But the critics were not yet ready for reconciliation and paid little attention.

The Christmas draft of the letter that Bennett saw in Latschar's office was finally dated May 15, 1998, from John Latschar to John Eline, the abridged contents of which appear in the citation below.[25] The letter was the first

---

24 "Hope for Peace at Gettysburg," *York Sunday News*, April 19, 1998.

25 Abridged contents of May 15, 1998 letter from Latschar to Eline: "1. NPS will include the following paragraphs in our management objectives: — Park visitors are actively encouraged to visit key sites and districts within the Borough of Gettysburg; the NPS will cooperate with the community and others who own and manage and operate historic resources… to ensure that those stories are told and are appropriately integrated into the Park's interpretive programs. 2. NPS will include the following action items in the draft GMP/EIS: — based upon the Historic Pathway Plan, the Park will assist the Borough and/or Main Street Gettysburg in developing a Borough interpretive plan; the Park will consult with the Borough and/or Main Street to revise our auto tour route and brochure, as a principal means of attracting more visitors to the downtown area; the Park will work to expand upon the successful start of the Historic Pathway program; the Park will work to physically mark the expanded Pathway; the Park will work to design, publish and distribute a new and expanded Historic Pathways brochure; based upon the above plan, and the assumption that the Train Station, Wills House, or other identifiable historic resources will become publicly owned and operated, the Park will consider stationing NPS personnel in a downtown visitor contact facility; if the Borough and the majority of Steinwehr Avenue property owners are interested, NPS will participate in discussions concerning the creation of a Steinwehr Avenue Improvement District, as recommended in the Historic Pathways Plan.

step taken by the NPS in over thirty-five years to rejoin the history of the Park and the town. The NPS actively encouraged the public to visit key sites and districts within the Borough of Gettysburg and promised to integrate the Borough's stories into the Park's interpretive programs. The letter came less than a month after Bennett's public remarks and eleven days after Eline declared Borough opposition to the Visitor Center project, and, coincidentally, a week after the Gettysburg National Battlefield Museum Foundation was founded. The GMP was in its final drafting stages. By offering to insert a laundry list of co-operative efforts in it, to bring the Park and the Borough closer together, Latschar raised the stakes for Eline. He reminded Eline that the new GMP was on schedule. There were windows of time available well before July 1, to identify, describe, and include in the GMP several objectives and actions that they could agree upon. Unsaid was Latschar's hope that Eline would endorse his offer and publicly support the GMP. There were reports that Latschar told the Borough that planning would have to move fairly quickly because the draft GMP would be available for public review around the end of June. Latschar was playing hardball, but the Borough insisted that all time constraints needed to be removed. Latschar would only agree that getting ideas into the draft GMP was flexible in terms of days or weeks, but not months.[26] Eline wouldn't take the bait, and while his window seemed to be closing, Latschar quietly left it open. Almost imperceptibly, all the items that signified a new and inclusive outreach from the Park to the Borough of Gettysburg, found their way into the final GMP without a formal town endorsement.

In the face of Bennett's pleadings and Latschar's attempt to engage the Borough, other activity on both sides of the project continued at a feverish pace. In June Congressman Miller addressed a letter to Director Stanton. The *Gettysburg Times* quoted him, "Stanton is merely continuing an established Park Service pattern of omissions and misleading statements about the Visitor Center project."[27] Stanton rejected Miller's accusations. He denied withholding any pertinent information from the public, and he offered to meet with Miller and discuss the issues with him personally.[28] The opponents even enlisted Senate Majority Leader Trent Lott's aid. Earlier in the

---

26 "Gettysburg Wants Park to Give it More Time," *The Evening Sun*, May 10, 1998.

27 "Congressman Renews Charges against National Park Service," *Gettysburg Times*, June 19, 1998.

28 Stanton to Miller, July 14, 1998.

year, Lott, hardly a familiar figure at Gettysburg, wrote Secretary Babbitt urging him to delay the GMP because, he said, it commercialized the very ground and principle they were striving to preserve. But Lott, after learning more about the project, subsequently acknowledged that the commercial nature of the venture would be largely invisible to the average visitor.[29] The Gettysburg Council asked Senator Arlen Specter to intervene, and they asked Goodling for help trying to extend the August deadline for the GMP.[30] Gettysburg business owners told Kinsley and the NPS to stop rushing their plans.[31] Kinsley and Latschar wouldn't budge.

Despite the incessant back and forth between the NPS and its critics, there were signs, beginning with the Friends' poll earlier in the year, that the tide was turning in the project's favor.[32] The NPS, claimed 85.7% public approval based on the Friends' poll and other surveys and responses. Latschar, choosing not to rely heavily on statistically uncertain data, merely said that the public is telling us to continue negotiations and work toward a project that benefits future Park visitors and the NPS, and that he knew this to be true from the letters he'd received.[33]

But in a true departure from past reportage, *The Evening Sun* told its readers that it was time to move past the war of words, that the arguments had become stale, and the public hearings pointless. The newspaper said that it was the same small group of naysayers that kept saying *nay* over and over, refusing to compromise on their position that a privately developed center "with—gasp!—commercial stores and eateries," is like sacrilege on the hallowed ground of the Battlefield. "That stubbornness is particularly frustrating in light of the significant compromises Kinsley made last month…."[34]

---

29 "Gettysburg," Harrisburg Sunday *Patriot-News*, Sept. 27, 1998. Trent Lott was a Republican Senator from Mississippi who served from 1988 to 2007.

30 "Borough to Ask Santorum for Public hearings on NPS Plan," *Gettysburg Times*, July 9, 1998. Specter was U.S. Senator from Pennsylvania who served from 1980 to 2010,

31 "Gettysburg Merchants: No Need to Rush Park Plans," *Gettysburg Times*, July 15, 1998.

32 In mid-February, the Friends announced that they had received a 29 percent response rate from 10,448 members; 88 percent of those responding supported "the public-private sector proposal recommended by a Park Service Evaluation panel and accepted by Director Robert Stanton last November 7." "Friends Survey Respondents Support Museum Project," *Gettysburg Times*, Feb. 16, 1998.

33 "Park Service Claims Public Support for Visitor Complex," *Gettysburg Times*, March 5, 1998.

34 "Move Ahead with Visitor Center," *The Evening Sun*, May 11, 1998.

The Evening Sun also wrote, "Scaling back the project has appeased some, but not all. Frankly the opposition seems to be coming from a select group of business owners fighting for their own interests and pocketbooks, but the NPS does not exist to keep shop owners and food vendors in business."[35]

A *Gettysburg Times* reader wrote that Gettysburg was the only place where the dead support the living. "It is totally incomprehensible to me why the merchants, Chamber of Commerce, *et al*, do not vigorously endorse the proposed NPS facility, which will ensure future visitor flow so that they may continue to be supported in the manner to which they have become accustomed."[36] One month later another reader wrote that, "The 5,900-acre Battlefield contains over 1,300 monuments and markers, four hundred cannons, and over 40,000 artifacts that are literally crumbling and rotting as each day goes by. As an eight-year volunteer at the Battlefield, I say it is criminal to allow this to happen. No one owes the business community a living. I have yet to hear them propose an acceptable plan of funding for a new Museum. In the interest of preserving this great Battlefield, they should put up or shut up."[37]

On July 20, 1998, the Foundation announced that it had signed a Letter of Intent with the NPS.[38] It was a four-page letter outlining project responsibilities of both sides. There were thirty-one items negotiated prior to the Letter being sent to Kinsley from Regional Director Rust on July 10, 1998, and countersigned by Kinsley on July 16. The Park Service still shared very few details about the project, only intentions, but that was, after all, the purpose of a letter of intent. The Letter said that the contractual agreement, still to be negotiated, would contain specific terms and conditions.

But there were nuggets of clarity and specificity to be found in the Letter of Intent: "museum collections will remain the property of the United States"; "all obligations of the NPS will be subject to the availability of appropriated funds" (usual annual Congressional funding); and "no increase in such funds shall be anticipated for purposes of construction, operation, or maintenance"—as Galvin had testified at both Congressional hearings. The Letter said, "the Foundation's activities at the facilities are subject to

---

35 "Palatable Plan," *The Evening Sun*, July 23, 1998.

36 "Lack of Support Incomprehensible," *Gettysburg Times*, July 23, 1998.

37 "Time for Museum Opponents to Put Up," *Gettysburg Times*, Aug. 25, 1998.

38 Information in this and the succeeding paragraph are drawn from the Letter of Intent, Marie Rust, NPS Northeast Regional Director to Bob Kinsley, July 10, 1998.

NPS approval"; "NPS shall exercise rate-approval authority"; and "the design and construction shall be subject to the prior written approval of the NPS." Clearly, the Letter of Intent was paving the way for a contractual agreement wherein the Foundation was to furnish expertise and funding to help build a Museum and Visitor Center at Gettysburg. But it was in no way an agreement by the NPS to cede its conservation or other responsibilities to the Foundation or to sponsor the building of an architect's dream. Several of the critics' worst fears about the partnership—for example, ownership of the collection, government funding of the project, or NPS approval authority—were put to rest by the Letter of Intent.

In mid-August 1998 the Park Service released the draft of the new GMP for public comment, unprecedented as it was for its scope and vision. It included the proposed Museum and Visitor Center that garnered most of the attention as well as most of the resistance. The recently delivered, NPS-sponsored, economic analysis of the GMP's likely impact studied visitation, length of visitor stay, and visitor expenditures; and plotted them against four Park rehabilitation alternatives, the first being "do nothing" and the other three representing increasingly robust building plans. The report concluded that as a result of the programs outlined in the GMP for all but the "do nothing" alternative, a visitor's average length of stay would increase, as would visitor spending, in all retail segments. The report expected spending in the community to decrease only if nothing were done. The Park Service's consistent message was that improved facilities were going to make things better, if not for everyone, then for most people. Conversely, stagnant facilities would lead to economic decay and everyone would suffer. Opponents of the study attacked its methodology and "predicted a new commercial zone" near the relocated Visitor Center, and the old commercial zone in crisis," a draconian forecast similar to Uberman's earlier prediction, and on its surface less believable than the NPS forecast.[39]

It was the landscape rehabilitation plan, however, that was the most stunning aspect of the draft GMP. It called for "cutting down 576 acres of trees … adding 150 acres of new woodland, developing 160 acres of orchards, and maintaining 65 acres of thickets," among many other items, all to restore the Park's landscape to its 1863 appearance. All in all, the proposed alterations to Gettysburg National Military Park in the draft GMP were breathtaking, both in their detail and in their scope on the ground, and in the potential for

---

39 "Report Cites Economic Impact," *Civil War News*, Dec. 1998.

rejuvenation of an iconic historic American place. It only seemed possible because of a remarkable vision and a philanthropic infusion of private capital and know-how. To keep the pressure on, NPS spokesperson Katie Lawhon said that August 17 "will be the first day of the sixty-day public comment period that closes October 17." Kinsley's Sardella added, "I think that we would like to see the schedule the Park Service has set up be followed."[40]

By September 1998 the Letter of Intent between the Foundation and the NPS had been signed (in July), and the draft GMP had been released for the sixty-day period of public comment. It was expected to be approved within a matter of weeks. But optimistic expectations underestimated the opponents' tenacity, which, ironically, was also beginning to draw unsympathetic national attention to it. As the general public gained familiarity with the facts, the interpretive virtues of the nationally significant, historic project emerged. The public began to recognize that the arguments against the project were largely being made around an array of different local special interests that, even if deemed valid, were of insufficient weight to win the day.

The Steinwehr Avenue merchants and other local opponents, who'd been vocal for years, were not the only adversaries. Others were appearing, perhaps fomented by a small coterie in Gettysburg, but, nevertheless, new and different. One new threat to the GMP's approval emerged without warning from within the NPS. It was the Cyclorama building, designed by renowned architect Richard Neutra, that the NPS planned to raze as soon as it was vacated. The Park Service determined in 1996 that the building was of no historic significance, and was not eligible for the National Register of Historic Places. The Pennsylvania State Historic Preservation Officer agreed. However, two years later, in the fall of 1998, the GMP was out for sixty days of public review, and friends of Neutra and the building petitioned the Keeper of the National Register, an NPS employee. The Keeper overruled the Park Service and the Pennsylvania Historic Preservation Officer, declaring that the building had "exceptional historic and architectural significance, and was therefore eligible for inclusion in the National Register."

Thus began a fifteen-year battle between the NPS and the nation's architectural community that raised Gettysburg's trademark ambiguity to another level. *The New York Times* headline read "Which of All the Pasts to

---

40 "Park Officials Stick to 60-Day Review on Management Plan," *Gettysburg Times*, Aug. 13, 1998.

Preserve?"[41] It was a classic showdown between two righteous forces. Both sides were preservationists. The historic new vision for the GNMP could not be fulfilled without the rehabilitation of Ziegler's Grove.[42] And the rehabilitation of Ziegler's Grove, one of the four primary goals of the GMP, could not get done without removing the Cyclorama building.

On the other side, the building had an eminent and respected list of defenders that included The Society of Architectural Historians and famed architects such as Norman Foster, Frank Gehry, and Robert Stern. They believed that the building embodied mid-twentieth century social and aesthetic values and was a monument to modernity.[43] Carter Brown, then Chairman of the U.S. Commission of Fine Arts and Director Emeritus of the National Gallery of Art in Washington, wrote, in a letter to the Advisory Council on Historic Preservation (ACHP), "The theme park concept of falsely re-creating a landscape that can never be put back to 1863 is an unconscionable intellectual travesty."[44]

Brown's assertion stood in sharp contrast to Boston University history professor Nina Silber's opinion that "changes to the Battlefield landscape [will enable] visitors to appreciate the Battle in its 1863 context."[45] And Latschar was as combative as Brown was. He referred to the building as the "the oil drum." He called the iconic Philippoteaux Cyclorama painting "the world's largest air filter" because of the building's air ducts that were located behind the painting and blew air through the canvas. He added that, "Only a California architect would put on a flat roof to protect a work of art in [snowy and rainy] Pennsylvania." Latschar pointed to the sliding glass doors that didn't work, spiraling indoor ramps that were too steep to accommodate handicapped visitors, dried up reflecting pools, and fractured concrete. Defenders accused the Park Service of letting the building go. Latschar asked, "Why would you invest in a dysfunctional building?" And on it went,

---

41   "Which of All the Pasts to Preserve?" *The New York Times*, Feb. 21, 1999.

42   "The mission of the GMNP is to preserve and protect the resources associated with the Battle of Gettysburg and to provide an understanding of events that occurred within the context of American history." General Management Plan and Environmental Impact Statement, June, 1999, 7.

43   "Which of All the Pasts to Preserve?" *The New York Times*, Feb. 21, 1999.

44   "Architectural Expert Calls Cyclorama Demolition Plans a 'Travesty'," *Gettysburg Times*, May 6, 1999. The ACHP, chartered in 1966, is the only federal agency that has the legal responsibility to help factor historic preservation into federal project requirements.

45   "Three Historians Add Their Support to Park Plan," *Gettysburg Times*, Nov. 1, 1998.

back and forth. For the moment, though, as a result of the Keeper's ruling, the Park Service and the State Preservation Officer needed to again review the building's historical significance. The Keeper's ruling stopped the GMP dead in its tracks. It could be discussed and reviewed, but it couldn't be approved. Concurrently, a separate effort was made to designate the building a historic landmark, but that failed when the NPS Advisory Board rejected the recommendation of the National Landmarks Committee to make that designation.[46]

Also, in a surprising development, Angie Rosensteel Eckert and eight other members of the Rosensteel family filed suit in federal court to repossess all of the enormous collection that her family gave to the NPS in 1971.[47] Rosensteel Eckert claimed that the NPS failed to keep its promise to care for the artifacts according to the highest standards, and she wanted the entire collection, all 38,000 artifacts, returned to her. Local observers may have believed that the NPS and Rosensteel Eckert were on good terms, but following Kinsley's selection and Monahan's removal from the picture, their relationship cooled and the lawsuit followed.

There were more than a few ironies surrounding the suit, not the least of which was that Rosensteel Eckert's husband, Larry, was chief curator of the collection for twenty-two years after the family's gift. Then, too, Latschar was touring the country exhorting Americans to support the public/private partnership as a means of taking better care of the collection. But at the same time, as part of his stump speech, and for emphasis, he declared time and again that the Park was "broke," and the NPS was "broke," all of which may have emboldened Rosensteel Eckert and/or her legal advisors. The lawsuit was no more than a nuisance, but it appeared at a time when there was a flurry of negative activity.

Nevertheless, there was also good news emanating from Gettysburg. The public learned in early October that three noted historians unanimously endorsed the GMP.[48] Their work had begun in early 1998, when Latschar heard from a friend who forwarded a message from Dr. Eric Foner, Professor of History at Columbia, and the pre-eminent American historian on Reconstruction. The message was that after Foner toured Gettysburg with

---

46 "Panel: Building Not Historic," unidentified newspaper article of unknown date.

47 "A True Gift Cannot Be Taken Back," *The Evening Sun*, Oct. 9, 1998.

48 "Three Historians Add Their Support to Park Plan," *Gettysburg Times*, Nov. 1, 1998. Also derived from the Latschar interviews on Nov. 20, 2013 and Feb. 17, 2014.

his daughter, she asked why she hadn't seen anything about slavery and that she had thought slavery had something to do with the Civil War. Latschar knew Foner was right. He knew that there was nothing about slavery at Gettysburg. Battlefield interpretation was traditionally about Battlefield action: "who shot whom, where." There was very little spoken about why the soldiers were fighting, or what happened after the fight. Again, Latschar saw an opportunity. He called Foner and told him he was aware of the problem. Latschar asked Foner if he would help and Foner said he would. He also reminded Latschar of the Park Service's agreement with the Organization of American Historians (OAH). That agreement, reached in 1994, allowed for the sharing of OAH resources, facilities, and information on subjects relevant to the National Park System. By this agreement, the OAH volunteered to help the Park Service open new historic parks, help with new GMPs, and evaluate interpretive programs or other operations that required the best in historical scholarship.

Latschar seized on Foner's offer. In the late summer of 1998, Foner, James McPherson, and Nina Silber came to Gettysburg and spent a solid week at the GNMP.[49] McPherson, in particular, the Pulitzer Prize winning Civil War historian, was a stalwart of the historian community, and he gave Latschar and the NPS his entire support. His words carried particular weight because of his close academic connection with Gettysburg. Latschar said, "They wrote a magnificent report telling us exactly what they thought we were doing wrong and could do better, and that report, in itself, was not only the beginning of our starting to pay real attention to our interpretive programs, but that team of three led to the Gettysburg Historians Advisory Committee that advised us on the storyline for the new Museum."[50]

In Silber's report that she drafted for the OAH, she wrote, "Our team of historians enthusiastically endorses the proposals in this Draft GMP, … which calls for the extensive changes to the Battlefield landscape, so that visitors can appreciate the Battle in its 1863 context, and for a new Visitor Center that can better convey the Gettysburg story." Aside from the report's intrinsic value, it was a political plus for any Park superintendent to have

---

49 McPherson is George Henry Davis '86 Professor Emeritus of United States History at Princeton University. He received the 1989 Pulitzer Prize for Battle Cry of Freedom. Silber is Professor of History and Director, American and New England Studies Program at Boston University.

50 Latschar interview, Nov. 20, 2013.

a panel of eminent historians on his side, and it was more evidence of the inevitability of the NPS's plan.[51]

Just fifteen months had elapsed since Kinsley received that fateful telephone call in the Colorado Rockies. On December 30, 1998, he drafted a letter to Dan Driver, his CFO and Treasurer of the Gettysburg National Battlefield Museum Foundation (GNBMF) that had a legal and a philanthropic purpose. Kinsley noted that Kinsley Equities and the Kinsley Family Foundation were entities owned by him and his family." He noted further that Kinsley Equities loaned $1,231,875 to GNBMF for costs that GNBMF incurred for the new Visitor Center and Museum, and that to help the project along, he would contribute $768,125 to GNBMF the next day. And he forgave the prior advance that then became a gift. He noted that the combined $2 million donation should help the project by paying for a portion of the land-acquisition cost.[52] The project had barely begun, and while some progress had been made, the GMP was on hold because of the Keeper's ruling. In spite of his considerable investment in the project, Kinsley had no contract with the NPS to build the Museum and Visitor Center complex, and even the new vision for Gettysburg was far from certain. Kinsley's generosity in the face of such uncertainty came naturally to him, it was seldom acknowledged, and it was precisely the philanthropic investment in Gettysburg that the NPS needed and that Congressman Goodling and Battlefield Guide Hawthorne claimed Kinsley would not make.

51 "Three Historians Add Their Support to Park Plan," *Gettysburg Times*, Nov. 1, 1998.

52 Robert A. Kinsley letter to Dan Driver, Treasurer, Dec. 30, 1998.

CHAPTER 6

More Combat, 1999 and 2000

Kinsley's surprise $2 million donation to the Foundation that closed the year 1998 was followed closely by the Foundation's $2.7 million acquisition of the LeVan parcel, the future home of the new Museum and Visitor Center that he had identified and recommended in his proposal to the NPS. When Kinsley contacted LeVan to buy the property, he believed they'd already agreed on the price. He was surprised and disappointed when LeVan denied that they had previously discussed price. But whatever was the cause of the misunderstanding, it was ironed out when Kinsley agreed to pay $57,000 per acre for the forty-seven acres. Gettysburg Borough Council President John Eline wondered how that would affect the price of real estate in Gettysburg.[1]

The purchase carried a risk for Kinsley. If he were unable to negotiate a contract with the NPS to raise the money and build and operate the complex, then he would own land that he couldn't use and didn't want. When asked what he would do, Kinsley cheerfully answered that he'd donate the land to the Park and take the tax deduction, which, of course, would hardly make him whole. But, he said, "I feel really good about this. It will be fun when we get it started and more fun when we hold the ribbon-cutting."[2] It was the first tangible step toward building the Museum and Visitor Center complex, an essential aspect of his new vision for the Park. Monahan called it "a very high-stakes gamble," which it would have been if Kinsley hoped to earn a profit.[3] But for the philanthropist and NPS partner, it was a lesser risk and a major step forward on the project.

The comprehensive draft GMP, released to the public for a sixty-day review in mid-1998, and at the time held hostage by the Keeper's ruling that the Cyclorama building was eligible for the National Register of Historic Places, seemed to provide endless opportunities for objections. For example, the *ad hoc* "Concerned Citizens for Gettysburg" continued its efforts to stop it

---

1 "Foundation Buys Land for Visitor Center," *The Evening Sun*, Jan. 9, 1999.

2 "York Developer Donates $2,000,000 for Museum Site," *York Sunday News*, Jan. 10, 1999.

3 Ibid.

and send it back to the drawing board. Their efforts, and those of the GBPA, Steinwehr Avenue merchants, and those opposed to the deer-herd reduction, led directly to a second Congressional hearing on February 11, 1999, that was chaired by Representative James V. Hansen of Utah. The declared subject of the hearing was the GMP and the Museum and Visitor Center project. The format called for a statement by the chairman and subsequent statements by Denis Galvin for the NPS, members of the Subcommittee and other interested parties. Chairman Hansen led off by scolding the NPS for withholding information about the "cut" and the National Tower; events that were nine and twenty-five years old, respectively.[4] Galvin's statement, an overview of the saga of the Gettysburg GMP, began the testimony. As it ended, his final point, made to a skeptical Congressional panel, related to Kinsley: "… the Kinsley proposal, and its spirit, and his flexibility in the face of what has been an arduous process, is admirable. He has been a most empathetic partner, and I believe he is doing this in a spirit of public good in support of the objectives of Gettysburg National Military Park."[5]

The committee's questions reflected a lack of familiarity with the GMP and sometimes related more to their constituencies at home than to Gettysburg. For example, Honorable Carlos Romero-Barcelo, the New Progressive Party delegate from Puerto Rico, asked Galvin what the Park Service would do if Kinsley couldn't raise the money for the project, and he asked questions about Davis-Bacon wage rates.[6] Congressman Walter B. Jones, Republican of North Carolina, asked, "Who owns the Gettysburg National Park?" as a preamble to stories of his own problems with the NPS in

---

4 Quotations in the next several pages are taken from the transcript of the Oversight (Hansen) hearing on Gettysburg National Military Park General Management Plan and Proposed Visitor Center before the Subcommittee on National Parks and Public Lands of the House Committee on Resources, Feb. 11, 1999.

5 Hansen hearing, Feb. 11, 1999, 9.

6 The Davis-Bacon and Related Acts, apply to contractors and sub-contractors performing on federally funded or assisted contracts in excess of $2,000 for the construction, alteration, or repair (including painting and decorating) of public buildings or public works. Davis-Bacon Act and Related Act contractors and subcontractors must pay their laborers and mechanics employed under the contract no less than the locally prevailing wages and fringe benefits for corresponding work on similar projects in the area. The Davis-Bacon Act directs the Department of Labor to determine such locally prevailing wage rates. It applies to contractors and subcontractors performing work on federal or District of Columbia contracts. The Davis-Bacon Act prevailing wage provisions apply to the "Related Acts," under which federal agencies assist construction projects through grants, loans, loan guarantees, and insurance.

North Carolina. Hansen questioned the adequacy of public participation in the Gettysburg process and whether the Foundation could raise $27 million to build the Gettysburg complex. Romero-Barcelo asked why the NPS hadn't requested special funding for Gettysburg, and why the NPS, probably Latschar, said that Gettysburg was broke, that the NPS was broke, and why the Park Service blamed Congress for not sufficiently funding the Park.[7] He said that if the NPS could accomplish their objectives at Gettysburg with private funding and if it didn't need Congressional funding, it shouldn't blame Congress for any lack of resources, thereby equating an NPS that was forced to seek outside assistance as in this instance, with an NPS that chose to seek outside assistance. His questions had little to do with whether the Gettysburg GMP was a good idea, or what might be done to improve it. Santorum submitted a lengthy statement urging the committee to move the GMP process forward. Hansen announced that he had more questions that he would submit in writing after the hearing.

There were six "witnesses" in attendance; two of them, Galvin and Kinsley, both for the GMP, were principals, not witnesses. Why the Subcommittee would not have called more interested parties is suspect because it was within their power to do so. Richard Moe, for example, President of the National Trust for Historic Preservation (NTHP), asked to testify and was refused. The NTHP is the largest and one of the most prestigious historic preservation organizations in the nation, and they were solidly on the side of the NPS. Gerald Bennett also comes to mind. The Subcommittee, judging by the questions it raised, seemed interested in exploring the NPS's relationship with the Gettysburg community, which would have made Bennett, Chairman of the GNMP Advisory Commission, a useful witness but one who endorsed the GMP.[8]

The second witness, Eileen Woodford, Northeast Regional Director of The National Parks and Conservation Association (NPCA), was well prepared. Her testimony was directed at the GMP and the approval process. Woodford described the NPCA as "America's only private not-for-profit citizens' organization, dedicated solely to protecting, preserving, and enhancing the U.S. National Park System." In the course of its work, the NPCA finds itself both advocating for and overseeing the NPS, or, stated more succinctly, either supporting or opposing the NPS on behalf of the Parks. She opened her testimony by describing the situation that Latschar faced when

---

7 NPS budget requests were made on a system-wide basis rather than park by park.

8 Information in this section regarding Richard Moe and the NTHP is derived from the Latschar interview, Nov. 20, 2013.

he first arrived at Gettysburg. She said:

> NPCA did not make this decision lightly to support the Museum proposal. We understand only too well what profound changes the proposal and the GMP will bring to the Park, but those changes are necessary. We can no longer tolerate mold and mites eating away at the Park's collection. We can no longer tolerate watching the paint chip off the Cyclorama painting. We can no longer tolerate visitors putting up with a second-rate experience. And we can no longer tolerate the intrusion of a wholly inadequate visitor center and a dysfunctional cyclorama building onto some of the most sacred ground in this country.

Woodford had summed it up. The NPS's plan dealt directly with the circumstances Woodford described. Woodford told the Subcommittee that NPCA supported the public/private partnership concept, but only a proposal "that passed the most stringent of tests and proved to uphold the highest of resource protection standards." And, as had the Adlerstein panel, NPCA found that Kinsley's original proposal was "highly unacceptable to us."

Woodford, in her oral testimony, also opined, "NPCA found the public planning process to be exceptional. At public meetings for both the Museum proposal and the GMP, the Park staff was willing to listen to a wide range of opinions and ideas. Additionally, the amount and detail of historical documentation presented in the GMP public meetings, was unparalleled in my four years with the NPCA."[9] Woodford's written testimony was also impressive. She alone among the witnesses in attendance, showed that she undertook a thorough examination of the related planning documents, especially the GMP.[10]

Walter Powell, representing the GBPA, followed Woodford, and he opposed the GMP. He said that the GMP was not about resource protection,

---

9 Woodford's comments, quoted in the prior two paragraphs, were drawn from the transcript of the Hansen hearing, Feb. 11, 1999, 20-22.

10 "To insure that the proposal was acceptable to us and met only the highest standards, we participated in nearly every single public meeting sponsored by the Park service. We examined all public documents and provided written comments to NPS stating our specific concerns. We met with both supporters and opponents of the Museum proposal to hear their points of view. We articulated strict, new standards by which to judge the appropriateness of related activities where none existed. We subjected the Museum proposal to extensive financial and economic analysis. We have given the draft proposal and general management plan the most rigorous of examinations, and we have concluded that they will significantly improve the preservation of historic resources and the visitor experience without compromising the integrity of the Park." Eileen Woodford, Ibid. 48.

but "the selling of the Battlefield to the highest bidder." He criticized the planning process for not offering sufficient alternatives; that, he said, was a clear violation of the intent of the National Environmental Policy Act. Powell sought alternatives to the NPS plan, and even suggested his own alternative that "might include demolition and rebuilding of the current Visitor Center, and if the National Tower is eventually acquired, the development of appropriately designed and screened facilities on the ground that has already been compromised." Taken literally, Powell was suggesting a site similar to that suggested by the LeMoyne Group, which would retain the NPS complex close to Steinwehr Avenue, which was not an NPS goal. Powell's suggestion underscored the difficulty of finding practical alternatives to the NPS's plan. Powell urged Latschar to halt the current plan and create a true partnership of "all the people, by the people, for the people," so that the Gettysburg Battlefield "shall not perish from the earth."[11]

The next witness, Ted Streeter, representing the Borough of Gettysburg, described the negative impact that he believed that relocation of the Museum and Visitor Center would have on the Steinwehr Avenue business district and on selected establishments in the district. He protested the Park's treatment of Gettysburg over the years, and he charged the Park Service with ignoring the town. But he offered no alternative to the NPS's plan.

Santorum, while absent from the hearing, submitted a lengthy statement urging Congress to move the GMP process forward. His testimony went directly at Hansen, after first arguing that the hearing would "help dispel many of the misperceptions of the GMP process." He reminded Hansen of his (Hansen's) letter to Secretary Babbitt. "I disagree," he said, "with the assertions and conclusions in your letter. I remain very personally engaged in this matter, and my staff has attended every public meeting and monitored every development in this process… I spent one day in Gettysburg to meet with a group of concerned citizens… I acknowledge that there is opposition to the GMP… [but] that input has been overwhelmingly positive. The majority of the constituents that have written [me] are from the Gettysburg area, including business owners, individuals, and families. I have received mail that expressed concern, and in some cases opposition [to the GMP], [but] the large majority of the input remains positive and supportive."[12]

11 Walter Powell's comments quoted in the prior paragraph were drawn from the transcript of the Hansen hearing, Feb. 11, 1999, 22-24.

12 Ibid. 46.

Hansen was a steadfast opponent of Latschar's, the NPS, and the GMP. He regaled his audience with tales of the "Sagebrush Rebellion," and Ronald Reagan's earlier admonishment of federal agencies that have a high-handed attitude. Hansen appeared to attribute the "attitude" to the NPS and perhaps to Latschar. In closing, Hansen again alerted Galvin that after the hearing he would "submit to you a pile of questions" in writing that he hoped Galvin would answer promptly.

Representing Galvin, Latschar's answers to Hansen's written questions arrived shortly after the hearing and they failed to satisfy the Congressman.[13] In fact, they seemed to irritate him. Hansen, teaming up with Miller, wrote a letter in early April to Stanton, asking Stanton to place a hold on the current draft GMP or withdraw it altogether, and develop a new draft, or a supplemental GMP.[14] They offered eight suggestions, the first of which was to "develop a full range of alternatives" for a new Visitor Center that would not be limited to "one predetermined location," thereby seeming to ignore thirty years of debate about the best place to locate a new Visitor Center at Gettysburg. Additionally, the idea of remodeling either the Cyclorama building or the interim Visitor Center would force the Park Service to abandon its goal of rehabilitating Ziegler's Grove at a site that the Park had analyzed and rejected four years before as being too small for the purpose.[15] But no one suggested a better alternative site for the Museum and Visitor Center. Hansen and Miller called on the NPS to "fully discuss" topics that had been debated publicly in Gettysburg for years.

Several days later, Hansen wrote Stanton to chide the Park Service for attempts to "dance around" questions posed to them after the Subcommittee's February 11 hearings, and he attacked Latschar for being arrogant and self-serving.[16] Later in the year, Hansen asked the General Accountability Office (GAO) to investigate the Park Service at the Battlefield, the Friends, and the Citizens Advisory Commission. The GMP was in its final stages of

---

13 "Park Service defends Battlefield plan," *The Evening Sun*, April 6, 1999.

14 "Congressman's Letter Urges Revision of Visitor Center Process," *Gettysburg Times*, April 2, 1999.

15 The 1995 DCP (p. 24) concluded that a smaller facility required a minimum of 8.2 acres and that "a maximum of 6.6 acres of land are available at the Visitor Center site." The new complex occupies approximately fifteen acres and is not visible from the Battlefield.

16 Hansen said, "Clearly, arrogant and self-serving statements as those made by Superintendent Latschar that 'there is nothing in our mission statement that says we're supposed to look out for businesses surrounding the park' are needless and unproductive in anyone's opinion." "Legislator Slams Park Official's Stance," *The Evening Sun*, May 11, 1999.

approval, and the investigation was into how the Friends used $29,000 in donations that were collected at the Visitor Center. The GAO found nothing unusual.[17]

On April 22, Earth Day, 1999, the National Tower at Gettysburg, the 300-foot behemoth that was adjacent to the High Water Mark, made a dramatic reentry into the public consciousness. By then, and as a result of the 1990 boundary legislation, the tower was within the new boundary of the Park. Coincidentally, the NPS realized that the Park never received 5 percent of the tower's net profits from Ottenstein because the tower appeared to have never earned a profit.[18] As spectacular a physical presence as it was, the tower may have been a financial flop. Less than a year before, the NPS provided a briefing for the Office of Management and Budget (OMB) on the GMP. After the briefing, OMB staff noticed that of the major issues facing the Park, only the tower remained, and they suggested that perhaps they should do something about that. The result was a $5.7 million entry in the President's budget for acquisition of the tower and certain other land parcels, in budget-speak, to eliminate adverse development and restore the historic integrity of the Park. This prompted an array of interested parties to spring into action. The National Trust for Historic Preservation, NPCA, Civil War Trust, and the Friends each contacted Congressional appropriation committees to urge their support for the budget; thus the tower removal found its way into the GMP. But the GMP was still up in the air because of the Keeper's ruling regarding the eligibility of the Cyclorama building for the National Historic Register.[19]

Secretary of the Interior Bruce Babbitt arrived in Gettysburg that April day to endorse the GMP that had been out for public comment since August of the prior year. There was a small ceremony near the Meade Statue in front of the field of Pickett's Charge. Then, totally unrehearsed, and a surprise to Latschar, Babbitt turned around and pointed to the tower and said, "We're going to get that thing down on my watch." Babbitt's watch ended eighteen months later, so "getting that tower down" became a secretarial initiative with everything on a fast track.

---

17 "GAO Finds No Evidence of Misuse of Funds by Friends of the National Parks," *The Evening Sun*, Dec. 20, 1999.

18 The agreement with the Department of the Interior that allowed the tower to be built, also provided that 5 percent of the tower's net profit would be paid annually to a foundation for the benefit of the Park.

19 Latschar, *The Taking of the Gettysburg Tower*, 85.

The *Gettysburg Times* reported a tantalizing exchange between Babbitt and Uberman after the ceremony:

> Uberman: Is it possible for you to meet with the community when most feel threatened and insulted by the GMP?
> Babbitt: We'll sit down when the plan is signed.
> Uberman: It's too late then.
> Babbitt: No, that's just the beginning.[20]

Uberman was right. Once the contract was signed, chances of his protest succeeding would be doubtful.

A month later Uberman filed a Freedom of Information Act request. Among other documents that he uncovered were fourteen interior and exterior photographs of his store that were taken two or three years before, that were to Uberman, "surveillance of his business" as well as "intimidation and harassment." A spokesman for the NPS said the photographs "were probably intended to show growth and development around the Battlefield."[21] Both statements invited skepticism. But it was an easy incident to criticize, and Goodling called for a review by Secretary Babbitt.[22] Hansen, by then ever alert, labeled pictures that were taken in broad daylight, of customers entering and exiting an open retail store, "an invasion of privacy," and he said he was "offended."[23] The brushfire went out almost as quickly as it flared. And in yet another very brief episode, Uberman was joined by Eileen Woodford of the NPCA on the *Today* show with Matt Lauer. The *Gettysburg Times* called it a "blistering debate," but no new ground was broken.[24]

In June, and adding to the consternation caused by the Keeper's ruling and the Rosensteel legal action, a third bolt came out of the blue when Representative Ron Klink, a four-term Congressman from the Fourth District in Western Pennsylvania, decided to try to unseat Santorum. Klink, from Altoona, was relatively unknown in Eastern Pennsylvania despite his seniority in the House. By all accounts, he needed to raise his name recognition

---

20 "Babbitt Promises to Topple National Tower," *Gettysburg Times*, April 23, 1999.

21 "Park Plan, Pictures Go Public," *Gettysburg Times* June 19, 1999.

22 "Park Photos Caught in Bipartisan Crossfire," *Gettysburg Times*, June 23, 1999.

23 "Key Congressman Calls Park Photos 'Invasion Of Privacy,'" *Gettysburg Times*, June 24, 1999.

24 "Gettysburg Businessman, Park Service, Debate on NBC "*Today Show*," *Gettysburg Times*, June 23, 1999.

across Pennsylvania if he were to defeat Santorum. Klink decided that the citizens of Gettysburg had not had sufficient input into the GMP process, that the community's tax base would "crumble" as a result of the implementation of the GMP, and that "This [GMP] needs to be postponed."[25] He introduced an amendment to an authorizing bill for two other battlefields that would have required Congressional approval for the construction of a new Visitor Center within the Gettysburg Park. The amendment was judged to be irrelevant to the authorizing bill so Klink withdrew it, but the die was cast.[26]

One month later Klink filed an amendment to the Interior Department's Appropriations Bill that passed in the House by a vote of 220 to 206 and, had it ever passed through the Senate, would have shut down the Gettysburg GMP for good.[27] It would have eliminated Kinsley's project and that, in turn, without any replacement, would have left the Park in a sorry state.[28] At that point, Goodling apparently thought that having no new Museum and Visitor Center project was not a good idea, and he voted against Klink's amendment. Santorum called the Klink amendment a "political stunt," and bluntly promised that the Klink provision would not be included in the Senate's Interior Appropriations Bill.[29]

Meanwhile, the GMP still languished in the arcane bureaucratic morass that involved the Park Service, the Pennsylvania State Historic Preservation Office, and the Advisory Council on Historic Preservation (ACHP), an independent federal agency.[30] In October 1998, the Keeper of the National Register of Historic Places had decided that the Cyclorama building was a historic structure, eligible for inclusion in the National Register, which, if allowed to stand, would prevent its removal by the NPS. In May 1999, in a seemingly contradictory action, the ACHP approved the GMP that

---

25 "Klink: Park Plan Would Crumble Business in Gettysburg," *The Evening Sun*, June 17, 1999.

26 "Klink Withdraws Visitor Center," *The Evening Sun*, June 23, 1999.

27 The amendment stated, "No funds made available under this act may be used to implement Alternatives B, C or D identified in the [GMP] for Gettysburg National Military Park, dated June 1999." Superintendent's Annual Report, Fiscal Year 1999. Also, "House Rejects Visitor Center Funding", *The Evening Sun*, July 15, 1999.

28 Ibid.

29 "Santorum, Klink Trade Accusations Over Visitor Center," *Gettysburg Times*, July 30, 1999.

30 Information regarding the ACHP was drawn from "About the ACHP: General Information." Retrieved from http://www.achp.gov/aboutachp.html

included provisions for the demolition of the Cyclorama building. The ACHP approval, therefore, cleared the way for the NPS to release the final GMP to the public, which it did on June 18, 1999, and for the three agencies to then begin working together to negotiate an appropriate mitigation for the destruction of the historic structure. On July 28, 1999, the three groups joined in an agreement based on the May ACHP report that provided for the implementation of the GMP and the demolition of the building and landscape rehabilitation.[31] To justify its action, the ACHP said:

> Gettysburg... represents... a turning point in national history... that has few if any rivals. It is of paramount importance historically. The rehabilitation of this key Battlefield site, so that the Battlefield can properly be interpreted must be regarded as a historic mission of the highest order... Neutra has a secure place in the pantheon of American architectural history. There are other Neutra buildings; there is only one Gettysburg Battlefield. The building must yield.[32]

Due to the architectural community's persistent dedication to preserving Neutra's work, and their willingness to continue to pursue legal remedies, however, the building's future remained unclear, but it no longer stood in the way of the GMP that called for the building's removal.

Even so, Congressmen and local opponents of the GMP, in spite of all the machinations that had worked against them, showed no signs of letting up. They were pitted in a desperate, last-ditch struggle against the Department of Interior, NPS, and GNMP, led by Babbitt, Stanton, and Latschar.[33] The former still seemed to be intent on delaying, sidetracking, or scuttling the GMP, the latter on implementing it. In June Monahan said, "I'm still of the opinion that the plan will never materialize in its current structure."[34]

But other developments marked the relentless forward progress of the GNMP's rehabilitation. The deer-herd reduction suit was wrapping up. It resumed in October 1999 because the stay that shut down the program was

---

31 "A Problem of Common Ground," Advisory Council on Historic Preservation, May 14, 1999.

32 Superintendent's Annual Report, Fiscal Year 1999.

33 The Gettysburg Borough Council voted to reaffirm its unanimous October 1998 opposition to the GMP by a vote of 5-1. Eline, having realized that Latschar was willing to work with the town, urged his colleagues to reconsider their vote and support the GMP. They would not. "Gettysburg Still Opposes Park Plan," The Evening Sun, Aug. 19, 1999.

34 "Gettysburg Park Plan Sees Light of Day," The Evening Sun, June 18, 1999.

lifted earlier in the year. The plaintiffs appealed to the D.C. Circuit Court in early 2000 to overturn the District Court ruling that had lifted the stay, but that Court reaffirmed the District Court ruling. The deer-reduction program that resumed in October after a two-year suspension continues today. Davis v. Latschar is a landmark decision upon which the NPS relies in its efforts to protect National Parks from overabundant wildlife.

In October, a House-Senate conference removed Klink's amendment from the Appropriations Bill just as Santorum said it would, and it wasn't restored. But after the Bill came out of conference, President Clinton threatened to veto it, even though he said he supported the Gettysburg proposal that it contained.[35] After more haggling before threatened deadlines, Clinton signed the Bill that drove the last nail into the Klink amendment's coffin and, again, propelled the GMP forward. Customarily, a thirty-day waiting period without public comment would follow the release of the final GMP before it went into effect. But Klink's machinations placed Interior Secretary Babbitt, a Democratic supporter of the GMP, in a bind. Rather than risk antagonizing the Democrat Klink, who was trying to unseat the Republican Santorum, by signing the GMP in July, Regional Director Marie Rust was asked not to sign it until the President signed the Appropriations Bill. That Bill contained positive language about Gettysburg that would provide some political cover for Babbitt:

> The Committees, through previous appropriations, have supported the preparation of a new GMP for GNMP to enable the NPS to more adequately interpret the Battle of Gettysburg and to preserve the artifacts and landscapes that help tell the story of this great conflict of the Civil War. Accordingly, the managers acknowledge the need for a new visitor's facility and support the proposed public-private partnership as a unique approach to the interpretive needs of our National Parks.[36]

So, on November 23, 1999, five months after the GMP's initial release in June, Rust finally signed the "record of decision" that signified the end of the planning process that began with the preparation of the 1995 DCP four years before and gave Gettysburg the go-ahead to build the Museum

---

35   "Congress Approves Gettysburg Fix-up Bill," *The Patriot-News*, Oct. 22, 1999; "Gettysburg Plan Headed for Veto," *York Daily Record*, Oct. 23, 1999.

36   House-Senate Appropriations Conference Report, Congressional Record, Oct. 20, 1999, H10542-43.

and Visitor Center.[37] But there was still work to do on a contract with the Foundation before Latschar's full attention could be directed toward landscape rehabilitation.[38]

Meanwhile, the Park's opponents shifted tactics, as their hopes for defeating the GMP dwindled. What began as a litany of attacks on the draft GMP became attacks on the planning process. When that failed, the criticism dropped down to personal attacks upon the Superintendent, under the assumption that if the Superintendent could be personally discredited, then the NPS might abandon the draft GMP.[39] A sympathetic *Civil War News* article posed leading questions about whether Latschar had a Park fence built just for his own horse or used Park funds to pay for his wife's trip to California. Or whether Latschar would soon close the Park to cars and force visitors to pay for a bus ride. The article concluded, "These were among a host of false allegations that have bedeviled the Park in the recent past... The charges often surface anonymously. Some make it into the pages of local and even national newspapers before deflating for lack of substance. Each time, Park officials issued denials and attempted to set the record straight." Latschar said, "There is always the vain hope that you can get a superintendent removed or transferred. Potentially more dangerous are [direct] appeals to members of Congress who may not be so well-versed on the plan."[40] But his constant fear that diminished day by day over the two years that he and Kinsley worked together was that at any time Kinsley might say he'd had enough. As time passed, those thoughts disappeared .

At the end of 1999, Kinsley wrote another letter, this time to Sardella, noting that he had advanced $1.5 million to the Foundation during the year and that he was converting the advance to a gift. He still had no contract with the NPS, his gifts to the Foundation were now over $3.5 million, and he stayed busy on a variety of Gettysburg projects. After taking title to the LeVan land, he researched its historical significance to the Battle to allay environmental concerns regarding its proposed use. No historical artifacts were found, and the work was submitted to the Pennsylvania Historical and Museum Commission for review and approval. Park historians confirmed the

37 "Gettysburg Restoration Marches On," *Washington Post*, Nov. 24, 1999.

38 "Latschar Copes With Critics' Charges," *Civil War News*, Sept. 1999; "Gettysburg Park Plan A Go," *The Evening Sun*, Nov. 24, 1999.

39 Superintendent' s Annual Report, Fiscal Year 1999.

40 " Latschar Copes with Critics' Charges," *Civil War News*, Sept. 1999.

location of Union artillery lines, but they were well away from the proposed construction. He worked on the contract with the NPS. He gave speeches and met with local officials. He met with hotel/motel owners, and they urged him to keep the Visitor Center open late so visitors would need to rent rooms. And he met with the restaurant/gift shop owners who lobbied him to close the Visitor Center early so they would shop in Gettysburg in the evening. Two years before, Senator Santorum had a similarly ambiguous experience while paying a visit to Gettysburg in a vain attempt to pour oil on troubled waters. Two newspapers wrote conflicting headlines. *The Evening Sun* ran with "Merchants Disgruntled after Santorum Visit."[41] The *Gettysburg Times* countered with "Officials Upbeat After Santorum Park Session."[42]

From the moment of his selection, Kinsley wondered how he would raise $30 million, which would require a new type of fundraising for him. A short sentence in the GMP stated that no construction of any part of the facility would occur until funds were secured, a clear indication that the NPS was worried about it too.[43] At the 1998 Senate hearing, Bumpers oozed skepticism about Kinsley's ability to raise the money. A year later, in the House hearing, Hansen seemed ready to wager Galvin that Kinsley would never raise the money. Meanwhile, Kinsley was trying to learn more about fundraising. He visited the Statue of Liberty where a restoration campaign led by Lee Iacocca had been spectacularly successful. He spoke with fundraising consultants from all over the country. Sardella said she was beginning to feel they needed help, and she thought Kinsley must have felt the same way. She thought they needed someone who'd done it before. Kinsley hired four or five staffers. And he also hired Dan Sherman, an executive recruiter.

That spring of 2000, the Rosensteel lawsuit was in discovery when in March the plaintiff's attorney asked for a settlement conference. The case was quickly settled, but questions remained.[44] In March of the prior year, the NPS had announced plans to build a $500,000 temporary storage facility for most of the Park's Museum collection, a central piece of Latschar's new vision for the Park.[45] The Park Service denied that the facility was related

---

41 "Merchants Disgruntled After Santorum Visit," *The Evening Sun*, Nov. 18, 1998.

42 "Officials Upbeat After Santorum Session," *Gettysburg Times*, Nov. 19, 1998.

43 General Management Plan and Environmental Impact Statement, June, 1999, 100.

44 Superintendent's Annual Report, Fiscal Year 2000.

45 "Park Confirms Plans for $500,000 Temporary Artifact Storage Facility," *Gettysburg Times*, May 6, 1999.

in any way to the Rosensteel lawsuit, which on its surface appeared questionable. But Latschar said that Stanton simply wanted to show the public that the Park Service was doing something constructive to take better care of the collection, and that Stanton personally authorized the expenditure. Seven months later, the plaintiff's attorney seemed to agree with the Park Service, saying that the storage facility really didn't affect their lawsuit.[46] By terms of the settlement, the plaintiffs agreed that the NPS had discretion to manage the Park's collection, and that included the ability to loan, trade, or de-accession items from the original Rosensteel donation. The settlement also legally confirmed the NPS's position that there were no legally binding conditions placed upon the original donation of the collection to the NPS.[47] By mid-summer 2000, the interim storage building was completed, and the Park Service moved ahead with the relocation of those portions of the Park's archival and artifact collections that were designated for the new facility.[48]

As late as May 2000, Hansen, apparently still convinced that the Cyclorama building was the linchpin of the "stop the GMP" effort, penned a letter to John Berry, an attorney at the Department of the Interior "strongly urging" that the Advisory Board "be directed to review anew the listing of the Cyclorama building as a National Historic Landmark."[49] Nothing came of it.

Concurrently, efforts to untangle the tower muddle progressed from failed negotiations with Ottenstein to condemnation and then a land taking on June 15, 2000. As the initiative to take the tower down advanced, its funding was suddenly problematical, both with respect to the mandatory owner's compensation for a taking and for the out-of-pocket cost of bringing the tower to the ground safely. The latter problem was resolved when Controlled Demolitions, Inc., of Phoenix, Maryland, offered to implode the tower, and clean up the site at no cost to the NPS. The owner's

46 "Battle Over Gettysburg Plans Will Go On Opponents Vow," *The Patriot-News*, Dec. 9, 1999.

47 Superintendent's Annual Report, Fiscal Year 2009.

48 "The final collection storage plan was completed, storage and furniture was purchased and installed, all of the textiles were treated and relocated, the archaeological collection was decompressed, culled and re-housed, archival materials were re-house, survey and assessment of diacetate negatives was completed, conservation of the bound manuscript collection was completed, and conservation of the collection and treatment of papers objects continued." Superintendent' s Annual Report, Fiscal Year 2000.

49 Hansen to Berry, May 16, 2000.

The National Tower falls

compensation was trickier, in that the amount would be determined by the Federal District Court in Harrisburg after the taking, and it could not be known until the Court acted.

On June 14, 2000, tower operators vacated the tower property. The NPS took possession the next day. On July 3 NPS Director Stanton and Secretary Babbitt made short speeches and led 10,000 people in a count-down to a ceremonial firing of two Civil War cannons. Three seconds later, the imaginary cannonballs flew to their target, and the real charge exploded. The 393-foot, two million-pound tower shuddered, tipped, and slid to the ground. Ironically, the tower was crowded with visitors before the demoli-tion. Opinions of the tower, like many things at Gettysburg, were far from unanimous. But most people believed that the Battlefield was finally made ready for the new GMP by the tower's removal. Ottenstein died one month later on August 7, 2000. The Court awarded his estate $3 million.

Kinsley's GNBMF and the NPS signed the General Agreement on June 30, 2000. It was eleven pages long, not including exhibits. It obligated the GNBMF to raise funds for, and design and construct facilities that would include collections storage, a Museum, and a Visitor Center with exhibits and interpretive venues. The GNBMF would restore the Cyclorama paint-ing and rehabilitate the historic appearance of Ziegler's Grove. It would also operate the facilities it built "and, at an appropriate time mutually agreed upon by the parties, donate the building and grounds to the Secretary of the Interior for the use of the Park."[50] It was the only contract of its kind with the Park Service—an historic occasion.

The contract revealed that the Visitor Center would be designed to accommodate 1,465,000 visitors per year, compared to 450,000 for the interim Visitor Center, all based on visitation estimates supplied by the NPS. The café that was originally proposed to seat six hundred, then three hundred, would seat two-hundred-fifty and would provide light food and beverage service, but no alcohol.[51] Bus groups needing full meals would be directed elsewhere. The contract nicely defined the lines of authority and responsibility between the Park and the Foundation. The Foundation had broad responsibility to operate the Visitor Center, but its purview was carefully overlaid with a lush carpet of required NPS approvals that assured NPS control. The Foundation "provided the funding for the proposed project," but only in accordance with the Fundraising Agreement with the NPS. That seven-page agreement was an administrative document that identified each party's responsibilities for accounting records and other items, but other than "conduct a fundraising campaign," there was very little in the Fundraising Agreement about fundraising.[52]

The General Agreement, however, sowed the seeds of tension that exist in most partnerships and that require extraordinary trust and leadership of both principals in order to succeed. For example, the Agreement states that revenues in excess of operating expenses, debt service, and reserves should provide donations to the Park. Donations from the GNMP are a key NPS objective. But if there is a shortfall, the maintenance of the customary level

---

50 General Agreement, June 30, 2000, 1.

51 The year before, in June 1999, Thomas Martin, economic consultant, conducted research into the economic impact of the Museum and Visitor Center on the Gettysburg area in response to local business opponents of the GMP, and amended his earlier work by estimating the impact of a new proposal to "change the Visitor Center food service from a three hundred-seat family-oriented cafeteria to an approximately two hundred fifty-seat limited menu food service facility. According to Martin, "because… there would be fewer seats available, the usage pattern of the food service would be reduced and the sales volume would be reduced." Martin said, "the annual amount available [for return] to GNMP is reduced to an estimated $298,000 from the $393,300 that would be possible under the assumption of a family oriented cafeteria." Finally, Martin concluded that the change… is estimated to have no impact on overall visitor spending… Some visitor spending on food would be shifted from inside the Park to outside the Park.

52 Fundraising agreement between Gettysburg National Military Park, NPS and Gettysburg National Battlefield Museum Foundation, June 30, 2000.

of visitor service will take precedence over donations to the NPS. In other words, the Foundation should take care of its visitors first. The level of operating expenses, therefore, becomes one determinant of whether the NPS receives donations from the Park. The annual operating budget is reviewed by the NPS. If the NPS has no comments on it, "the budget in its entirety shall be deemed to be approved," the unwritten corollary being that if the NPS does have comments on it, the budget shall be deemed to be not approved.[53] It would appear to be a very short jump then from budget approval that might be withheld, to discussions of operating expenses, or to changes in the way the Visitor Center is operated by the Foundation. Ordinarily, when the NPS encounters a financial shortfall, its instinct is to cut expenses. Conversely, the Foundation's natural instinct would more likely be to increase expenses in an effort to increase revenue. The Foundation spends money in order to raise money. But the potential conflict presents itself if the NPS feels it needs to reduce expenses in order to protect its donation. But the Agreement also states, "In the event there is a shortfall in the revenues necessary to meet operating expenses, debt service, and reserves, there will be no requirement on the part of the Foundation for a donation of funds to the Park or to the NPS for any purpose."[54]

To further complicate matters, salary scales are higher in the private sector, the Foundation, than they are in the public sector, the Park Service. The public partner works regular hours while the private partner may not. If the Foundation's fundraising activities are underfunded or if the Foundation is unable to hire the best people, then the resulting inadequate spending may depress the amount of funds raised, and that, too, will decrease cash to other parks or so goes the logic. In reality, it's tenuous, and the idea of the public/private partnership that benefits both partners is tested every day, especially if there is a financial shortfall.

While the tower was coming down, Kinsley was still pondering how to deal with the enormous fundraising project that he'd volunteered to lead. In his words, "I hired a headhunter and we interviewed some people. None of them fit the bill. But then we learned that Bob had just left the Williamsburg Foundation." "Bob" was Robert C. Wilburn, past President and CEO of Colonial Williamsburg.[55] "When we found Bob, I called John Latschar and

53 General Agreement, June 30, 2000: Exhibit C, Operations Plan: E, 2, 4.

54 Ibid. III, D, 3, c.

55 Colonial Williamsburg is a living-history museum and private foundation presenting part of a historic district in the city of Williamsburg, Virginia, USA.

said I want you to meet somebody."[56]

Latschar remembers the call:

The 1997 Regional Superintendent's Conference was at Williamsburg. Bob Wilburn was CEO and he was on the program. I heard him speak and he was impressive. But I was most impressed by the amazingly complex way they had brought the story of slavery into Colonial Williamsburg. I can still remember some of the living history demonstrations that I saw down there, so I was doubly impressed by what Wilburn had done at Williamsburg. I'd never seen or heard of him since. Then Bob Kinsley called me and said, "I've got a guy I want to hire as the first President of the Foundation, and I want you to meet him." I said, "Great, who is it? He said, "Bob Wilburn from Williamsburg." I said, "I don't need to meet him. Hire him. Hire him as quickly as you can."[57]

One man was from government and the other was from the private sector. But never were two men who had more in common brought together to do a job. Without knowing it, they shared a vision for Gettysburg, and this was the start of their work together.

56 Kinsley interview, Nov. 21, 2013.
57 Latschar interview, Nov. 20, 2013.

CHAPTER 7

The Foundation Takes Shape

It was two-and-a half years between Kinsley's selection as the NPS's preferred partner in November 1997 and the signing of the General Agreement in June 2000. During that time, aided largely by broad national support for the plan, the NPS overcame a torrent of local opposition to the GMP. And while Kinsley was hardly idle, the Foundation itself remained an ambitious concept: a good idea that was far from being realized. The job of the private partner in a public/private partnership is to raise money for the public partner. Kinsley had no prior national fundraising experience. No outside money had been raised. What made the Gettysburg partnership unique in the NPS was that the private partner, in addition to fundraising, had a long-term contract to build and operate the major facility. The arrangement is replete with both opportunities and potential conflicts. But after Kinsley hired Bob Wilburn in the summer of 2000, the Foundation, as well as the partnership, began to come together.[1]

Bob Wilburn has a brilliant, and most unusual, entrepreneurial resume. He was born and raised in Western Pennsylvania. His father was a welder and a union organizer at Westinghouse Electric. From the very beginning, Wilburn's mother insisted that young Wilburn bring home all A's on his report card. When the time came for college, Wilburn applied to top-ranked schools—Columbia, for example, where he was admitted with a full scholarship. But New York intimidated young Wilburn, and when he received an appointment to the Air Force Academy, he accepted it.

Wilburn did well at the Academy although his poor eyesight kept him off the pilot track. He earned his degree in Engineering and Economics in 1965, and he did well enough to earn a full scholarship to Princeton's Woodrow Wilson School, where he received his Master's degree in Economics and Public Affairs. After two years at Princeton, Wilburn was assigned to an issue-oriented staff group in Washington, D.C. and began fulfilling his five-year military obligation.

---

1 Biographical information about Bob Wilburn in this section and elsewhere in this chapter is drawn from an in-person interview with Wilburn on Sept. 21, 2015, and a telephone interview on April 6, 2016.

While there, he produced a thick report on the impact on the Air Force of an all-volunteer military. That report caught the eye of the White House, and it led to a staff assignment to the President's Commission on an all-volunteer armed force that included such luminaries as Milton Friedman, Alan Greenspan, General Lauris Norstad, and Roy Wilkins. To this day, Wilburn recalls it as "an incredible eye-opening experience." When the assignment ended in 1970, Wilburn, well armed with the fruits of his labor of the prior two years, returned to Princeton and earned his Ph.D. in three months, only the second Ph.D. that the Wilson School had ever given out. From there, he completed his military obligation as an economic advisor to Defense Secretary Mel Laird.

In 1972 Wilburn began a four-year stint at Chase Manhattan Bank where he headed Operations Research and wound up as a senior officer in the Treasury Department, responsible for determining the bank's daily liquidity needs and running its foreign-exchange position. But by spring of 1976, at age 32, Wilburn was restless. By chance, he saw an advertisement in *The New York Times* for the presidency of Indiana University of Pennsylvania, just a few miles from where he was born, and he knew immediately that he was the right man for the job. Apparently the University, then with about 13,000 students, thought so too. "I wrote them in May, interviewed in June, and greeted the incoming freshman in August." He was at Indiana for three years, where he earned a reputation as a fund-raiser and a leader who was somehow able to solve previously intractable labor disputes.[2] As the youngest university president in the nation, Wilburn attracted attention, and in 1979, Dick Thornburgh, the newly elected Pennsylvania Governor, named him Secretary of Budget and Administration, arguably the second most powerful position in the Commonwealth.

In 1983 Wilburn moved on. Thornburgh persuaded him to become Secretary of Education, and after two fulfilling years there, he left government to assume leadership of the Carnegie Institute in Pittsburgh. The Institute oversaw two museums as well as Pittsburgh's public library. During Wilburn's tenure, the Institute merged with the Buhl Science Center to form the new $40 million Carnegie Science Center, and then constructed the new Warhol Museum that raised the number of the Institute's museums to four. The

---

2 Wilburn said, "When I went there we had all these lawsuits—collective bargaining problems. It really was so simple… We had hired this negotiator who seemed almost to enjoy stoking fires. After…[one]… meeting I asked him to come into my office and I told him he was fired. He said you can't fire me. I was hired by Governor Shapp. I said that's fine. I'm firing you. I may reinstate you if the governor calls me, but he's going to have to call. I knew the governor wouldn't call, so that worked out well."

core of the Warhol Museum's collection was the Warhol collection, 1,000 paintings reportedly valued at between $800 million and $2 billion, and it came to the new Museum as the end result of Wilburn's negotiations with the Warhol Foundation. For all this, Wilburn was voted Pittsburgh's Man of the Year in 1992. After Carnegie, he was named President of Colonial Williamsburg, where, in his seven-year tenure, he revitalized that institution and oversaw a $300 million capital campaign. When Bob Wilburn arrived at Gettysburg in 2000, he had already raised substantial sums for Indiana University, Carnegie Institute, and Colonial Williamsburg.

When Kinsley became aware of Bob Wilburn's qualifications, Wilburn was fifty-six years old. He had a wealth of relevant experience at not-for-profit institutions, raising money, and building museums. He was well known in Pennsylvania; the only question was whether Kinsley could convince him to come to Gettysburg. Kinsley's pursuit began in May 2000 with the softest hard sell imaginable, skillfully orchestrated by Dan Sherman, Kinsley's soft-spoken, go-to, executive recruiter. Sherman talked to Wilburn about Gettysburg's history, about how Kinsley could use his help, and how rewarding it would be to assist in Gettysburg's rejuvenation. Wilburn knew well the historical significance of Gettysburg. But he hadn't envisioned a full-time commitment. Sherman's immediate goal was simply to arrange a meeting with Kinsley, which he did. Both Kinsley and Wilburn recall it. It was mid-summer 2000.

Kinsley says:

We dogged Bob. When I found out about him—knew his credentials— we would almost try to know where he was every day. So finally he was coming to York County in the middle of the summer with his wife, Pat. They were actually camped about a mile and a half from my home. Bob rode his bicycle on the rail trail through a tunnel on our farm that was there when Lincoln's funeral train went through. That evening he left his bike over there and walked across the lawn. He was probably here for two and a half or maybe three hours, and we talked and had dinner on the porch. We talked about a lot of things.[3]

Wilburn recalls, "We had recently begun camping, because we had two Great Danes, and with a small trailer, we could go with our big dogs wherever we wanted. There was a show of Scottish Highlands nearby. We had a small herd of them at our farm and we wanted to see the show. We were

---

3 Kinsley interview, Nov. 21, 2013.

camping near Kinsley's home." Anne Kinsley remembers, "He rode his bike up and then walked across the lawn… He looked like the right person."[4]

She must have felt Wilburn's utter lack of pretense at once: his openness and honesty. People trust Bob Wilburn. And trustworthiness is the essential quality and a common trait of the best fundraisers. Wilburn continued, "I went over to dinner, I met Anne, and we three had a pleasant conversation. Bob Kinsley was pretty persuasive in talking about what should be done and could be done at Gettysburg. He was in a full court press to get me. He wasn't putting me in competition with others either. That was important at that point in my career. But by the end of dinner, I had pretty much decided that I was going to be full-time."

In succeeding weeks, Wilburn and Kinsley went back and forth through Sherman. Kinsley put together a financial package for Wilburn that was essentially nothing more than Wilburn had originally received from Colonial Williamsburg eight years before, although the GNBMF was riskier. There was no endowment and no revenue. But Wilburn, nevertheless, became increasingly comfortable with the idea of totally committing his energy and experience to Gettysburg. Kinsley did all the right things, including agreeing to Wilburn temporarily remaining in Washington, D.C. Wilburn credits his wife, Pat, for doing a lot of the convincing. She thought he was uniquely qualified, given his background and interest in Pennsylvania. With Pat Wilburn's unqualified support, Bob Wilburn joined the GNBMF on August 21, 2000. But when Wilburn asked Kinsley to defer the announcement, Kinsley worried that he was having second thoughts. Kinsley thought Wilburn had other business opportunities that he was still considering. He also thought Wilburn was concerned that he and Kinsley might not get along. Wilburn thinks Kinsley misunderstood him. He appreciated Kinsley's enthusiasm, but he felt he needed time to put his past activities behind him and adjust to the idea of a full-time commitment before he began speaking publicly on behalf of the Foundation. They announced Wilburn on October 24, 2000. Local newspapers carried the news, referring to Wilburn as "nationally recognized."[5] Years later, Anne Kinsley said, "If Bob Wilburn hadn't come along when he did, I'm not sure we would've made it through all this."[6]

At that moment, six years after Latschar's arrival, and three years after Kinsley's selection by the NPS, the project's operational leadership was finally

---

4   Anne Kinsley interview, Feb. 17, 2014.

5   "Gettysburg Project Head Finds Perfect Fit," *The Patriot-News*, Dec. 4, 2000.

6   Anne Kinsley interview, Feb. 17, 2014.

John Latschar, Bob Wilburn, Bob Kinsley in front of old (interim) Visitor Center

in place: Kinsley, the entrepreneurial philanthropist, the engine driving the project that was geared to upgrade Park facilities and improve and broaden the educational experience of Gettysburg; Latschar, the soldier, historian, and public servant, whose vision for Gettysburg's future became the NPS's vision that both Kinsley and Wilburn shared; and Wilburn, combining many qualities of the other two, but uniquely possessing the experiential and political resources, the resilience, and the restless energy that was required to line up the funds they needed to drive the project to its completion. When Wilburn came aboard, Kinsley and Latschar were already like brothers. Wilburn's relationship with Kinsley, his employer, was respectful, and it warmed as time passed, as they came to appreciate what each other could do. Kinsley says he had a very good relationship with Wilburn. Wilburn says he always thought, given Kinsley's commitment and passion for the project, that you couldn't possibly have a better chairman, not to mention his expertise in building, which was what they were doing. If there was any surprise, it was that Wilburn and Latschar, so respectful of each other's talent, worked in perfect tandem.

On Wilburn's first day, he might have been forgiven if he were at a loss to decide where to begin. The challenge he faced differed significantly from the challenges he had faced at Indiana, at Carnegie, and at Williamsburg. For Gettysburg, he needed to raise funds from donors who had not been identified, to fund a project that had not been defined. There was no donor list of past supporters whom he could rely on; nor were there architectural plans that pinpointed the building they would build. There were multiple questions to be answered, and obstacles to overcome, each of which cried out for his attention, and they all had top priority; most were connected to each other, and there was no obvious place to start. Wilburn simply had to begin, and "begin" he did. From his small, temporary, rented office in Washington, he studied the project, what it was going to cost, and how to pay for it. Throughout Kinsley's selection process, the project was often referred to as a $43 million project, although negotiations with the Park Service eliminated several of Kinsley's commercial venues in response to the public's resistance to commercialism at Gettysburg, and the estimated cost fell to just over $39 million. Wilburn thought differently. He'd overseen museum construction at Carnegie and at Colonial Williamsburg. He knew that the special requirements of museums differed from less costly commercial or residential buildings. Wilburn knew from the beginning that they would not be able to build what they needed for $39 million.

Fortuitously, the perfect vehicle for communicating Wilburn's ideas was simply awaiting his input: the Fundraising Agreement that Kinsley had agreed to with Park Service Director Robert Stanton at the signing of the General Agreement in June 2000. It obligated the Foundation to "conduct a fundraising campaign," which was no surprise, and to develop a financial management plan, no later than 120 days after the agreement became effective that would identify costs, and how those costs would be paid. The financial plan would become part of the fundraising plan.[7] The first person Wilburn talked to about fundraising was Jack Hills. John M. Hills was Vice President of External Affairs at The Brookings Institution for twelve years before he went out on his own. Wilburn asked Hills to do the feasibility study. Working quickly, Wilburn, Hills, and Dan Driver, Kinsley's CFO, put together the financial management plan that the Foundation agreed to prepare, and, after obtaining a thirty-day extension, delivered it on November 29, 2000.

The five-year, pro forma analysis showed a 2003 groundbreaking for the project, a 2005 completion date, and a total project cost of $67.2 million,

7 Fundraising Agreement, June 30, 2000, Article III, B. 2 and 5.

not $39.2 million. The $39.2 million figure had included no fundraising expenses or design costs, and several spaces in the new Visitor Center were assumed to be self-financing, that is, the user of the space would pay for its construction and would own it. For example, the bookstore, the restaurant, and the theater were assumed to be built and owned by others, and they were not included in the $39.2 million construction estimate. But to Wilburn, it was essential, for operating reasons, that the Foundation own and control these venues. And, as previously noted, Museum space is more expensive to build than commercial space, so he added $4.5 million to the cost of the project for those two items. Wilburn also added his own estimate of $5.5 million to restore the Cyclorama painting. In a masterful piece of understatement, the plan read, "… It appears that the cost of preparing a plan and study for the restoration of the Cyclorama painting, performing the restoration, and relocating the painting, will be more than originally anticipated."[8] He added $3 million to rehabilitate Ziegler's Grove after the Cyclorama building was razed because the final scope of the project had not yet been defined, $5 million for exhibits, $10 million for endowment, and it all added up to $67.2 million.[9]

As to why the initial estimates were so low, the NPS was, in the project's initial stages, locked in a heated political battle with their local critics and with Congress, and they could not have wanted the project to appear to be more costly than necessary. Politicians like Congressman Goodling and Senator Bumpers, had wondered if sufficient funds could be raised even for a $40 million project. Wilburn, holding the opposite point of view of a fundraiser, knew that large potential donors would size their gifts to the size of the project. They would donate larger gifts to larger projects and smaller gifts to smaller projects. To him, it was counter-productive to advertise the cost of the project as less than it actually was because less money would be raised. He calculated further that with about $12 million of borrowings combined with over $3 million of earnings from deposited donations, he would need to raise $52 million to complete the $67.2 million project, nearly twice the earlier calculation of $27.4 million.[10]

---

8 Fundraising & Financial Management Plan submitted on 11/29/002 to the NPS by the GNBMF, approved by the NPS, Dec. 19, 2000, 4.

9 Ibid. 16.

10 Fundraising Agreement, June 30, 2000, Article I, D. The fundraising agreement stipulated that no more than $11.925 million of debt could be assumed for the $39.2 million project. The allowable debt was not increased as the size of the project expanded: "Gettysburg Group Seeks $52 Million," *The Patriot-News*, Jan 16, 2001. "Visitor Center Done Deal," *The Evening Sun*, July 6, 2000.

Kinsley's original proposal, criticized for being too commercial, was designed that way for a reason. Kinsley wanted the project to pay for itself. When, through negotiations with the NPS, Kinsley eliminated several revenue sources from the original plan, he looked for sources to replace them, such as parking fees, which were also discarded. Kinsley knew that without the commercial venues, and with no fee for Museum admission, it would be difficult to break even. With prospective revenue curtailed, the sheer size of Wilburn's $52 million campaign attracted attention. Washington politicians were afraid that they would have to come up with the money if Kinsley didn't. Kinsley believed in Gettysburg, and America's love of it, but he could have had no idea where $52 million would come from. At the time of his selection in November 1997, when he first spoke publicly about the then-$40-to-$43-million project, he said that they expected to raise 65 to 75 percent of the money from sponsorships, grants, and donations; and that the rest of the construction funds would come from loans to be paid off in twenty to twenty-five years, before the facility reverted to the Park Service."[11] He made no mention of government funding.

When Denis Galvin testified before the Thomas Subcommittee in February 1998 he said, "… One of the criteria here is that there will be no additional cost to the taxpayers, not even operating costs."[12] One year later, before the Hansen Subcommittee, Galvin said "the proposal would allow us to preserve the Park's archives, collections, and the colossal Cyclorama painting. Gettysburg would be able to provide much improved interpretation of the causes, course, and consequences of the Gettysburg campaign. Moreover, thanks to the generosity and entrepreneurial spirit of private sector partners, [Kinsley], NPS could accomplish this at no cost to the taxpayers.[13] There was no confusion about what Galvin said. Therefore, an announcement in October 2001 that Congress appropriated $2.5 million for rehabilitation of the Cyclorama painting was met with consternation by the project's critics.[14] "No cost to the taxpayer" became their rallying cry. Constantly probing for weaknesses in Latschar's program, they insisted that anything short of "no cost to the taxpayer" was a betrayal and a failure. To this

11 "Kinsley Outlines Vision for Park Complex," *Gettysburg Times*, Nov. 8, 1997.

12 Thomas hearing, Feb. 24, 1998, 10.

13 Hansen hearing, Feb. 11, 1999, 9.

14 "Funds OK'd for Painting Restoration," *The Evening Sun*, Oct. 22, 2001. The story behind this government funding appears in Chapter 10.

day, the project's critics point to government funding as evidence of its failure.

This was not clear to Kinsley, however. He made his original statement before his initial proposal was altered by the NPS in negotiations. And as the identifiable costs of the project rose, he never wavered even though he couldn't have known where the money would come from. That was why, three months after Galvin's appearance before the Thomas Subcommittee in 1998, and nine months before his appearance before the Hansen Subcommittee in 1999, Kinsley's spokesperson publicly acknowledged that "changes in the proposal, as a result of public concerns [about commercialism], raise the possibility that the Museum and Visitor Center complex cannot be built without federal money." Yet the *Gettysburg Times* reporter continued to insist that from their first presentation, NPS officials pledged that the project would not receive "one dime" of federal money.[15] After Kinsley's negotiations with the NPS altered his original proposal neither he nor the Park Service drew attention to whether or not federal money would be involved even though Kinsley had made it clear, publicly, that federal funds would be welcomed and might be needed. That story was under-reported and then lost.

State funding was another matter. Neither Galvin, nor anyone associated with the project, mentioned not soliciting funds from Pennsylvania. Galvin, in his capacity as Deputy Director of the NPS, could only have been referring to normal Congressional funding of the NPS when he stated "no cost to the taxpayers."[16] So when the *Gettysburg Times* reported that the Foundation requested $10 million from Pennsylvania for construction of the complex, and that opponents of the public/private partnership were indignant, Wilburn was unmoved.[17] It seems unlikely that anyone, supporters or critics, gave any thought to state support of a national park until Wilburn did. He had been the Commonwealth's Secretary of Budget and Administration and Secretary of Education for six years. There were very few senior government officials in Pennsylvania whom he did not know. One can only imagine that even as he was considering accepting the Foundation presidency and assuming responsibility for raising funds for Gettysburg that he could have not thought that he would seek state funding. Wilburn knew that the state program he had in mind was set up precisely for a Gettysburg-type project and that it had enormous value

15 "Federal Funds 'Welcome' for New Visitor Center," *Gettysburg Times*, May 30, 1998.

16 Hansen hearing, Feb. 11, 1999, 9.

17 "Foundation Seeks $10 Million from State," *Gettysburg Times*, Oct. 26, 2002.

statewide. He was not part of the initial discussions that led some in the community to believe that no public money would be used to construct the complex. "It was always my intention to try to get state support. I thought about it the moment I took the job."[18]

The fundraising portion of the financial plan was less detailed than the financial analysis. There was mention of plans to study the feasibility of raising $52 million, although a feasibility study for a Gettysburg-type project was nearly impossible because most capital campaigns, whether for hospitals, schools, museums, or other not-for-profits, begin with a list of past funders, upon whom the institution relies for financial support and whose reaction to an imminent campaign can be measured. Nevertheless, the Foundation's study was based on interviews with over sixty individuals and potential supporters, and it identified twenty-seven prospects with the capacity to give at the $5 million level, and another twenty-five who could give at the $1 million level.[19] But capacity to give is a far cry from a commitment to give. The GNBMF began its campaign with no past donors, only a blank sheet of paper. What that meant was the success of the campaign was more uncertain, and it would take longer to finish than would normally be the case in a capital campaign. Wilburn and Hills, the Foundation's consultant, thought it would take five years, and it took eight years.

The feasibility study was based on interviews with potential donors as well as leaders of the Gettysburg community. They were looking for suggestions and insights that would sharpen their solicitations.[20] Some particularly apt and constructive advice emerged from one of those meetings, advice that would alter the trajectory of the capital campaign. It had been the Foundation's intention to focus its efforts on Civil War buffs, individuals who studied, and were seriously interested in the Civil War. A potential donor told Wilburn that he was missing the point, that Civil War buffs won't be interested in Gettysburg. He said that they were interested in preserving battlefields and that in their minds, Gettysburg was preserved. He advised focusing on people who were interested in education. It was good advice

---

18 Ibid.

19 Oversight (Radanovich) hearing before the Subcommittee on National Parks, Recreation, and Public Lands of the Committee on Resource, U.S. House of Representatives, March 21, 2002, Hoffman testimony, 19. Hoffman was Deputy Assistant Secretary for Fish and Wildlife and Parks, U.S. Department of the Interior.

20 Fundraising and Financial Management Plan, 9.

although it was just what Kinsley and Latschar had believed from the beginning. Children's education was Kinsley's original motivation. And as we
shall see below, Latschar's work on broadening the Battlefield interpretation
at Gettysburg to include the causes and consequences of the Civil War was
always about education.

The fundraising plan listed the people who would be soliciting funds, it
disclosed that they were identifying Board candidates, and it included the
new Foundation's bylaws. The plan said the fundraising process would include invitations to visit Gettysburg, customized guided tours, and special
events.[21] It said that they were identifying donors, and that they would be
focusing on prospects with the potential to contribute $1 million or more to
the Foundation.[22] With the new $52 million figure now firmly planted in
their minds, they went to work. Wilburn, Kinsley, to a lesser extent Latschar,
and others, began meeting with possible donors, and they explained the
Gettysburg project, urged them to visit Gettysburg, and asked them for suggestions of others whom they might contact.

And there were others, mostly critics, who were looking at the larger
cost estimate of the project. As it was probed and dissected, more attention
was directed toward more aspects of the imaginative project, details emerged
from more analysis—and those details were expensive. It wasn't so much
that the costs of the project rose over time, although they did; it was that a
segment of the real costs of the unknown project had not been identified.
They were always there, but they emerged only as the project was scrutinized.
As costs were identified, some observers were uneasy about how Gettysburg
could attract such enormous sums. Senators were skeptical. Local opponents
were heartened, as they perceived that Latschar's ambitions might just be
pie-in-the-sky. Two years before, Congressman Goodling pointed out that
Kinsley's scaled-back proposal and his original proposal were as different as
day and night. Goodling had observed ironically that he wouldn't start selling tickets for the groundbreaking. Elaborating further, he said, "When the
Superintendent talks about the original [proposal], and you don't need any
funds from the federal government, and then you look at what they have to
do after they pared it down, it is a bigger loss to the person [Kinsley] who is
trying to do it."[23]

---

21   Ibid. 10.

22   Ibid. 9.

23   "Goodling Not Optimistic About New Proposal," *Gettysburg Times*, April 20, 1998.

So that's where matters stood in early 2001. The NPS and the Foundation were silent about their sources of funding, but critics didn't let it go. Uberman, for example, in late 2002, said, "I think the Foundation should keep its word to the taxpayers."[24] A year and a half later at a public meeting, he "asked Wilburn whether the Foundation and NPS have an 'ethical responsibility' to honor what he described as their 'promises' not to use tax dollars for the project...." Wilburn replied that at some point he'd need to "get over it."[25]

The Foundation was focused on more than actual fundraising. It also helped develop the interpretive "storyline" that visitors would read and hear at the new Museum. Perhaps more than any other, this particular task went on in close concert with, and under the leadership of, the NPS that had begun the work years before, following the Silber Report.[26] Traditionally, battlefield interpretation at National Parks, and at Gettysburg, reflected both battlefield action and the national memory of reconciliation: the Blue and the Gray shaking hands over the stone wall at the Bloody Angle. But as historian David Blight points out, "Race was so deeply at the root of the Civil War's causes and consequences... that it served as the antithesis of a culture of reconciliation. The memory of slavery... never fit well into a developing narrative in which the Old and the New South were romanticized..."[27] The interpretive policy rankled many of the superintendents at historic Parks, who believed that visitors to their Parks, in addition to learning about battle action, should also learn about why the two sides were fighting, and the consequences of the fight. At the root of it was the NPS's interpretive policy toward slavery, which was to ignore it.

In a speech Latschar gave in Texas in April 2003, he recalled that when he began his tenure as Gettysburg Park Superintendent, he was asked to speak on the topic of *Gettysburg: The Next 100 Years*. He observed then that while Blacks should be intensely interested in the Civil War, they are not. He attributed that circumstance in part to the fact that battlefield interpretation

---

24 "State May Aid Visitor Center," *York Dispatch*, Nov. 4, 2002.

25 "Foundation Still Needs $21 Million to Break Ground," *Gettysburg Times*, May 7, 2004.

26 The Report, authored by Nina Silber, prepared in 1998 by Eric Foner, Jim McPherson, and Silber, under the auspices of the OAH.

27 David W. Blight, *Race and Reunion* (Cambridge and London: The Belknap Press of Harvard University Press, 2001), 4.

avoided mentioning what the Civil War was fought for. "For Blacks," said Latschar, "it has always been abundantly clear that the Confederacy was created to protect and preserve the institution of slavery," and that until the Park Service made that connection, "they could not hope to make the Civil War battlefields relevant to them."[28]

Latschar's speech triggered more than 1,100 postcards from Southern heritage groups to the Department of the Interior asking that Latschar be dismissed or reprimanded for "rewriting history."[29] But Interior didn't dismiss or reprimand him. He was part of a larger movement within the Park Service, among historians, and within the Congress, that had begun several years before. In a carefully worded letter, written in 2000 to Robert Thomas, an influential amateur Confederate historian, Latschar traced the movement back to the 1990 Boundary Act, in which Congress instructed the NPS "to interpret" the Battle of Gettysburg in the larger context of the Civil War and American history, including the causes and consequences of the Civil War."[30] He further traced it through the Park's Strategic Management Plan of 1997, and to a 1998 conference of Civil War Park superintendents held in Nashville, Tennessee.[31] His point was that whatever changes were afoot were not new. In 1998 there was a debate going about whether the NPS ought to be interpreting the causes and consequences of the Civil War on our battlefields, and most of [the Civil War community] was saying 'no.'"[32] They believed that the battlefields were sacred sites, memorials to the brave soldiers who fought and died there. They believed that to engage in a discussion of causes and consequences of the Civil War would be like discussing politics in church. And they believed that there was a time and a place for everything, and a Civil War battlefield was not the place to talk politics, and invite reopening the old wounds of the Civil War.

There was a group of superintendents of historic Parks, however, who believed that it was important to examine, on the battlefield, why the soldiers

28 National Counsel on Public History, Houston, Texas, April 24, 2003.

29 "The Last Battle," *Baltimore Sun*, July 1, 2001.

30 Latschar to Thomas, Aug. 2, 2000. Robert Thomas was Commander of the Robert E. Lee Camp of the Sons of the Confederate Veterans in Sandford, NC. He also led the fundraising effort for the Longstreet monument at Gettysburg.

31 The meeting was called by the Regional Directors from the Northeast and National Capital Regions of the NPS.

32 Latschar interview, Nov. 20, 2013.

were fighting and dying, as well as the larger results of the battle.[33] This meant adding content to waysides, the interpretive signs that dot the battlefields, and, more importantly, to the interpretive talks that rangers share with visitors every day. These superintendents adopted four principals at the 1998 Nashville, Tennessee, meeting of National Park Superintendents. One of these was that the NPS needed to talk about the causes and consequences of the American Civil War, not just the battle action, at all of our Civil War sites. The principles were submitted to the Park Service, they were approved, and in 1998 the NPS began to expand and deepen its interpretive stories at National Parks.

In Latschar's letter to Thomas, he patiently developed the idea that the Park's interpretation would concentrate not only on slavery, but it would develop other themes new to Park interpretation: Lee's military strategy; the background and experience of the soldiers; the impact of the Battle on citizens of Gettysburg; the wounded; women, especially Southern women, who fought their own battles at home; and other broad themes. To hammer his point home, he wrote that in 1861, the nation's political system failed, and that "we have to understand why our system of government failed, or each of those boys will really have died in vain." He wrote that the Park would develop these themes by letting the words of the participants themselves describe their feelings. He would let Alex Stevens and Jefferson Davis explain in their own words why their states determined that it was necessary to secede from the Union; and Abraham Lincoln explain in his own words why he determined to fight a war to preserve the Union; and Johnny Reb and Billy Yank describe their own experiences in their own words. Latschar's letter was a masterpiece, and by the time he and others had written or spoken about what the Park Service was doing at the historic Parks, and the new Museum opened its doors, most citizens appeared to accept, even embrace, the new interpretations.

When the Foundation welcomed the Gettysburg Museum Advisory Committee back to Gettysburg on January 8, 2001, for their second meeting, Park historians were sufficiently prepared, even at that early date, to speak for over three hours on the particular segments of the draft story line, from *Why We Went to War* through *The Gettysburg Address* and *The Results of the*

---

33 Robert K Sutton, Holding the High Ground: Interpreting the Civil War in National Parks, 47. Retrieved from. http://www.georgewright.org/253sutton.pdf Also Martin Gegner and Bart Ziino (Editors), *The Heritage of War* (London and New York: Routledge, 2012.

War.[34] When the Foundation began fundraising in earnest, they would need to be able to talk to donors about what would be written, seen, and heard in the new museum in order to stimulate interest in the project. Wilburn had not been in his new job for six months before he knew that enough work had been done by the Park Service and the Advisory Committee to satisfy him.

Meanwhile, the Friends, allied with the Foundation and the NPS, worked actively and effectively to prevent the development of the tourist-based commercial zone that critics predicted adjacent to the planned entrance to the new Visitor Center. The Civil War Trust had identified the Gettysburg Battlefield as one of ten battlefields most endangered by urban sprawl.[35]A spokesman for the Trust voiced concern that the new Visitor Center would create conditions along the Baltimore Pike corridor similar to those on Steinwehr Avenue—a jumble of tourist-oriented stores, punctuated with fast-food outlets.[36] The Friends bought three homes on the Baltimore Pike, resold two of them with conservation easements on them, and donated the third to the NPS. Then the Foundation acquired several parcels including a recreational vehicle business, and razed the building, returning the site to grassy open space. Critics of the project had long insisted that the new Visitor Center would attract the makings of a commercial strip. The Foundation, the NPS, and the Friends, bent on proving them wrong, were off to a good start.

Along with the important work to develop the storyline, and the landscape rehabilitation efforts around the site of the future entrance to the new complex, the Foundation also moved forward on the construction of the complex itself. In August 2001 they announced the selection of the project architects, Cooper, Robertson & Partners of New York, a firm, said Wilburn,

---

34 The original members of the committee were: Gabor Boritt, Gettysburg College; Eric Foner, Columbia University; Gary Gallagher, University of Virginia; Olivia Mahoney, Chicago Historical Society; James McPherson, Princeton University; Robin Reed, Museum of the Confederacy; Nina Silber, Boston University; and Dwight Pitcaithley, NPS. The eleven segments were, in order: *Introduction: The Beginning of your Journey*; *Pre-War: Why We Went to War*; *The Gettysburg Campaign: Invasion of the North*; *Battle of Gettysburg: Battle*; *The Aftermath of the Battle: The Human Consequence*; *The Civil War to June 1863: "War!"*; *The Gettysburg Address: A New Birth of Freedom*; *The War Continues: 1863 to 1865*; *The Results of the War: Union and Freedom (?)*; *Post War, 1865 to 1913: Battleground Memorialized*; *1913 to Present: The Symbol of Gettysburg*; Program, Gettysburg Museum Advisory Committee, Jan. 10, 11, 2001; Meeting Agenda.

35 The Civil War Trust is a charitable organization whose primary focus is the preservation of American Civil War Battlefields.

36 "Demolition Signals Change to Come," *York Sunday News*, April 1, 2001.

noted "for its extensive experience and dedication to maintaining the 'authenticity of place' in its design work."[37] Simultaneously, Wilburn announced that Gallagher and Associates of Washington, D.C., would be the exhibit design firm for the new Museum. In keeping with what would quickly become the closest possible working relationship between the Foundation and the NPS, as well as Latschar's duty to keep the public informed of it, he added that the Park worked closely with the Foundation on the selections, and that two staff members were present at the meetings in which each firm was selected.[38]

At the same time NPS announced its intent to lease Sherfy House to the GNBMF to be used for meetings and overnight quarters for members of the Foundation staff, Board of Directors, and personal guests, while they were in the Gettysburg area for business.[39] Joseph Sherfy's house lies about one mile south of Gettysburg on Emmitsburg Road, where in 1863, Longstreet's Confederates smashed into Sickles' Union troops on the second day of the Battle. It was home to a fifty-acre farm that included Sherfy's famous Peach Orchard—right across the Emmitsburg Road from the house.[40] It's the original house, a smallish, single-chimney and clapboard affair, built in the 1840s. Bullet holes pockmark its external brickwork and pierce the walls within, signs of the fierce fighting that took place there on July 2, 1863, and they bear witness to the building's authenticity. It's the perfect spot to teach and win over prospective donors amid the physical presence of our nation's history. Wilburn observed that when he was in Williamsburg, they had guesthouses, and so they suggested to the NPS that it would be nice to have a guesthouse at Gettysburg. The NPS said they were willing to lease Sherfy House to the Foundation. While the Friends expressed concern about using Sherfy House for fundraising years later, Barbara Finfrock, a past President of the Friends, said that she believed that the Friends wouldn't feel that way today.[41]

In fact, Sherfy House was the ideal vehicle for guided tours, special

---

37 "Firms Selected to Begin Work on Visitor Center," *Gettysburg Times*, Aug. 3, 2001.

38 Ibid.

39 "Friends Unsettled by Foundation's Plans for the Sherfy House," *Gettysburg Times*, Aug. 15, 2001.

40 The Peach Orchard, at the intersection of Wheatfield Road and Emmitsburg Road, was the scene of intense fighting between Longstreet's Confederate soldiers and Sickles' Union troops on July 2, 1863.

41 "Friends Unsettled by Foundation's Plans for the Sherfy House," *Gettysburg Times*, Aug. 15, 2001; Also, from a personal interview with Barbara Finfrock at Sherfy House, May 22, 2014.

events, and donor education, regarding the historic significance of the Battle of Gettysburg. Fundraising, as more and more people associated with the Foundation began to realize, was a more complex process than quiet meetings and twisted arms. It was about educating donors, and there could be no better venue than Sherfy House for educating donors about the sacrifices that were made at Gettysburg. Kinsley and Latschar realized this. Bob and Anne Kinsley generously agreed to rehabilitate and redecorate Sherfy House for its new purpose.

Wilburn had been on the job for a year, and while he hadn't raised large sums of money, the Fundraising plan, the Museum's story line, land rehabilitation around the new entrance to the complex, a nationally known architect and an accomplished exhibit designer, and the Sherfy House lease were tangible accomplishments that fed into the nascent capital campaign, all steps the GNBMF needed to take before a persuasive case could be made to donors.

CHAPTER 8

Reality Revealed

Another talented member of the leadership team was Rob Kinsley, Bob Kinsley's youngest son, who, after Wilburn's arrival in late 2000, rejoined the project on a day-to-day basis.[1] At times young Kinsley appeared to be everywhere—at board meetings, staff meetings, working on the Cyclorama, working on exhibits, and more. Robert A. Kinsley, II ("Rob"), the fifth son of Bob and Anne Kinsley, was born in 1970, and, in 1997, when his father was selected by the NPS he was twenty-seven and at his father's side from the beginning of the Gettysburg project. He said he was there, first, because he was family, but second, "because I think we knew that my father was very emotionally attached to Gettysburg. I think we knew [the project] was a good idea. I think we were a little apprehensive, maybe even more than he was in the beginning, because we had a sense that this was a big thing, and could go on for a long time." At this writing, nearly twenty years after Bob Kinsley was selected, Rob Kinsley is now CEO of Warehaus, Inc., the successor of LSC Design, the Kinsley-owned architectural and design firm, originally founded in 1980 as Land Survey Consultants. Over the years, the firm, which now employs about eighty professionals, developed a practice that includes architecture, interior design, civil engineering, land planning, and landscape architecture, and while it was not clear at the time, LSC was destined to play a leading role at Gettysburg.

In the spring of 1997, Rob Kinsley was a newly minted graduate of the University of Pennsylvania's three-year Master's Degree program in architecture. His route to Penn is revealing about him, about his father, and about his family. Kinsley studied art and anthropology at Colorado College in Colorado Springs, and after his graduation in 1991, he went to work on a ski mountain in Colorado. Reflecting on his circumstances at the time, he said, "I could barely afford to live there. I was working six days a week, and I didn't have time [to do what I wanted]. After a year on the mountain, he fielded a telephone call from his brother Patrick who said, in a nutshell, "Rob, we're

---

1 Biographical information about Rob Kinsley in this chapter derives from an in-person interview at his office, May 21, 2014.

all here working our tails off and you're out there being a ski bum. We're not okay with that anymore. We're giving you an ultimatum. We need you, we need your help, and you need to come back now, and if you don't [come back now], we're not going to let you [rejoin the family business]." It's remarkable that the call came from brother Patrick and not from father Bob. But Bob Kinsley leads by setting direction. He seldom interferes or involves himself with details. For the moment, this was a detail, an important detail, but a detail nevertheless. Rob told Patrick, "I'll be back." Then after two years working at Kinsley Construction and LSC, Rob enrolled in Penn's architectural program where he earned his advanced degree in architecture in 1994.

In 1997 Rob's father was one of a handful of volunteers who answered the Gettysburg RFP. The architectural rendering that he submitted to the selection committee was, according to Rob, "very space-ship-like… what I would expect a science center to look like in an urban center. I didn't feel it was appropriate." Continuing, he said, "We didn't have a close relationship with the architect; it was very rushed and they were not providing any site planning." His father asked him to take the size and the shape of the building and place it on the LeVan site that they had selected. He produced site renderings—laid out parking, the entrance, circulation— "basically to show that the land was credible, feasible." But after spring of 1997, Rob had a three-year hiatus from Gettysburg during a busy time there. Bob Kinsley was selected by the NPS later that year; he established the Gettysburg Foundation in 1998, he acquired the LeVan land for the Museum and Visitor Center in 1999, and he negotiated an agreement with the NPS in 2000. During all that time, Rob Kinsley was working at the family business, and gaining valuable experience that would soon stand him in good stead on the Gettysburg project.

Kinsley says that when Bob Wilburn "came on board in August 2000, I got involved again [with the Foundation] in a big way. We all realized that we needed to find a new architect," and the management of the selection process fell to Rob almost by default. It's tempting to attribute Rob's selection to an accident of birth, but that's not Bob Kinsley's style. Rob Kinsley was surely young and inexperienced, but he was also a recently trained architect from a top school, and he had a good head on his shoulders. No one else at the Park Service or at Kinsley had comparable qualifications. Both Wilburn and Latschar liked him. Latschar, in particular, was suspicious of architects, and every day, Richard Neutra's Cyclorama building reminded him why as he passed it by on his way to work. Latschar knew that the Museum and Visitor Center complex needed to blend into the landscape and the history of the region, and, above all, it couldn't be a monument to the architect. He told Kinsley, "I want a building that looks like it's of this place, and that people who drive by think that it's always been there, and almost miss it."[2] He knew he'd have as much influence on a selection process that was run by Rob Kinsley as anybody else.

Kinsley began by organizing a selection committee, composed of himself, his father, John Latschar, Bob Wilburn, Debbie Darden, and Darden's husband, Richard Segars. He researched architectural firms from across the country that had previous relevant experience and a portfolio that demonstrated the capacity to execute a project of the size and scope of the Museum and Visitor Center. They sent a "Request for (each firm's) Qualifications" (RFQ) to roughly sixty firms, and about half of them responded. Robert A. M. Stern, the nationally known architect, who was superbly qualified for the Gettysburg project, disqualified himself on the grounds that he was opposed to the removal of the Neutra building that the NPS proposed, and he felt, therefore, that his firm should not participate. As the review process wore on, the list narrowed to fifteen or so firms. RFP's were sent to those fifteen, and after responses were received and analyzed, the list was narrowed down to five or six firms—old and new, large and small.

Kinsley suggested that the committee visit each firm in their own office for the final interview to see how they operated in their own space. Wilburn liked that idea and says today, "We got a much better sense of each firm by doing that."[3] Kinsley says, "One of the things that narrowed the field rather distinctly was that we needed an architect who was willing to do a building that was contextual to the site. The architectural world, at the time, was pushing toward the idea that it was the architect's duty to do original, contemporary, modernist work. There weren't a lot of architects willing to do work that looked old. Stern was one of those and we were disappointed by his recusal." Cooper, Robertson was another.

When the interviews were over, two firms emerged as the favorites: Cooper, Robertson & Partners of New York; and a smaller regional firm, headquartered in Philadelphia that Bob Kinsley favored. According to Rob, his father was attracted to the smaller firm "because he felt they were good,

2   Latschar interview, Nov. 20, 2013.

3   Wilburn interview, Sept. 21, 2015.

they would be committed to the project, and it would be their top priority." Wilburn, who had dealt with architects before, and who was most responsible for raising funds for the work, wanted a firm with a national reputation because he thought it would help fundraising. In the end, and over Bob Kinsley's vote, Cooper, Robertson & Partners won the competition. To this day, Kinsley revels in telling the story of how he was out-voted on his own project.

Cooper, Robertson was well known for creating sensitive designs that fit into historic landscapes. Wilburn relates that Jaquelin "Jaque" Robertson, a principal of the firm, told him that after 9/11, he began driving, rather than flying, to Gettysburg to avoid the airport hassles. As he drove through the rich, rolling, historic farmland of Eastern Pennsylvania, the idea for the conceptual design of the Museum and Visitor Center building came to him. For budgetary reasons, the Foundation retained Cooper, Robertson only to render a schematic design—no more than that—an arrangement that would end before construction began.

As the architect selection process was proceeding, the Foundation was also selecting an exhibit designer using a similar process. The selection committee decided that they would hire both architect and exhibit designer at the same time to place them on an equal footing, and avoid the idea that the exhibit designer ranked below the architect in the project's hierarchy. They sent out RFQs, and then RFPs, but there weren't as many exhibit designers as there were architects, and they didn't visit the designers' offices. Patrick Gallagher, whose young firm had designed major exhibits for the Smithsonian Institution that included the then-recent American Presidency Exhibit at the National Museum of American History, made a positive impression on the committee, and his firm was selected.[4]

Kinsley's crisp, creative, and methodical management of the selection process favorably impressed both Latschar and Wilburn. Latschar, especially, had gained confidence in young Kinsley during the selection process, calling him the "master translator and arbitrator," and that the NPS's ideas for the project "were heard and got through" to the design team.[5] After the selections, the Foundation again hired him, this time to manage the design process. For two years, Kinsley went to every meeting. He went to design meetings. He went to exhibit meetings. The storyline was well along at the start of 2001. But it still needed to be refined, and Kinsley went to every

---

4 "Firms Selected to Begin Work on Visitor Center," *Gettysburg Times*, August 3, 2001.

5 Latschar interview, Nov. 20, 2013.

historians meeting. There may have been several people who knew more about individual aspects of the project, but very few people knew more about the entire project than Rob Kinsley.

The stream that ran through the site, and the associated wetlands, made siting the building particularly challenging. Latschar said, "There were numerous meetings between the Park, Foundation staff, consultants, the Corps of Engineers, the Pennsylvania Department of Environmental Protection, and Adams County, to discuss wetland impacts and mitigation. By the end of the year, the site design for the complex was modified to reduce potential wetland impacts to less than one acre."[6] That one acre was replaced by four acres of wetlands that resulted from breaching the man-made ponds on the adjacent *Fantasyland* site, and restoring the historic stream bed. Wilburn noted that typically you have to return two or three acres of wetlands for every acre that you destroy, and the Foundation returned almost twice that.[7]

As Rob Kinsley recalled later, "The storyline was being developed, the building was being developed, the site plan was being developed," and the results were "plans and renderings of the building, the site, and the exhibits." One of the sparkling, tangible rewards that emerged from the design phase were three spectacular watercolor renderings of the prospective new Museum and Visitor Center. When they were first unveiled at the Gettysburg Hotel in January 2002, they were the first public look at what the Foundation intended to build, and they were stunning. Jaque Robertson said, "This was a profoundly interesting job without exaggeration. This building looks like it belongs in this place. It doesn't look like a big set of boxes left by FedEx the night before."[8] By this time, much of the local Gettysburg opposition to the project, although not all, was melting away.

But Bob Kinsley was as anxious as ever about fundraising, as he had been since he was selected in 1997. Wilburn said, "I spent 25 to 30 percent of my time raising money, but almost one hundred percent thinking about it." In 1997 Kinsley had volunteered for a $40 million project that could carry $12 million in debt, and he'd have to raise the balance of less than $30 million. In the intervening four years, the challenge of funding the project had risen dramatically. He'd investigated the possibility of doing a national campaign,

6 Superintendent's Annual Report, Fiscal Year 2003.

7 Wilburn interview, Sept. 21, 2015.

8 "Battlefield Visitors Will Get a Sense of History, Rural Life in Adams County," *Gettysburg Times*, Jan. 12, 2002.

led by a nationally known figure, just as Lee Iacocca had done for the Statue of Liberty. But there were differences between Gettysburg and Lady Liberty. As powerful a symbol as Gettysburg is, it's not as powerful as the story of America's nineteenth-century immigrants. And the Statue is in America's metropolis, not rural Pennsylvania. It was difficult identifying a potential leader for the campaign, especially from the Black community, which would have been ideal.[9] After all, as Latschar had pointed out, slavery was barely mentioned at the Battlefield. Kinsley's inevitable conclusion then was that somehow he'd have to raise the money himself.

With Wilburn's arrival in 2000, Kinsley became more comfortable about the capital campaign. But by the beginning of 2002, the amount of money that was needed was growing fast; very little had been brought in, and there seemed to be no end to the escalating need for funds. A year earlier, Wilburn's fundraising plan identified $67 million in project costs that required that $52 million be raised.[10] But by 2002 the size of the project had risen to $95 million, and that implied that $75 or $80 million was needed, nearly three times the amount that Kinsley originally proposed. In its fourth year, the Foundation had raised $8.4 million: $5 million from Kinsley that was growing daily, in lock step with the Foundation's expenses that he underwrote; $2.5 million from Congress; and another $900,000 in gifts.[11] Gettysburg, the mounting cost and the expanding gap between what was needed and what had been raised, was bound to attract the attention of Congress, and it did. Three years after Congressman Hansen's hearing in February of 1999, Hansen had advanced to Chairman of the House Committee, and his place as Chairman of the Subcommittee on National Parks, Recreation, and Public Lands was taken by Congressman George Radanovich, Republican of California. What was to be the final Gettysburg hearing was called to order on March 21, 2002. The most pertinent issue at hand was whether the larger, more expensive Museum and Visitor Center project had deviated from the GMP sufficiently to necessitate a new, revised, time-consuming, and expensive GMP.

At the time of the hearing, there was no question that the project's external metrics, particularly its size and its cost, had changed dramatically.

---

9   Foundation Board members reached out to Bill Russell, Bill Cosby, and Black Entertainment Television executives, all to no avail.

10   Project costs of $67,234,014 were offset by $12 million in borrowings and contributions and earnings from contributions. That left approximately $52 million still to be raised.

11   This initial government funding is described in greater detail in Chapter 10.

Internally, however, the use and the content of the new complex were un-changed. It was still a Museum and Visitor Center, albeit a larger one than had originally been planned. Specifically, the GMP that was released in June 1999 and approved in November of that year, described a 118,100 square-foot building to be built for $39.3 million, with no less than $27.36 million of funds raised for the purpose, and no more than $11,925,000 of borrowed funds.[12] Three- and-one-half years later, in early 2002, the comparable num-bers had grown to a 139,000 square-foot building that would cost about $65 million. An additional $30 million of non-building related expenses boosted the total to $95 million for the project.[13] The allowable amount of borrowed funds remained unchanged at just under $12 million.

The hearing proved to be the least contentious of the Congressional hearings that were held to oversee the Gettysburg project. That was due in part to a relative lack of Congressional zeal, and in part by the preparedness of the witnesses: Senator Santorum, Paul Hoffman, from the Department of the Interior, and Wilburn, and their ability to satisfy the committee. At the outset, Radanovich listed three items that concerned him: (a) "legal ques-tions regarding the adequacy of the environmental protection process …," (b) that the General Agreement of June 2000 "may violate the 1998 Park Concessions Act, Federal procurement laws…," and could require an amend-ed GMP and (c) that the General Agreement… "is unclear as to when, or even if, the complex will be turned over to the Park."[14]

Following opening statements, Santorum led off by reciting his long relationship history with Gettysburg to establish his credibility with the Subcommittee.[15] He anticipated Radanovich's questions, such as the cost of the project, and whether there was substantial deviation in the current project from the project that had been approved in the GMP. But when the questions turned to the old issue —was there a consensus that the Visitor Center needed to be removed?—Santorum dismissed them. He was only willing to acknowl-edge that businesses located within walking distance of the interim Visitor Center were not happy, but he believed there was a favorable consensus among the rest of the Gettysburg business community. Said Santorum, "the bottom

---

12   General Management Plan and Environmental Impact Statement, Gettysburg National Military Park, June 1999, 92, 99.

13   Radanovich hearing, March 21, 2002. Hoffman testimony 15, 31.

14   Ibid. 6.

15   Ibid. 9-13.

line was, that with regard to the businesses that were located near the interim Visitor Center, no matter what changes we made to accommodate them, those folks didn't want to move the Visitor Center." When the questioning turned to speculation about what to do if sufficient funds weren't raised, Santorum responded that he was very confident they were going to raise the money, and then he repeated that he was supremely confident that they were going to raise the money. He wouldn't back down. He was an excellent witness, and when he was through, Radanovich thanked him and asked unanimous consent to allow the Senator to join the Subcommittee on the dais for the rest of the hearing, a sign of respect that Santorum accepted.

Hoffman, too, was well prepared.[16] During the course of his testimony he emphasized two ideas. First, he regretted that the then current cost estimate of $95 million was two- and-a-half times the original, inaccurate estimate of $39 million. He referred to the $39 million figure as an abysmal attempt to forecast the cost and that as a consequence made the $95 million cost appear excessive. Second, he detailed the changes that were made to the complex, all in the interest of improving the visitor experience, not in the interest of adding back commercial assets that had been eliminated during negotiations with the NPS. That would have required a new GMP.

Hoffman divided the $55.7 million increased cost ($95 million less the original estimate of $39.3 million) into five categories: general inflation, which added $7.6 million or 14 percent of the total increase; increased space, a larger building that added $8.5 million; enhanced exhibits and visitor ex-perience that added $19.6 million; administrative and fundraising" costs, which added $10 million; plus another $10 million for an endowment to be used to maintain the facility and preserve the Park's collections.[17] It added up to $55.7 million that when combined with the original $39.3 million, 86 percent of which were omissions from the original budget, went towards improving the quality of the project and enhancing the visitor experience. As to the "increased space," the building in the original Kinsley proposal was over 140,000 square feet, and that included an IMAX theater, street retail shops, and a larger restaurant that were not put back in the project.[18] Instead, the design team recommended, and the Foundation agreed, to enlarge the Museum exhibit space, increase public circulation space across the board in

---

16 Ibid. 14-22.

17 Ibid, 21-22.

18 Ibid. 32. Testimony of David Hollenberg, NPS Staff.

order to provide a more peaceful and reflective experience for visitors, and add administrative space for the Foundation's staff.

Wilburn was the next witness.[19] Regarding $19.6 million of "enhanced exhibits and visitor experience" that Hoffman had just identified, Wilburn pointed to the most significant items in this category which included the restoration of the Cyclorama painting. Serious work on it had not yet begun, but, according to Wilburn, the budget "increased from the original estimate of $1 million to $5.5 million [not only for restoration] but to replace parts of the original painting that were lost over the years." Another example was the caliber and cost of the architect. Initially the Foundation estimated that it would pay $2.9 million in design fees to the architect that increased to $6.4 million for Cooper, Robertson.[20] And Wilburn added a third item. "In developing the plan," he said, "it became apparent that it would really be better if we included the *Fantasyland* site owned by the NPS as well as all the land owned by the Foundation. We [plan] to use both parcels and to add parking on both."[21] This added $4 million to the cost of the project.

Wilburn, too, was confident that the money would be raised. Like Hoffman, he took pains to differentiate between a preliminary estimate that was based on a $39 million generalized plan that proved to be grossly inaccurate, and a budget, which reflected detailed conceptual plans and a careful study of specific program elements that would cost $95 million. For those Congressmen who continued to fret about the size of the project, he pointed out that Monticello was in a campaign to raise $100 million, the Constitution Center and Independence Hall Visitor Center in Philadelphia had as their campaign goal $225 million, and Colonial Williamsburg was in the midst of its first capital campaign, and they had set a goal of $500 million. When asked if he didn't feel that his fundraising was somewhat slow, Wilburn replied, "It is deliberate. It is deliberate, as we had planned."

The hearing ended hurriedly, but on an agreeable note. The General Agreement of June 30, 2000, provided that the Foundation turn all of the facilities over to the NPS when all debt incurred by the Foundation had

19   Ibid. 23-29. Testimony of Bob Wilburn, President of the Gettysburg Foundation

20   "Visitor Center: $95 MM by 2006," *The Evening Sun*, Feb. 3, 2002.

21   "The overlay area (for the Museum and Visitor Center project) also included the *Fantasyland* tract which was purchased by NPS to provide a suitable building site for its administrative and visitor service needs." General Management Plan and Environmental Impact Statement, Gettysburg National Military Park, June, 1999, 96.

been paid, estimated to be twenty years from the date of completion of the project, or at some other appropriate time to be mutually agreed upon.[22] This was understandably not good enough for Radanovich because it provided no date certain when the NPS would own the facility. Wilburn and Hoffman agreed to fix the problem. That was good enough for Radanovich so he adjourned the hearing.[23]

Two months later, in May 2002, the Subcommittee staff apparently decided that the rigor of the uneventful hearing was insufficient, and in May they sent the NPS thirteen—and the Foundation six—additional requests for information.[24] Most of the questions had been gone over before and during the hearing, and they related to whether there was sufficient environmental analysis, as well as whether the project was deviating from the GMP that was a product of significant public input. In exasperation, and rather than responding to the questions, the NPS obtained a solicitor's opinion that confirmed that the 1999 environmental impact statement was legally sufficient, and that changes in the size and cost of the facility did not require the preparation of a supplemental EIS.[25]

At last the hearing was put to bed in November 2002 when the NPS and the Foundation revised the General Agreement to provide that all property would be handed over to the NPS, debt-free, no later than twenty-five years from the date of the original General Agreement, June 30, 2000, or twenty years from the completion of the project, whichever is longer.[26] The revised agreement also changed the language in the original agreement regarding funds that were needed to be raised before construction of the project could begin, an item of interest to anyone who thought the Foundation would have difficulty raising the money. The original agreement provided that the project "may not begin until the NPS and the Foundation agreed that sufficient funds are available to complete the planned construction project."[27] The revised agreement was more thorough in that it listed nearly twenty

22 General Agreement, June 30, 2000, Article IV: Ownership, A.

23 Radanovich hearing, March 21, 2002, 42.

24 Superintendent's Annual Report, Fiscal Year 2002.

25 Ibid.

26 Revised General Agreement between Gettysburg National Military Park, National Park Service, and the Gettysburg National Battlefield Museum Foundation, November 4, 2002, Article IV: Ownership, A. The language tracked the language of the original agreement, Article V: Term of Agreement.

27 General Agreement, June 30, 2000, Article VIII: Required Clauses, D.

specific aspects of the project, all of which would need to be funded before construction could begin.[28]

And in another development the Foundation engaged the services of the art conservation firms Olin Conservation of Great Falls, Virginia, and Perry Huston Associates of Fort Worth, Texas, in September 2002 to at last assess the condition of the Cyclorama painting that had been deferred for years because of a lack of funding. When the consultants reported their findings, in June 2003, Latschar said, "Everything we feared about the condition of the painting was confirmed, and some aspects of its condition are worse." He added that the cost of restoring the painting "would top out at $9 million," a significant increase over the most recent estimate of just six months before of $5.5 million.[29] But they still didn't know just how much the rehabilitation of the Cyclorama would cost.

With the hearing finally out of the way, the year 2002 ended on a positive note. Governor Mark Schweiker announced that Pennsylvania's redevelopment assistance fund would be the source of a $10 million award to the Gettysburg project. "I can't say that I started singing, but I did work up to a wide grin," said Latschar, when he was told of the award. Announcement of the grant apparently moved Uberman to declare, "The Foundation's hands are in the taxpayers' pockets."[30] Several weeks earlier he told the *York Daily Record* that all that Gettysburg needed was the "renovation of the Cyclorama building and possibly the reconstruction of the current visitor center..." This was one idea out of several ideas that Uberman and others, nearly five years after Kinsley's selection, continued to promote that the NPS had rejected in the GMP.[31]

---

28   The revised agreement provided that "construction of the new museum and visitor center complex (may begin) only after sufficient funds have been raised to complete the core physical components of the new facility, including purchase of land; final design costs; museum, visitor center, theater, classrooms, and circulation space construction; utilities, roads, parking lots, trails and landscaping; restoration and reinstallation of the Cyclorama painting; installation of the electric map theater; construction of exhibits and displays; relocation of NPS collections; construction and fit out of retail and food service space." The "electric map theater" was a planning term carried throughout the GMP for what eventually became the movie theater. The term described the "purpose" of the theater; i.e. to give visitors at least as good an orientation to the 3-day Battle as the electric map did. Revised General Agreement, November 4, 2002, Article III: Framework for Accomplishing the Project, C, 5.

29   "Cyclorama Restoration Could Reach $9 Million," *Gettysburg Times*, June 20, 2003.

30   "Visitor Center Gets Boost from State Funds," *The Evening Sun*, Dec. 31, 2002.

31   "Site Central to Dispute," *York Daily Record*, Dec. 6, 2002.

But in spite of the good news, fundraising concerns continued to loom over the project. In July 2003 Wilburn tried to be upbeat, although if one read between the lines he seemed concerned. "'On schedule,' is how [Wilburn] describes the effort to raise $95 million…" "We plan on groundbreaking at the end of 2004," which was a year later than he forecasted in the Financial Plan of November 2000. "Depending on how commitments come in, we may have to slip it by a month or two."[32] There was $27 million committed to the project, and that included the $10 million from Pennsylvania. Governor Schweiker made that commitment in the waning days of his administration, but when Governor Ed Rendell came to office in January 2003, he placed that grant, and many others across the state, on hold. Wilburn was optimistic that it would be restored, but at that moment it was in limbo. Another $5 million had come from Congress, along with about $6 million from Kinsley, which meant that approximately $6 million had been raised from other private sources.[33] But there was $68 million still to be found, a tall order. In conversations that Wilburn and Latschar had with the *Gettysburg Times*, Wilburn said that "the cost of wetland mitigation has been reduced," but that was not enough to make a difference.[34] Latschar mentioned the possibility of reducing the endowment if costs continued to increase.[35] One casualty of the rising costs and sluggish fundraising results was the architect, Cooper, Robertson.

By all accounts Cooper, Robertson did an exceptional job on the schematic design, successfully fulfilling their contract. Before the schematic was finished in May 2003, however, the Foundation began asking the firm for their prices to complete the project. The quotation ran into millions of dollars at a time when day-to-day operations were hand-to-mouth, funded primarily by Bob Kinsley. The uncertainties of the fundraising effort added to the difficulty of the decision. With fundraising success not yet assured, costs rising, and Congressional and local critics always lurking in the background, the question of possible alternatives to Cooper, Robertson had to be asked. Latschar, Wilburn, and Bob Kinsley were interested in how much it would cost to have LSC Design complete the project. They asked Rob Kinsley, and he said that LSC would cost about half as much as Cooper, Robertson.

32 "Visitor Center 'On Schedule,'" *Gettysburg Times*, July 3, 2003.

33 See Chapter 10 for a discussion of Congressman Murtha's role in the Gettysburg project.

34 "Visitor Center 'On Schedule'," *Gettysburg Times*, July 3, 2003.

35 Ibid.

Wilburn's dilemma was whether to change architects, go with an unknown firm without the cachet that he had wanted to help with fundraising, or continue with Cooper, Robertson who had done excellent work.

Rob Kinsley remembers a meeting with Latschar and Wilburn when a general conversation about the project turned specific, and one of them asked Kinsley whether he couldn't just finish it. Couldn't he take it from here? LSC had the requisite technical capabilities and capacity to complete the project. But it didn't have a portfolio of previous experience on similar projects, and that posed a risk. Nevertheless, sometime in mid-2003, Bob Wilburn asked Rob Kinsley and LSC design to assume responsibility as lead architect and complete the project. There can be little doubt that the partners of Cooper, Robertson were let down by this unexpected turn of events. But in spite of their disappointment in the commercial outcome of the assignment, they might have taken solace in the knowledge that the distinctive, handsome Gettysburg Museum and Visitor Center that exists today is their design, and that they played a prominent role in the historic rehabilitation of Gettysburg National Military Park.

The year ended with the crucial approval by another body whose interest was piqued by the size and trajectory of the cost of the Gettysburg project. The NPS Design Advisory Board (DAB) was made up of executive-level NPS employees and external advisors whose job it was to review design and construction projects for cost effectiveness and the responsible use of NPS construction monies. The Museum and Visitor Center was to become the NPS's largest visitor center. Latschar explained that it held a Museum and a Cyclorama painting that other visitor centers didn't, but there was no denying its size.

Whether or not the DAB had jurisdiction over a project on which no federal government funds were spent was a moot point.[36] Wilburn was advised not to cooperate with them but Latschar advised otherwise, and the Foundation's decision to cooperate was never in doubt. Latschar's knowledge of NPS protocol was critical at this juncture because an approval fight with any arm of the NPS would have been disastrous for the fundraising effort. Latschar advised that the DAB most cared about whether the Foundation had considered a range of alternatives before reaching its conclusion. He

---

36 The federal funds earmarked for Gettysburg went toward the restoration of the federally owned Cyclorama painting. It was not for the construction of the Museum and Visitor Center. See Chapter 10.

also pointed to the fact that the aging interim Visitor Center was sized to accommodate approximately 450,000 visitors per year. The new complex would accommodate annual visitation of 1,465,000.[37] Rob Kinsley said that if you looked at the building on the basis of square-feet built per visitor, it was actually more efficient than the old building."[38]

There was a highly unsatisfactory October conference call with the DAB's Washington office construction management staff.[39] Afterwards, Regional Director Marie Rust helped engineer a constructive meeting in Washington between Wilburn and Fran Mainella, Director of the NPS. At that meeting, Mainella agreed to attend the Foundation's presentation to the DAB on November 4, 2003. At that meeting, Rob Kinsley delivered a persuasive PowerPoint presentation that was greeted with enthusiastic support by the DAB, although there was no denying the positive impact of the Director's presence at the meeting.

The project was going well, but considering the slim fundraising results, the Cyclorama painting, that historical icon of the Gettysburg story, was emerging as a black hole. Its estimated cost to rehabilitate, that at the time stood at $9 million, had nearly doubled in the prior six months, and yet, still, in 2003, no one knew exactly how the painting could be restored to its original splendor, or what it would finally cost.

---

37 General Agreement, June 30, 2000, Exhibit A, B. General Program for Facilities, Orientation and Information.

38 Gettysburg visitation as reported by the NPS, peaked in 2002 at 1.9 million; it had risen fairly steadily from about 1 million in 1979. In 2000, the year before the architects were retained, reported attendance was about 1.6 million.

39 Superintendent's Annual Report, Fiscal Year 2004.

CHAPTER 9

Cinderella

To have seen the Cyclorama painting in 2002, hanging free as it did in the old cement building before its rehabilitation, was to be a witness to that short period between the time when an old creature becomes defenseless and the Grim Reaper takes its final toll like a crippled old bull elk, surrounded by a pack of wolves, proud, defiant, and utterly helpless. It was hanging on for dear life: billowing canvas folds, draped loosely from thirty feet in the air, with dirty, crusted, cracked paint and frayed edges. The gigantic oil painting, created over one hundred years before, depicted the High Water Mark of the Confederacy—that split second on the afternoon of July 3, 1863, when the Confederate Army, following a mounted General Lewis Armistead, swept over the stone wall near the Bloody Angle atop of Cemetery Hill, only to be swallowed up by the defending Union Army.[1] General Robert E. Lee can be seen in the distance, observing what was quickly to become one of the foremost disappointments of his life. After that, the Battle of Gettysburg was over, but somehow French artist Paul Philippoteaux captured the Battle's climax. From the floor, the decrepit painting roused feelings of disbelief, sadness, and a tinge of hopelessness.

The word *cyclorama* combines the word *cycle*, a circular arrangement, with the word *panorama*, a complete view of an area in every direction.[2] Webster's defines *cyclorama* as "a large pictorial representation encircling the spectator and often having real objects as a foreground." Cycloramas were popular in Europe during the late eighteenth and early nineteenth centuries and were brought to America in the late 1870s. The Gettysburg Cyclorama painting is a remarkable American artifact. Its provenance is the stuff of legend. Philippoteaux began work on his first of four Cyclorama *Battle of Gettysburg* paintings in 1882 that went on display in Chicago in 1883. His

---

1   Philippoteaux depicted a mounted Armistead leading the Confederate charge. By all accounts, Armistead led the charge on foot. He died at the temporary military hospital that was set up at the George Spangler Farm at the GNMP.

2   Information on the subject of the Cyclorama painting presented on the succeeding pages is taken from Boardman and Porch, *The Battle of Gettysburg Cyclorama*. Boardman now heads the GNBMF's Leadership Program.

second Cyclorama painting, completed in 1884, hung in the Boston Cyclorama building for seven years after it was first shown there in December 1884. That painting was destined for Gettysburg and for rough treatment for nearly one hundred twenty years after its Boston showing ended in 1891. The artist completed his third and fourth Gettysburg Cycloramas for Philadelphia and New York in 1886. After Boston closed, that painting went to Philadelphia and then to Chicago, where it replaced the Chicago version that was, by then, in no condition to be displayed and embraced by the hordes of Civil War veterans who were expected to visit Chicago for the Columbian Exposition of 1893. The promoters assumed that if the Cyclorama were exhibited, the veterans would want to see it, and if they paid to see it, it had better be good. Union General John Gibbon visited the Chicago Cyclorama in 1893, and he later wrote to his former artillery chief Henry Hunt, "The perspective and representation of the landscape is simply perfect, and I say nothing more than the truth when I tell you it was difficult to disabuse my mind of the impression that I was actually on the ground."[3] There are only a handful of professional art conservators in the world who know how to hang a cyclorama correctly.

After Chicago, the painting returned to Boston around the turn of the century, where it was ignominiously discarded, packed in a pine box, and left in a vacant lot. Various 1901 Boston newspaper accounts of the neglected artifact mentioned sleet, snow, sun, rain, warping, and cracked boards; boys tearing boards off the box; two or three fires; and firemen soaking the flaming box with water. All that notwithstanding, nine years later, in 1910, there was another flurry of interest in the painting. It was unpacked, unrolled, and found to be in two long strips: one nineteen feet wide, the sky; and one twenty-six feet wide, the horizon and landscape below it. From there, a new entrepreneurial owner sent the painting on an eastern tour of venues in Newark, New Jersey; New York City; Baltimore, Maryland; and Washington, D.C. It finally landed in Gettysburg in 1912 where an unheated building was built for it, one hundred twenty feet in diameter and twenty-eight feet high, and that was the painting's home for the next fifty years. There it hung, incorrectly, straight down the wall as a mural or a shower curtain would hang. The building's height indicated that somewhere between Boston and Gettysburg, the painting lost its sky. And the remaining canvas was cut into sections, tailored to fit the nooks, crannies, and openings in the several places where it hung, with entrances cut out and sections moved.

3 Boardman and Porch, *The Battle of Gettysburg Cyclorama*, 26.

The essence of a properly displayed cyclorama is illusion—the three-dimensional illusion that the viewer is actually at the scene in the midst of the action. The illusion is created by several techniques, foremost of which is the manner by which the cyclorama painting is hung. A cyclorama is correctly hung only from an upper circular beam at the top of the painting, and a circular pipe on the bottom, each running the length of the painting; the top is fastened near the ceiling, and the bottom, heavily weighted, hangs a few feet above the floor. The weighted hanging of the painting causes its center to bow inward, and creates a taut, hyperbolic shape. The horizontal center of the painting draws a foot or two closer to the viewer than it is either at the top or the bottom. The peculiar shape adds a three-dimensional perspective to the painting when it's viewed from the level of the painting's horizontal center. The illusion is enhanced (a) if the top of the painting is well lit, ideally by an aura of natural light from a source hidden by an outcropping above the viewer; (b) if the bottom of the painting is a diorama, a seamless joining of the painting to a realistic, three-dimensional setting displayed on the ground; and (c) if the surface of the painting is flat and even, thereby preventing unnatural visual distractions. In other words, if the painting is hung as a hyperbola, so the horizon is closer to the viewer at eye level, is enclosed beneath a sky that has no visible edge, joins the ground realistically and seamlessly, and has a smooth surface that's visible in every direction, then the illusion is complete. When nineteenth-century visitors viewed a cyclorama, it was the closest thing there was to virtual reality.

From 1913 until 1962, the painting remained on display in Gettysburg, privately-owned until about 1942 when it came to the NPS. The NPS continued to display it in the same building and in the same incorrect manner until it moved it to the NPS's new Cyclorama building in 1962, where it still simply hung on the wall. When a cyclorama is hung correctly, the canvas fibers are free to expand and contract as atmospheric conditions change, without stressing the canvas. Incorrect hanging stresses the canvas. For ninety years, therefore, from 1913 until 2003, the painting deteriorated, in part because of how and where it was hung. The combination of incorrect hanging in an unheated building for fifty years without climate control for ninety years, very nearly destroyed it. But in spite of the neglect by its private owners and by the NPS, the enormous work of art retained its iconic stature because of what it represented, the High Water Mark of the Confederacy, and the defeat of the Confederate Army at Gettysburg.

Creating a cyclorama painting was a specialized and elaborate enterprise. It began with the rendering of a detailed, full-color miniature of the finished work of art. The word "miniature" is used loosely here because it was drawn to a scale of one to ten, and was, therefore, about five feet wide and forty feet long. The images on the small version were systematically transferred, first traced onto paper using pen and ink, then photographed onto glass plates, and finally projected onto the large canvas on which the artists drew the larger images, precisely as they were drawn on the miniature. The finished painting is longer than a football field. When the painting was completed, sections of the huge finished canvas were rolled onto large spools and transported to the site for installation. The entire operation took about a year to complete and involved teams of up to two dozen artists.

From his first days at Gettysburg, Superintendent Latschar knew the Cyclorama painting was a pivotal cultural resource. From the beginning, he planned to remove the Cyclorama building; rehabilitate the ground it occupied; and remove, restore, and rehang the painting. But as he learned more about cycloramas, he recognized the difficulty of delivering on his vision because of both the enormity and the complexity of the painting. Latschar's first conservator told him that the painting was on the brink of cataclysmic decline. He later reached out to art conservator Perry Huston, who was known to have a familiarity with cycloramas, and who, at Latschar's request, submitted a *Proposal for Moving and Conserving the Gettysburg Cyclorama*.

Huston addressed Latschar's plan and what he believed it would entail. He began with a candid understatement: "The project is an enormous undertaking." He noted several problems that included the condition of the canvas that was surely damaged by incorrect hanging and rolling the painting each time it was moved; the added tension caused by the sky's removal and the painting's consequent hanging from its horizontal center; and uncertainty regarding the materials and methods used in prior restorations. He presciently speculated that a section of the bottom of the original painting was missing. Huston knew how a cyclorama was supposed to hang, and he described it on the first page of his report. But he clearly doubted, because of the years of neglect, that the painting could ever be correctly rehung again. He referred to its long history of abuse and noted that it could not now be predicted with any degree of certainty how the painting would respond to the conservation steps necessary to move it. He reiterated that everything possible would need to be known about prior restorations before treatment methods could be recommended. He cautioned that it was quite possible that the painting had been through too many variables in tension and forces to place it again under tension from hanging. And finally, he estimated that the project he foresaw would require nearly 4,000 man days from a nucleus of a five-conservator team, administrator, administrative assistant, and augmented as appropriate by a carpenter and conservation assistants.[4]

At the time that Huston submitted his report, the fight was on over the recently released draft GMP, and the Keeper had just determined that the Cyclorama building was eligible for the National Register of Historic Places. After Huston's report, the NPS might have given up on the painting. But the RFP was released the year before, and it was explicit. Beneath the overarching Park Service Goal I were "four objectives that define this goal," the second of which was "Preserve the Cyclorama painting." Then, further, it noted, "Provide adequate facilities for the long-term preservation and display of the Cyclorama painting." That was the NPS's charge the proposers answered. But neither they nor the Park Service knew just what the words meant, and they certainly had not the remotest idea of what "preserving and displaying" the painting would cost. When in October 1997 Adlerstein wrote to Director Stanton recommending that Kinsley be selected for negotiation, he made no mention of any aspect of the Cyclorama painting as a factor in the selection process. The words "long-term preservation" unwittingly involved proper hanging of the painting, but no one knew that at the time. Beyond that there was no obligation for the prospective partner to do anything more than clean and repair the painting and rehang it the way it was hung for ninety years.[5] Who knows how those who answered the RFP and were not selected would have responded had they been confronted with the "long-term preservation" of the Cyclorama?

From the beginning of the project, there were various estimates made of the cost of restoring the painting that were initially as low as $1 million and rose quickly to $4 million after the first Huston report. The *Fundraising and Financial Management Plan* of December 2000 included an allowance for

---

4   Perry C Huston, *Proposal for Moving and Conserving the Gettysburg Cyclorama*, November 1998.

5   Latschar says that the NPS knew the painting was hung incorrectly and would not have accepted it re-hung as it had been before. This may be true but it appears to beg the question of how the picture would have been hung. The General Agreement only required "reinstallation of the painting." It did stipulate that the gallery was to be "designed to ensure and display [the painting] appropriately," but it `makes no further mention of the painting.

Cyclorama restoration of $5.5 million. Wilburn says that the cost to restore the Cyclorama painting kept inching up, and it reached a point where he knew he needed to get some firmer estimates from conservators around the country as to what they would do and what it would cost.[6] That led to the September 2002 retention of the Olin and Huston firms mentioned in the previous chapter.

The Foundation selected Olin and Huston to assess the painting's condition, based on their joint response to the Foundation's RFP that was released in June. There was only one other responder, from California, and distance alone would have made that firm's participation difficult. No conservation firm was willing to assess the painting's condition without being paid. And the Foundation wouldn't pay one conservator for an assessment and then choose another conservator to do the restoration. So when Huston and Olin were selected to do the assessment, it was tantamount to being selected to do the restoration.

The conservators' uncertainty with regard to how the painting would be reinstalled, led later to time-consuming trials to find other ways, even while they tried to coax the original shape out of sections of the old painting. Their *Response to the June 5, 2002 Letter*, submitted in July 2002, said that it was possible that the painting would be mounted to a solid support that may have to accommodate a change in shape from the shape the painting has presently assumed—an ominous speculation.[7]

Aside from the damage done to it from years of incorrect hanging and exposure to the elements, the painting was also damaged by restorations that were generally done according to best practices of their time, but proved later to be destructive. There were five restorations, the first taking place in 1912 and 1913, when the painting arrived in Gettysburg. "Canvas was added to the… damaged bottom edge, holes and tears were mended, and there was significant over-painting." In 1948, an attempt was made to repair areas damaged by roof leaks and unheated conditions. "The treatment caused significant dimensional distortion, resulting in serious puckering and radiating folds, with subsequent serious damage to the paint layer." Subsequent restorations in 1959–1961, 1975–1976, and 1984–1989 aimed at "flattening out surface distortions by relining the canvas with new canvas and wax resin,

6 Wilburn interview, Sept. 2, 2015.

7 Perry Huston & Associates, Inc., Olin Conservation Inc., Response to June 5, 2002 letter, July 9, 2002.

Cyclorama painting damage

Assessing the Cyclorama painting

removing canvas to eliminate folds, and attaching folds to wooden slats, taping the bottom edge to the floor." These efforts did nothing to stabilize the painting and did incalculably serious damage.[8]

Both David Olin and Perry Huston were experienced and capable art conservators. Huston had some experience with cycloramas. Sue Boardman, co-author of a history of the painting and a staff volunteer, said that Huston had a pretty good idea of what a cyclorama was supposed to do.[9] Olin was the younger of the two and he had a great deal of expertise—a chemistry and conservation background—but he hadn't worked with cycloramas. They were enthusiastic about their assignment and from the outset they were excited about bringing the billowing old wreck back to its original radiance. But they knew it would be expensive. Huston, having seen a cyclorama hung

8 Information on restorations is from Brigid Sullivan, Chief Conservator, Collections Conservation Branch, Northeast Regional Conservation Center, National Park Service, *Report*, Nov. 24, 1998.

9 Information from or about David Olin contained in this chapter is from a telephone interview with Olin conducted in the Spring of 2016, or from an in-person interview with Sue Boardman at Rupp House in Gettysburg, Sept. 23, 2015.

properly, was on the lookout for opportunities to show his team the painting's potential. Boardman recalls a day in 2005 when Huston was on a scaffold at eye level with the horizon of the painting, and he was suddenly transfixed by the three-dimensional effect. He called to anyone who would listen. "We all ran up and wow! What a difference it made when you viewed it properly. You could imagine what it could be."[10]

Restoring the painting was sophisticated, technical work. The initial effort, for example, included "a detailed analysis and identification of layers of added and accumulated materials and the tedious removal of altering layers."[11] The conservators needed to learn as much as possible about the ways the painting had been cleaned in the past and the cleaning materials that were used. Their work revealed the delicacy of the original painting and the tenacity of the added layers of paint and dirt. And while they knew that the fabric was meant to assume an irregular hyperbolic shape that was itself misshapen by years of hanging incorrectly, and that the canvas needed to be returned to its original shape, they didn't know how to do it.

There were decisions to be made throughout the rehabilitation process, and some of them had outsized financial consequences. After the initial assessment, some people may have assumed that the painting would be reconditioned and rehung incorrectly, as it had been since 1912. But there were also strong feelings that there was more that could be done. A comprehensive restoration would improve the visitor experience. The painting was far and away the NPS's best known and most distinctive artifact, and if it were restored improperly, it would have dolefully hung in the new gallery like a broken mirror in a new home, to say nothing of the fact that it would prolong the painting's deterioration. Olin and Huston believed that the painting should be fully restored to appear just as it did on the first day that it was hung in Boston in 1884. And they tried to bring Latschar and Wilburn to the same conclusion. Latschar was torn between his extraordinary vision of a restored Gettysburg, on one hand, and his long career as a parsimonious Park Service veteran on the other. He was unusually proficient at doing more with less. Happily, it appeared to be Wilburn's decision because whatever the cost, the Foundation, not the Park Service, would pay for it. Wilburn wanted to do things correctly, and he was generally optimistic that if it was the right

10 Boardman interview, Sept. 23, 2015.

11 Unknown author, *Restoration of the Gettysburg Cyclorama*, late 2005. Believed to be an adaptation of a memorandum authored by David Olin.

thing to do, the money could be raised to do it. But in a matter of this importance, he didn't feel he could proceed without Kinsley's blessing. Kinsley, in turn, generally supported things that were good quality and good history.

Someone needed to make a decision. Olin and Huston were consultants, not principals. Latschar, too, in this matter lacked standing. Kinsley could have stepped in, but he wouldn't. It was Wilburn, the Foundation's CEO and chief fundraiser who had to decide, and he approved it. He said, "John [Latschar] was thrilled. He loved the idea. But he wasn't willing to ask us to come up with that kind of money. If I remember correctly, at the time, the number to take the painting back to its original presentation was $9 million rather than $5 million—another $4 million. I felt pretty strongly that if we were to spend that kind of money on it, we should do it right and offer a really unique experience. And so that's what we did, and I think it was a good decision." *The Evening Sun* reported "Cyclorama Cost Almost Doubles" and the pressure on Wilburn to raise the money continued to mount.[12] Of the $26.6 million raised, $10 million was put on hold by Governor Rendell, and that left only $16 million committed to the $95 million project at the time.[13] And before the restoration was completed, the total cost of restoring the Cyclorama would accumulate to over $15 million.

The Cyclorama building closed for work on the painting on November 6, 2003, and America's largest, single art restoration ever attempted was underway.[14] The first phase was carried out in the Cyclorama building because there was no other space large enough to hold it. That had to wait for the Foundation to build the new building. Rob Kinsley and Steve Schrum, Kinsley's project manager, had a keen interest in the Cyclorama restoration. Whether or not the painting was longer than 356 feet, whether they would add the sky, whether there would be a diorama, and how they would hang it, impacted the new building's architecture and construction. A diorama required props such as wagon wheels, canvas stretchers, fence rails, guns, canteens, grass, rocks, and dirt that added depth and perspective by visually blending into the bottom of the painting and recreating the foreground. A diorama disguised just where the painting and the floor came together. But, stated simply, Kinsley couldn't draw the building, or Schrum build it, before they knew the size of the painting. And to make matters more pressing, said

---

12 "Cyclorama Cost Almost Doubles," *The Evening Sun*, June 20, 2003.

13 "Cyclorama Restoration Could Reach $9 Million," *Gettysburg Times*, June 20, 2003.

14 "Restoring Glory," *The Patriot-News*, Nov. 25, 2003.

Kinsley, "We had to keep working the schedule because we had to frontload getting that big gallery built and the climate in there stabilized." Olin couldn't conserve and reinstall the painting until they did. It was the end of 2003, and the grand opening was scheduled for spring 2008— four-and-a-half years. And Huston and Olin still didn't know how to properly rehang the painting.

When the old building closed, the conservators began their research work on two sections of the painting, each about thirteen feet wide, to analyze the paint's composition and determine what cleaning treatment would work. They cleaned the panels, secured loose flakes of paint, and applied an opaque supportive facing to their surfaces that tended to stabilize them. In mid-January 2004 the building re-opened and remained open, on and off, throughout the cleaning process so that the public could observe the conservation team in action. The building closed again in early February while the team removed the two panels that each weighed about three hundred pounds. Philipoteaux's original painting consisted of fourteen sections. Olin and Huston subdivided the canvas into twenty-seven sections. Huston selected the two sections to be analyzed because they were sturdy enough to travel, and they were representative of the problems plaguing the entire painting. Each section had been tacked onto a large frame. The team removed the tacks, wrapped the sections in plastic, carefully wound each section around a four-foot diameter cylinder, wheeled them to a truck, and loaded them carefully in full view of a hushed conservation team that was taking its work seriously. They then drove two hours to an undisclosed conservation laboratory in Virginia.[15]

At about the same time, team members, still uncertain of the painting's right size, traveled to Boston to the original Cyclorama building, still in use after 120 years, for squash matches, antique shows, and a variety of other entertainments. The surviving Gettysburg painting was 356 feet long and 26 feet high. The team's objective was to measure the Boston building to get an indication of the painting's original dimensions from the dimensions of the building. But before they could take all their measurements they hit pay dirt. Still suspended from the beam that encircled the inside of the building near the ceiling were the original rings from which the painting was hung in 1884. From that they calculated the original length of the painting, 377 feet,

---

15 "Gettysburg panels to be Renewed, Reunited In 2006," Gettysburg Times, Feb. 18, 2004.

Cleaning the painting

and other dimensions that they needed to know.[16]

Six months later, a newspaper article appeared that described the work on the first two sections that were by then almost fully restored.[17] The professional conservators used Q-tips and solvents to clean the two panels, testing materials and techniques before they used them on the rest of the picture. Everything the conservators did was reversible, so that if improved or more cost-effective techniques came to market in the future their work could be reversed without damaging the painting. They removed most of a waxy adhesive that was used in a prior restoration, to attach backing that was holding up the canvas. What emerged from the conservators' experimentation in the laboratory was an impressively orderly, assembly-line cleaning system; impressive because of the compressed time schedule under which they operated. It was mid-2004, and by the spring of 2008, just under four years, they needed to clean and restore the mammoth painting, move

16 Boardman interview, Sept. 23, 2015.

17 "The Big Picture: Cyclorama Restoration is Long, Tedious Job," *The Patriot-News*, July 23, 2004.

it, and somehow reinstall it in another building that was yet to be built.[18] There was no time to waste.

The conservators' extreme disappointment was that they were unable, in the laboratory, to persuade the two newly restored sections to return to their original shape. They were using specially designed wooden shaping tables to restore the painting's original hyperbolic shape. Olin said that most of the wrinkles in the fabric of the canvas that he had hoped the shaping table would remove still remained. But he hoped that future treatment would remove more of them.[19] In spite of the positive results from the cleaning tests, the conservators' prolonged uncertainty about how to reinstall the painting was beginning to cast doubt on the entire project.

Restoration of the other sections of the painting began in earnest in August 2004 after the conservators finished their work on the first two panels.[20] The first team of conservators, augmented by volunteers, worked from scaffolds, removing surface grime, dirt, and recent repaints, and producing the flattest, smoothest, surface possible. Boardman recalls being part of a volunteer team that "left the office at five o'clock and worked until nine."[21] They did light cleaning. The second crew followed the first, and they worked on more tenacious, embedded, harder to remove materials, and they too focused on leaving a flat, even surface. They tried to remove everything but the original paint, and by the end of 2005, their cleaning work was over. Olin said that starting in November they'd be taking down each section and removing the old lining.[22] The lining was stuck to the reverse side of the painting and while it restricted the canvas and was, therefore, destructive, it was also what supported the painting. Tests showed that without the lining the canvas weighed far more that it had the ability to support.

Professional conservators removed the lining after tests proved that its removal would not damage the original material. They peeled it off in narrow strips; even the angle of removal was prescribed to reduce distortion and stress in the original canvas. Then volunteers scraped off the wax adhesive, inch by inch, with a scalpel, until the canvas was clean. After that, the

18 Superintendent's Annual Report, Fiscal Year 2005.

19 "The Big Picture: Cyclorama Restoration is Long, Tedious Job," *The Patriot-News*, July 23, 2004.

20 "Restoring Glory," *The Patriot-News*, Nov. 25, 2003.

21 Boardman interview, Sept. 23, 2015.

22 "Gettysburg Cyclorama Restoration Begins," *Civil War Courier*, February 2005.

conservators began to identify Phillipoteaux's original seams in the canvas. They flattened all the seams before they applied a thin, strong interleaf that allowed the canvas to breathe, and at the same time provided the support that the canvas would need when it was reinstalled.[23]

But the mystery of how to reinstall the canvas still loomed over the project, and it was unsettling. They were, in 2005, no closer to determining how to install the painting than they were in 2003, and it was two-and-one-half years until the scheduled Grand Opening. Huston, always

Removing the lining

doubting that the beaten old canvas, if hung correctly, could reemerge in its original shape, focused on creating a solid support system. But it finally became clear that a solid support system wouldn't work.[24] Sometime during 2005, Huston decided that for health reasons as well as the difficulty of regular travel between Fort Worth and Gettysburg, he would withdraw from the project.

Olin had given up on the solid support system earlier in the year. He embarked on an intensive effort during 2005 to learn all he could about cyclorama conservation. He visited twelve cycloramas, most of them in Europe, but also in China and Canada. He developed relationships with conservators around the world who had relevant knowledge and experience. He sought out members of the International Panorama Conference, a global network of artists, restorers, and historians. The organization's goal is to stimulate research and communication about the medium, and all of Olin's inquiries ultimately led him to Ryszard Wojtowicz of Wroclaw, Poland. Olin's sources told him that two of the most damaged and, subsequently, two of the most successfully conserved cycloramas, were the Raclawice Cyclorama in

---

23 Unknown author, *Restoration of the Gettysburg Cyclorama*, late 2005.

24 A solid support system upon which the painting was mounted on a hard surface prevented the canvas from "breathing" and was proven to be destructive.

Wroclaw, and the Feszty Cyclorama in Opusztaszer, Hungary. Wojtowicz and his team led the conservation of both, and they used the suspension method described on page 169.

Olin contacted Wojtowic directly, visited him in Poland, introduced himself, and told him about the Gettysburg restoration. The two art conservators hit it off immediately. After Olin returned to the United States, a four-page note surfaced, probably originating with Olin, that urged the Foundation to hire Wojtowicz and his team.[25] In it, the author asserted that they were uniquely qualified to assist in the effort to reestablish and preserve the Cyclorama to its original form, reverse previous restorations, and re-create the painting's proper form.

The note explained that determining the exact size of the canvas was necessary to fabricate the support and that the Gettysburg canvas's exact dimensions had been "elusive." It said that the answer lay in the original seams, which retained the original curve of the original shape. The means to recapture this information was to be gained only by experience. Wojtowicz had it, and he was the only conservator in the world to have successfully employed the suspension method on large, damaged paintings such as the Gettysburg painting was.

In the note, the author asserted that the suspension method recreates the hyperbola by exerting a certain amount of tension on the canvas, to help it "remember" its original shape, and will pull out the undulations that were introduced into the painting over the prior ninety years. Too little tension and the original shape wouldn't recur. Too much tension might damage the canvas, perhaps irretrievably. It had to be just right. If ever there were a need for experience, this was it. The author concluded that the team of Polish conservators who had directed the successful restorations were willing and available to direct efforts at Gettysburg.

In January 2006 Bob Wilburn had another decision to make. But before he made it, he decided to go to Poland to meet Wojtowicz. He asked Rob Kinsley, who was working on construction of the new gallery as well as with Olin on the restoration, to go with him.[26] The trip was a three-day whirlwind. After the trans-Atlantic flight to Munich and a change of plane for Wroclaw, Poland, Wojtowicz, the Mayor, a few dignitaries, and a small band

---

25 Unknown author, *Restoration of the Gettysburg Cyclorama*, late 2005.

26 Information about the Polish trip was derived from the Rob Kinsley interview, May 21, 2014 and the Wilburn interview, Sept. 26, 2015.

were there to meet them. The next day they visited the Raclawice Cyclorama that depicts the 1894 Battle of Raclawice.[27] Wilburn and Kinsley arrived believing they were interviewing Wojtowicz, but they quickly realized that they were also talking to his restoration team: his wife Danuta, his sister Wictoria, and a fourth conservator, Wieslaw Kowalczyk. They had dinner at the Wojtowicz' home that evening and left the next morning. In Kinsley's words, "We felt this was the guy we needed. And we trusted him. On top of that we didn't have any choice."

The idea that accomplished professionals from Poland—each with lives, relationships, and business backlogs of their own, with virtually no advance notice and little prior knowledge of Gettysburg—were willing to put their lives on hold for two years, speaks volumes about their liking for the people they met from Gettysburg and for the project at hand. There was no question that with just over two years left to complete it, and little likelihood that it would be completed on time or even at all without them, the Foundation needed to make a generous offer to secure their services.

On April 17, 2006, Bob Wilburn signed a contract with Ryszard Wojtowicz: to employ Wojtowicz and his wife Danuta, each at $222,000 annually, and two assistants, Wieslaw Kowalczyk and Wictoria Wojtowicz Janowska, Ryszard's sister, each at $144,000 per year.[28] Wojtowicz would earn an additional $200,000 "upon successful completion of his work" by May 2008, in about two years. He was addressed in the letter as "Head Restorer of Feszty and Raclawice Panorama and Chairman of the Society of Lower Silesia Restorers." The contract stated that the Wojtowiczes were being "engaged because of [their] international reputation in having developed a treatment strategy, and having successfully conserved two of the most damaged cycloramas in the world." It stated that their "role is further described in the enclosure, entitled *Restoration of the Gettysburg Cyclorama* that has been referred to herein." The group brought with them twenty-five years of experience, advanced degrees in arts conservation, and a long list of awards, accomplishments, and publications, as well as two young sons in their early teens. They would add another $2 million to the cost of restoring the Cyclorama. They also brought a unique and essential capability to the project.

---

27 The Battle of Racławice, April 4, 1794, was one of the first Battles of the Polish Kosciuszko uprising against Russia. Wikipedia.

28 Wilburn to Ryszard Wojtowicz, April 17, 2006.

Meanwhile, on June 2, 2005, the Foundation formally broke ground for the long-planned Museum and Visitor Center complex amid ceremony and celebration of the big event. The first real work began the day before, when the Foundation signed a $400,000 contract to return the adjacent Guinn Run, a waterway that was dammed for use by *Fantasyland*, to its Civil War-era condition.[29] The groundbreaking signified the beginning of a new home for the dilapidated Cyclorama painting that was still being cleaned in the old building, but was well on its way to becoming the Cinderella of Cycloramas.

As construction began, the contractors were asked to seal and acclimatize the gallery that would house the Cyclorama first, before they started on other sections of the complex. That meant that heating, cooling, humidity control, power, and fire suppression systems, *et al* would be installed, all before the rest of the complex was even closed in. So while the restoration was ongoing, Rob Kinsley was timing the escalators, planning the coordination of crowds of visitors that would move, first, from one of the two theaters, up to the Cyclorama, and then out, and—alternately, the same routine from the other theater. Kinsley recalls spreadsheets and hours and hours figuring out the timing of the film, the escalators, and the light show that went with the Cyclorama. And the gallery had not only to be measured perfectly, but it needed to be equipped with specialized equipment such as pipes, rollers, pulleys, and weights, for use in hanging the painting.

The gallery was ready in April 2007 and by the end of June, the painting was carefully removed from the old Cyclorama building, and carried down the Baltimore Pike to its new home. Before it could be hung, about fourteen feet of canvas was added to its top surface to create a single canvas its original size.[30] In August one of the original fourteen sections was raised to the top, triggering "applause, tears, hugs, whoops, and handshakes" from the assembled art conservators and other bystanders.[31] From June, when the painting was moved to the new facility, until the grand opening of the new complex in September 2008, each section of the painting was raised into position, the original seams painstakingly and precisely stitched together just

---

29 "Battlefield Restoration to Begin in Stream," *The Patriot-News*, June 2, 2005.

30 "Massive Painting Survived Decades of Neglect," The *Washington Post*, May 12, 2007. Fourteen feet of surface was approximately equivalent to the nineteen-foot strip that was found in Boston in 1910 after allowances for overlapping the bottom edge, and winding the top edge around the upper beam to secure the mounting.

31 "Big Step for the Big Picture in Gettysburg," *York Sunday News*, Aug. 12, 2007.

Finishing touches

as the original seams were joined, to form a continuous image. Then, slowly and surely, the magnificent old painting, gradually placed under tension, adjusted, readjusted, pushed and pulled, lifted and lowered, all ever so carefully, slowly regained its shape and the historic hyperbola emerged.

After the sections were hung, the missing section was filled first by moving a large piece of the painting that was cut out and moved decades before, and returning it to where it belonged. Then, using photographs of the original painting as a guide, the original images were painted in. The sky was another matter. According to Boardman, their first intention was to paint computer-generated sky onto the new canvas. But just as had happened with other aspects of the restoration, a collective conscience turned to the idea that everything else was restored to its original state: why not the sky? On a research trip to the Chicago History Museum, Boardman was searching for artifacts to borrow for display in the new Gettysburg Museum. Looking through the card catalog, Boardman came upon a card labeled "Philippoteaux Paintings." Out of curiosity she asked to see what they had. Before long she was studying the artist's original miniature "with all that brilliant sky." She telephoned Olin and sent him digital pictures that revealed the previously unknown sky. The Cyclorama's sky is now a re-creation of Philippoteaux's original work.[32]

In June 2007, Gallagher began fabrication of the museum's exhibits. A contract for the construction of the diorama was expected to be awarded. Another contract for food service was already signed. Shooting for the principal film, as well as for a half-dozen films for the exhibits, was about to begin. And while the finished restoration of the Cyclorama was not yet achieved, it seemed that the Olin-Wojtowicz art conservation team had the project well in hand even though time was short. The one challenge that was not yet answered was financial, and regardless of the many directions in which Kinsley and Wilburn were pulled, they never lost their focus on fundraising.

---

32 Boardman interview, Sept. 23, 2015.

CHAPTER 10

Finding the Money

The date was March 21, 2002. Bob Wilburn had been on the job since August 2000.[1] He was testifying before the Radanovich Committee, facing skeptical questioning from Donna Christensen, a non-voting Congressional delegate from the Virgin Islands.[2] The Foundation had raised $8.4 million, most of it from just two gifts, $5 million from Kinsley and $2.5 million from Congress. Ms. Christensen asked rather naively, "So you don't feel that your fundraising is somewhat slow?" Wilburn, who may have raised as much not-for-profit money for museums as any one in the world, responded, "It is deliberate, ma'am. It is deliberate as we had planned."

The original fundraising plan that was approved by the NPS in December 2000 had as its goal $52 million, which was a significant increase at the time it was announced and did not include borrowed funds. That goal had risen further by the time Wilburn encountered Ms. Christensen. But the plan was clear, consistent, and well laid out. Before there were funds raised, there would be a board of directors recruited, a project design approved, a campaign brochure designed and written, and donors identified and cultivated, each of which was an important preliminary step that needed to precede fundraising. No capital project of any sort that began without any list of prior donors could have meaningful fundraising results in nineteen months.

Preparatory groundwork was well underway. The first brochure was done in sepia tones, dignified and powerful, and it was stunning. After recounting events at Gettysburg in words and pictures, it closed with an appeal to support the project "for those who gave their lives so that our nation might live." The architect and the exhibit designer, both selected nine months before, were hard at work. The architect, two months before, had unveiled the dazzling schematic renderings of the barn-red silo that would house the Cyclorama painting.[3] A credible board of directors, an immediate task, was

1   Information about Bob Wilburn in this section and elsewhere in this chapter derives from an in-person interview with Wilburn on Sept. 21, 2015, and a telephone interview on April 6, 2016.

2   Radanovich hearing, March 21, 2002, 39–40.

3   "NPS Unveils Visitor Center Plans," *The Evening Sun*, Jan. 12, 2002.

taking shape too. When donors become aware of a possible new charitable interest, one of the first things they will do is find out who is on the board. A less-than-credible board can discourage a potential donor before their cultivation begins. A credible board may act in the other direction. Prospective donors, with the potential to make large gifts, are often asked to join a board. But a good board is generally a blend of donors, workers, and others who provide a variety of talents, and a reputation that reflects well on the institution.

Kinsley and Wilburn were making progress recruiting directors. Just one week before the hearing, the Foundation announced seven new board members to join board Chairman Kinsley. The group included: former Pennsylvania Governor Dick Thornburgh; noted historian Gabor Boritt of Gettysburg College; retired Army General Dan Christman, also past Superintendent of West Point; and three businessmen—Tom Petrie, an investment banker and West Point graduate from Denver; Christine Toretti, chairwoman of S.W. Jack Drilling Co., of Indiana, Pennsylvania; and David LeVan, a Gettysburg native who was past Chairman and CEO of Conrail, the same LeVan who sold his land to Kinsley. Syndicated columnist George Will was also named to the board, along with Wilburn. During the hearing, Wilburn told Christensen that he hoped she would agree that they had gathered a distinguished group of individuals on their board, and that they were building on that.[4] Three months later, well after the hearing, they named five more new directors that included four businessmen: John Cooke of Los Angeles, Clyde Tuggle of Atlanta, David Remington of Boston, and Wes von Schack of Albany, New York, as well as actor Morgan Freeman of Los Angeles. And within a few more years, Craig Cogut, the founding partner of Pegasus Capital; Kay O'Rourke, an amateur historian and heiress to the Winn-Dixie fortune; Turney McKnight, a retired lawyer and head of his family's foundation; and Richard Edelman, CEO of the public relations company Edelman, joined the board.

As to developing a prospective donor list, identifying individuals who have the financial capacity to give is not particularly difficult. Some are household names. To winnow out those who might have an interest in American history, or the Civil War, or in the history of race relations in America, or in educating America's children, or in Gettysburg, is more difficult and takes time. And then, to bring those whom the Foundation might view as potential donors to a point where they are willing to commit their

---

4 Radanovich hearing, March 21, 2002, 40.

capital to a new project is hardest of all. It requires a clear, often visual, idea of the project, trust in those who are seeking support, a donor's motive for giving, good salesmanship and communication, and often a more-than-can-be expected amount of good luck.

Fundraising professionals, like salespeople, call the identification of potential donors "prospecting." After donors are identified, that period of time between when a donor is first identified, and then asked for a gift, is called a "cultivation" period. A gift request is an "ask." Cultivating a prospect may take weeks or it may take years. It often requires patience, persistence, many meetings, and other conversations. Most prospects never become donors. Some donors appear when they are least expected. The aim of the solicitor, just as a salesperson, is to have an open, trusting, personal relationship with the prospect. Conversations generally revolve around the needs and goals of the institution and to what extent they mesh with the philanthropic needs and goals of the prospective donor. Ordinarily, the solicitor doesn't ask for a gift until it has been pretty well established that the institution's needs match the prospect's goals. Once an ask is made, it's usually not a matter of a simple "yes" or "no." Most asks are heavily strategic, generally larger than a solicitor expects to receive, and often accompanied by a recognition opportunity that the solicitor hopes will appeal to the donor. Often a well-thought-out ask will result in a polite negotiation between the solicitor and the prospective donor, who might want more recognition, or who might like the funds applied differently than the solicitor would like. Some times solicitors have to say no, and that may quash the gift or it may not. Sometimes donors are not asked for a gift for a considerable period of time. Sometimes they are never asked, but a gift simply appears. Some such gifts are perfect. Some others are preemptive; small gifts that a donor might make to avoid being asked for a larger one. It is no wonder that Wilburn told Christensen that he was being deliberate. He knew the campaign would get off to a slow start because he had no list of past donors to Gettysburg whom he might rely on to start it, as a college or a hospital might have.

Many of the gifts that ultimately came to the Foundation were the result of interesting solicitations as well as good luck. One such enormous donation fell out of Wilburn's twenty-five-year acquaintance with Democratic Congressman, John "Jack" Murtha. When Wilburn was President of Indiana University in Indiana, Pennsylvania, he found that Murtha was an enthusiastic supporter of the University. While not an alumnus, Murtha took graduate courses at Indiana. He had served in the Marines Corps in Vietnam, and he was the first Vietnam veteran to be elected to Congress, in 1964. Two days before he died in 2010, he became Pennsylvania's longest-ever serving Congressman. Murtha was a colorful character, and throughout his forty-four-year career, he was involved in some heated political contests. Over the years, his opponents accused him of various improprieties, including the embellishment of his war record, but nothing was ever proven, and his constituents reelected him, time and time again. Murtha's record in Congress is well beyond the scope of this book, but he was a sincere, dedicated, and effective supporter of the Gettysburg Foundation.

Indiana University was an important institution in Murtha's Congressional district. Wilburn, when he was President of the University, cultivated Murtha, and at one point, he seriously considered naming a building in his honor. As luck would have it, Murtha suddenly was linked to a political scandal, and, while Wilburn remained at Indiana, the campus naming never took place.[5] When Wilburn left Indiana to join the Republican Thornburgh administration in Harrisburg, he was on the opposite site of the political fence from the Democrat Murtha, but he saw him, maintained the relationship, and knew him when he (Wilburn) was at Carnegie.

In October 2000, after the Foundation announced that Wilburn was its new president, the first Park Service function he attended was a meeting of Eastern U.S. Park superintendents held in western Pennsylvania. Congressman Jack Murtha, who by then had emerged as Chairman of the House Defense Appropriations Subcommittee, was the keynote speaker. Murtha was opposed to the public/private partnership at Gettysburg, not because he had anything against Gettysburg; in fact, the opposite was true. Murtha was a soldier and a great fan of Gettysburg. He believed in Gettysburg and he respected John Latschar. He was opposed to the partnership, first, because, as a Democrat, he believed that whatever was done at Gettysburg should be done by the federal government, and second, because he had no confidence that sufficient private funds could be raised for a federally funded National Park like Gettysburg.

---

5 In 1980, Murtha was caught up in the "Abscam" (short for Arab scam) investigation that targeted dozens of congressmen. FBI agents posed as agents of foreign nationals, hoping to bribe their way into the United States. Murtha was videotaped meeting with them, responding to an offer of $50,000. Murtha said, "I'm not interested... at this point. [If] we do business for a while, maybe I'll be interested, maybe I won't." The U.S. Attorney's Office reasoned that Murtha's intent was to obtain investment in his district and he was never charged.

Wilburn remembers the superintendent's meeting well, but to this day, he doesn't know if Murtha knew he was in the large audience of Park Service personnel. When Murtha began to speak, he checked off the reasons he opposed the Gettysburg partnership until he came to his skepticism that private funds could be raised. No one was more surprised than Wilburn to hear Murtha say, "But, of course, if anyone in the country can raise [the money] Wilburn can." Of course, Wilburn took it as an enormous public compliment. If he had not been in the audience that day, the story surely would have unfolded differently, but at that moment, whether he knew it or not, Murtha became a prospective Gettysburg donor. Wilburn would cultivate him assiduously. He framed his cultivation around the simple proposition that the Congressman from Pennsylvania would want to be briefed on a major Pennsylvania project. Wilburn never requested federal funds. He didn't have to. Murtha was an elected Democrat who believed that government had a role to play. He wanted to play a part in the rehabilitation of Gettysburg, and he wanted his country to play a part in it too. He thought it was important.

Wilburn met with Murtha every six months or so. He would just make an appointment and go see him. Murtha never had anyone with him. Wilburn said that when a Congressman meets with you, he'll typically have an aide with him to follow up if something arises, or to take over the meeting if he has to leave. As Wilburn kept Murtha abreast of the project's progress, when the time came, events fell into place, in part because Murtha loved Gettysburg, and in part because he trusted that Wilburn would deliver a successful project. Both were necessary, but neither was sufficient.

In October 2001, a year after Kinsley announced Wilburn's hiring, the House of Representatives voted to allocate $2.5 million (see Chapters 7 and 8) for the restoration of the Cyclorama painting at Gettysburg that was, of course, a federally owned artifact.[6] The NPS credited Murtha for providing leadership that led to the gift. It was an "earmark," a term that had become politically toxic and a Congressional practice that allowed Murtha to insert a provision in the Appropriations Bill; and the entire bill, not any single item, was voted on by the House.

A year later, Congress approved another $2.5 million to preserve the painting. The next year, 2003, Murtha inserted a third $2.5 million for Gettysburg into the Appropriations Bill, but House-Senate budget negotiations ended with an across-the-board cut in the Interior Department's

6 "Funds OK'd for Painting Restoration," *The Evening Sun*, Oct. 22, 2001.

budget. Gettysburg funding was lowered to just under $2 million. At that time, the estimated cost of restoring the Cyclorama painting had reached $9 million. Murtha said he thought that the nearly $2 million, in addition to the $5 million that was approved in prior years, would be enough to keep the project on track.[7] In June 2004 Congress allotted another $5 million to restoring the Cyclorama, raising the total federal allotment to Gettysburg to just under $12 million. Finally, in late 2007, the House Appropriations Bill passed a final appropriation of $3.8 million for the Gettysburg Cyclorama.[8]

The odd $3.8 million amount came about because of a mistake made by a Congressional staffer. During one of Wilburn's briefings with the Congressman, Wilburn recalls Murtha picking up the phone and calling the chief of staff of the Appropriations Subcommittee. He asked him to allot $3 million to the Gettysburg project. The problem, which turned out to be Wilburn's and Gettysburg's good fortune, arose when whomever Murtha had spoken to, forgot to make the entry. When the Appropriations Bill was finalized, there was no funding for Gettysburg. Murtha was irate and embarrassed. He called Wilburn sheepishly and asked how much it would take to finish the restoration, to which Wilburn replied, "$3.8 million." Murtha admitted to Wilburn that he'd been taking a lot of heat regarding earmarks, and that because this latest request would be out of order, tacked on at the end, it would undoubtedly draw attention. His name, therefore, would not be on it. The appropriation would be "staff directed" rather than "member directed." Wilburn, of course, agreed to keep Murtha's name out of it, but he forgot to tell Latschar. Local Gettysburg newspapers attributed the allocation to Murtha, and Latschar publicly expressed his gratitude to the Congressman. Fortunately for Wilburn, Latschar's attribution failed to reach the Washington newspapers.

The federal government was not the only government supporter of the Gettysburg project. Tourism was an important part of Pennsylvania's strategy to boost its economy, and Gettysburg was an important state tourist asset. A dismal Gettysburg National Military Park would not do. The state was eager to support its rehabilitation. Wilburn had his eye on state funding from the start of his Gettysburg tenure because he knew the program, and he knew the people who ran it. In late 2002 Pennsylvania Governor Mark Schweiker,

---

7 "Congress Makes Third Gift to Cyclorama," *The Evening Sun*, Nov. 20, 2003.

8 "Taxpayers to Shell Out Another $3.8MM for Cyclorama Project," *Gettysburg Times*, Dec. 20, 2007.

Governor Tom Ridge's replacement, opened the door for a $10 million state grant for Gettysburg by signing off on a list of eligible projects, which included a request from the Gettysburg Foundation.[9] That was followed closely by Schweiker's formal approval of the grant one month later as he neared the end of his term. Wilburn feels that the success of that request was related in part to his personal relationships with Commonwealth officials. In May of 2003, however, newly elected Governor Edward Rendell, temporarily suspended $350 million of project grants pending a more rigorous review of their economic development value that included the $10 million for Gettysburg.[10] Ordinarily, a suspension for further review would not be good news. Wilburn, however, relying on the experience he gained from his earlier life in politics, saw it differently. Said he, "I told somebody that I thought we'd get [a second $10 million] because the government was going to change. I thought the second Governor [Rendell] would want to have as much recognition as the first Governor [Ridge]."

The earliest gifts lent impetus to the fundraising effort. Gettysburg Tours, for example, an operator of bus tours on the Battlefield, was an early supporter.[11] The announcement of their first gift of $500,000 was the first public notice of private non-Kinsley funds coming to the Foundation. The gift was not only early, but it was doubly positive, as it reflected a local company's belief that the project was going to benefit the entire Gettysburg economy. The company's announcement said, "We all win with the successful completion of this project." Clearly the bus company profited from added activity on the Battlefield, but it would be a while before profits from bus tours made back the $500,000 gift that would become $1 million before the project was finished.

Every gift told a different story. One very significant contribution came from board member Kay O'Rourke, heiress to the Winn-Dixie fortune, who lived in Florida and traveled to board meetings by train. O'Rourke was a generous supporter of Colonial Williamsburg during Wilburn's tenure there. He briefed her on his newest project, and she later joined the Gettysburg

---

9   "State May Aid Visitor Center," *York Dispatch*, Nov. 4, 2002. Ridge served as Pennsylvania Governor from 1995 to 2001. He was Assistant to the President for Homeland Security from 2001 to 2003, and he was the first U.S. Secretary of Homeland Security from 2003 to 2005.

10   It was not unusual for newly elected governors to review grants made by prior governors, especially if the prior governor were of the opposing party. "Rendell puts Visitor Center and Majestic Funding on Hold," *Gettysburg Times*, May 17, 2003.

11   "Foundation Receives $500,000 Donation from Gettysburg Tours," *Gettysburg Times*, Jan. 13, 2003.

board. Wilburn never asked her for a gift to Gettysburg, until one day when she asked him if he had given any thought to creating a tavern at Gettysburg as they had done at Williamsburg; she implied that she would support it if they did. O'Rourke was interested in food and food service. Wilburn told her they had not considered a tavern, but he said they might create a "themed cafeteria," and he gave her examples of other themed cafeterias around the country. She was interested. And she was very interested in helping to create what would become the "Refreshment Saloon" that was inspired by refreshment saloons of the Civil War era. She was drawn to the selection of the chairs for the saloon. She identified a sample, shipped it to Gettysburg, and then had it reproduced at her expense. She studied the murals on the walls. She and Boardman studied books of murals. Almost overnight, O'Rourke was identified with the Refreshment Saloon. Wilburn always knew she was a prospective donor, and both he and Hills spoke with her often. But rather than asking her for a gift immediately, Wilburn briefed her on the project and waited patiently to see if some aspect of it would engage her. When it did, he reacted quickly. Kay O'Rourke's gifts to Gettysburg ran into the millions of dollars, and they were undoubtedly magnified by her genuine interest in the history of food in the Civil War, rather than what might have been a more sterile and less responsive reply to a premature, outright, "ask" for a gift.

Another generous donor was asked to sponsor an exhibit gallery that would be named for him. He answered affirmatively, but the amount he wanted to give was half of what the Foundation had determined was the price for naming the gallery. Wilburn thanked the donor profusely for his generosity before reminding him of the price. He said that he would look for another donor to fill out the gift. The gallery would be named jointly in honor of both donors. The first donor, after not too much thought, increased his gift considerably so that he could retain the exclusive naming opportunity. In this case there was cultivation, there was an "ask," and there was a short negotiation before the final gift was agreed to.

In early 2004 Governor Rendell announced that Pennsylvania would invest $20 million in the [Gettysburg] project through its Redevelopment Assistance Capital Program.[12] Wilburn explained that what Rendell did was cancel the first $10 million and then appropriate $20 million. By then, two years after Christensen questioned the Foundation's fundraising, which

12 "Foundation Gets to $54MM for Museum, Visitor Center," *Gettysburg Times*, April 24, 2004.

stood at $8.4 million—most of it from two gifts—fundraising results went straight up, to $41 million by the end of 2003 and to $54 million by April 2004, just two years after the hearing.[13] By that time the state and Congress had, together, invested nearly $27 million, about one half of the approximate total of $54 million that had been raised. The other half was represented by $12 million in bank borrowings and $15 million from 130 gifts from private foundations, corporations, or individuals.[14] As prospects were identified, the Foundation built relationships through staff or board members or both. The project was sold, the need documented, the importance proven, and gifts that rewarded Wilburn's deliberate approach to cultivating prospects began to flow. The entire process moved forward relentlessly, until in mid-2004, it almost ground to a halt. From April through November 2004, for some inexplicable reason, donations slowed to a trickle. And the pressure was unrelenting to maintain the flow of donations coming in. While the total amount raised grew from $54 million in April to $62 million at the end of November, a rate of about $1 million per month, it included a $5 million grant from Congress for the Cyclorama. Even at a $1 million per month pace, however, the groundbreaking would have been delayed until early 2006. But in December, several other patient solicitations bore fruit. A group of donors that included the Pew Foundation of Philadelphia, which announced a $1 million gift, and Gettysburg Tours, which upped its gift from $500,000 to $1 million, made contributions that totaled $5.5 million for the month and raised the 2004 year-end total to about $67.5 million.[15]

The Foundation's contractual obligation to the NPS regarding how much money needed to be raised before it commenced construction, eschewed a set dollar amount, but required sufficient funds available to cover core elements of the new Visitor Center: to build a viable building. The Foundation's conservative estimate to fulfill that obligation was $75 million, so it set that as its own non-contractual goal that they intended to raise before they broke ground. That number had remained unchanged even as the date for breaking ground was deferred twice, from December 2004 to March 2005 and then

13 "Gruber: Gettysburg Center Gets $41 MM in Pledges," *The Evening Sun*, Nov. 2, 2003. Elliot Gruber was Chief Operating Officer of the Gettysburg Foundation, reporting directly to Bob Wilburn.

14 "Foundation Gets to $54MM for Museum and Visitor Center," *Gettysburg Times*, April 24, 2004.

15 "Museum Foundation within 90 Percent of Funding Goal," *Gettysburg Times*, Feb. 1, 2005; "Gettysburg Group Nears Fund-Raising Goal," *The Evening Sun*, Feb. 1, 2005.

to June 2005, because fundraising slowed during most of 2004. At year-end 2004, the scheduled groundbreaking was six months away, and they were more than $7 million short of the goal.

The Foundation's consultants were pressing. In addition to JMH Associates, Jack Hills' firm, the Foundation had retained the services of Odell, Simms of Virginia, to assist in turning up potential donors. Their Tony Lynch led the charge. Through Lynch's efforts, the Foundation made contact with the McCormick Foundation, former owners of the *Chicago Tribune*. McCormick announced a $1 million grant in early 2005 that reduced the funding gap to $6 million. A McCormick ancestor, Major William H. Medill, died of wounds sustained at Gettysburg, and the gift honored his service and his sacrifice for his country.[16]

One prospective donor, who would have been on any list of prospective Pennsylvania donors, was H. F. (Gerry) Lenfest of Philadelphia. Lenfest matriculated at Washington and Lee University, as had Foundation board member Beverly "Bo" DuBose of Atlanta. After Lenfest graduated from Columbia Law School, he began his career practicing law in New York City, and then joined Triangle Communications, a Walter Annenberg company. In 1974 he founded Lenfest Communications, a cable company that was sold to AT&T in 1999. Lenfest was wealthy and he was generous. Before the Foundation reached out to him, DuBose invited Lenfest to Gettysburg in April 2005. At that time, the Foundation still needed $6 million to break ground, and the groundbreaking was still scheduled for June. There were three months to go.

Lenfest arrived at Gettysburg, toured the Battlefield, and asked a lot of questions about the project. Among other things, he learned that an attractive stone facing, as well as a metal roof, both on the main building and costing $3 million, were being omitted from the project to hold costs down. At dinner, Lenfest said that he thought the omissions were mistakes and that both should remain. He proposed a $3 million, one dollar for two dollars, matching gift to pay for the restoration of both the facing and the roof to the building. That meant that if the Foundation raised $6 million before June, Lenfest would donate $3 million. Lenfest thought that $3 million would pay for the roof and the facing, items that he and the Foundation wanted, and that his challenge would help raise the $6 million they needed to break ground.

---

16 "$1M Donation made to Visitors' Center," *York Sunday News*, Jan. 23, 2005.

Wilburn put on a game face, but the way he looked at it, the inclusion of the facing and the roof at Lenfest's expense left the Foundation no closer to the $6 million that they needed to break ground. Wilburn was focused on the groundbreaking, not the roof or the facing. He was initially reluctant to accept the gift, but by the end of the evening he retreated, thanked Lenfest for his generous offer, and asked him to forgive his initial reluctance. He realized that it would be a superior building with the facing and the roof, but he still worried about the $6 million that eluded him, even though he must have realized that the partial match might help.

Lenfest, though, spent the night doing some thinking of his own. He is a true philanthropist, who had confidence in the partnership, and he wanted very much to help the project. He also believed in matching gifts. By morning, he'd crafted a new proposal to increase his challenge from $3 million to $4.5 million, which would be earned through a dollar for dollar, not a one dollar for two dollars, match. That is, if the Foundation raised $4.5 million by June, it would earn the gift, still $9 million in total, but configured quite differently and far more beneficially for the Foundation. First, Lenfest's gift was larger. That meant that if the Foundation raised $4.5 million dollars, not $6 million, they would have, along with $1.5 million from Lenfest, the $6 million they needed to break ground. Second, the match, while still difficult to achieve, was decidedly easier by $1.5 million. Instead of having to raise $6 million to earn a $3 million gift, they had to raise less money, $4.5 million, to earn a larger gift of $4.5 million. It was a generous, demanding, and exciting offer.[17]

Tony Lynch was one of those who was motivated by the Lenfest challenge. Knowing that William Ford, President of Ford Motor Company, had a Civil War interest, Lynch had been attempting to reach the Company's charitable foundation to make a proposal, but he was getting nowhere. Learning of Lynch's frustration at Ford, a Gettysburg Foundation Board member happened to know a Ford Motor Director, who, he knew, had a long personal relationship with William Ford. The Foundation Board member asked his friend for advice, and the Ford Director, being an amateur historian himself, was sympathetic and offered to help. The Foundation Board member reported his conversation to Lynch who was suddenly able to enter doors at Ford that were previously closed to him. The result of Lynch's persistence

---

17 "Meeting Lenfest's Challenge Could Put Foundation Over Goal," *Gettysburg Times*, April 30, 2005.

was a $3 million gift to support Battlefield learning at the Visitor Center's educational facilities that would be known as the Ford Educational Center. Lenfest's match was two-thirds earned with the Ford gift. Lynch's hard work paid off, but who could have predicted the way it would happen and the indispensable role of Lady Luck.

Ford wasn't alone. The History Channel, Boeing, Coca-Cola, and the Sumner T. McKnight Foundation, controlled by Foundation Board member Turney McKnight, each chipped in $1 million.[18] As it turned out, the Foundation raised $9 million—and more than earned the $4.5 million matching gift in the allotted time. Nothing motivates donors more than a deadline or a match. The Foundation had both. The total funds raised by June 30, 2005 approached $80 million.

On June 3, 2005, the groundbreaking, the beacon that had guided the Museum and Visitor Center project for nearly a decade, finally took place near the intersection of Hunt Avenue and Baltimore Pike. Kinsley, Latschar, and Wilburn were there, as were Paul Hoffman of the Department of the Interior, new Congressman Todd Platts, Senator Santorum, and NPS Director Fran Mainella, all wielding ceremonial shovels. It was a milestone, and there was a celebratory, festive atmosphere among the hundreds of supporters on that hot day in June, but it would be three more years of hard work and millions of dollars more to be raised, before the job was finished.

Ten months after the groundbreaking, the GNBMF and the Friends announced that effective June 30, 2006, they would merge into a new entity to be named Gettysburg Foundation (GF). The combination would affect Foundation fundraising for years to come. A forceful proponent of the merger, Latschar attended the board meetings of both organizations. He'd seen the wisdom of combining the two groups for years, because, while their tracks ran parallel, it was inevitable that if they remained apart, one day there would be a collision. Both groups raised money, both groups supported the NPS at Gettysburg, and both groups looked for different ways to enhance the Park that included land purchases.

The Friends of the National Parks at Gettysburg was founded in 1989. Its work had had a broad, positive impact on the GNMP since its founding. The Superintendent's Report for Fiscal 1995, for example, lists the Friends activities for the year: cash donations of nearly $40,000; initiation of a long-term cannon carriage rehabilitation program; application and receipt of grants

---

18 "Passing on the Legacy," *The Evening Sun*, June 3, 2005.

Bob Wilburn, Friends Chair Barbara Finfrock, and John Latschar

totaling $58,000; staffing major volunteer efforts; raising nearly $300,000 to bury utility lines around the Park; and the completion of two land transactions that totaled approximately $175,000. Fiscal 1995 may or may not have been a typical year, but it seems clear that the GNMP could hardly have had a better friend than the Friends.

At the announcement ceremony, Latschar observed that "the Museum Foundation has been able to go out and find people who have been able to write us five, six, and seven figure checks. Then on the other hand, there are the Friends, and they've had the ability to make wonderful contacts with folks who continually write us two, three, four, and sometimes five figure checks."[19] That said it all. The Gettysburg Foundation was able to access the largest donors. But the Friends had many more donors of lesser amounts, many of whom gave year after year; and gave as well, their indispensable volunteer efforts— "free" labor for a myriad of essential Park projects. The Friends' activities were very important for the future of the Park. They would be the public face of the Foundation. It was strategically critical for the combined organization's future success that the Friends feel good about

19 "Park Service Groups Merge," *Gettysburg Times*, April 25, 2006.

the combination, and for that reason the "merger" aspect of the combination was underscored. Any idea that the Friends were "taken over" was anathema. The question that has been asked, however, is when the Gettysburg Foundation was founded, which was in 1998 by Bob and Anne Kinsley. By all conventional measures, the Museum Foundation was the acquiring entity and its founding date of May 15, 1998, governs.[20]

Following the groundbreaking in June 2005, fundraising slowed as the Foundation's "pipeline" of prospective donors recovered from the extraordinary efforts that were made to reach $75 million by the June 5 date of the groundbreaking. But that was all that slowed. The groundbreaking unleashed pent-up energy in every direction, as one deadline after another rose and fell. It was a dizzying pace, but the completion date was set for spring of 2008, and the grand opening was scheduled several months later, in September, after the Cyclorama was installed. Those dates needed to be met. They had already been moved back twice. Further delay would add cost, delay revenue, and place the project at risk.

As the deliberate fundraising effort resumed unabated, new donors were uncovered and funding slowly began to grow again. Less than two years later, in April 2007, the total fundraising reached $93 million.[21] In August 2007, Foundation Director Tom Petrie and his wife Jane issued a challenge to the Foundation wherein the Petries would match every dollar given by a new donor, dollar for dollar, up to a maximum of $1 million, thereby yielding a potential gift of $2 million. Petrie was a Green Beret graduate of West Point, who, after building a business and selling it to Merrill Lynch, became Vice Chairman of Merrill Lynch. By then, the Foundation had split its $125 million total fundraising goal between the first phase; $103 million for everything related to the Museum and Visitor Center; and $22 million for everything else, including the rehabilitation of Ziegler's Grove and a $10 million endowment. At that time, the Foundation was about $8 million

20 Prior to the combination, the GNBMF Board of Directors had twenty members, each of whom became a member of the new Foundation's board. The Friends board had ten members three of whom became members of the new Foundation's board. The board of the new Foundation was composed of twenty former GNBMF directors and three former Friends' directors. The GNBMF's Chairman, Bob Kinsley, became the Foundation's Chairman. The Friends' Chairman, Barbara Finfrock became Vice-Chairman of the new Foundation. GNBMF President Bob Wilburn became President of the new Foundation. Barbara J Finfrock, *Twenty Years on 6,000 Acres: The History of The Friends of The National Parks At Gettysburg, 1989-2009,* (Gettysburg: Barbara J Finfrock), Appendix A.

21 "Gettysburg Foundation Secures $93 M for Campaign," *Civil War Courier,* April 2007.

short of its first goal.[22] The brunt of the fundraising was behind them, but the prior two years and the year that lay ahead, were, and would continue to be, challenging. While the work went on at a feverish pace, critics remained, new opponents appeared, and a new division emerged that revealed fresh ambiguities within the partnership and threatened its fabric, and even its long-term ability to survive.

22 "Challenge Issued to Raise Money for Foundation," *The Evening Sun*, Aug. 28, 2007.

CHAPTER 11

Mission Accomplished

The festive groundbreaking ceremony that took place on June 2, 2005, marked the end of the beginning and the beginning of the end of the eagerly awaited Museum and Visitor Center project. It had been eleven years since John Latschar arrived in Gettysburg with a new vision for the GNMP that quickly collided with an NPS admission that his vision could not be funded currently or any time soon. He knew it would be hard, but he could not have known how difficult the road ahead would prove to be. Fast forward to 2005: the arduous and demanding work of constructing the enormous complex had begun, but as it pushed ahead at a dizzying pace, the wrangling that marked the project from its beginning seemed as if it would never end. The Grand Opening, which would feature the first public display of the restored Cyclorama, was scheduled for September 2008, and the schedule needed to be met.

The first phase of the construction project was the restoration of the Guinn Run corridor. Guinn Run, a small stream that flows southeast from its source on Cemetery Hill, was dammed in the late 1950s to create three ponds that were part of the *Fantasyland* amusement park. In 2005, the dilapidated and collapsing dams remained. Plans called for their removal and the return of the stream to its pre-Civil War condition. In some areas, new roads and/or parking lots disturbed the existing wetlands that were replaced with more wetlands than were destroyed. The second phase, begun late in the year, involved clearing the site, removing stumps and vegetation, building access roads, and installing utilities, water, and sewer lines.[1]

The third phase, foundation work that also began in the fall of 2005, proceeded apace, and one year later, in the autumn of 2006, steel beams were poking their heads out of the ground. Sixty workers were on site five days a week. The steel beams framed the giant silo that would house the massive Cyclorama painting, and it needed to be erected and closed in before winter.[2] Adding to the likely time and expense to build the complex was a

---

1 "Foundation Eyes Second Phase Of Visitor Center Project," *Gettysburg Times*, Sept. 12, 2005.

2 "Visitor Center Complex," *Gettysburg Times*, Sept. 20, 2006. "Battle Museum's New Home," *The Evening Sun*, Sept. 20, 2006.

geo-thermal heating system that an enthusiastic donor persuaded Wilburn to include. It would take longer to install, but in the long term it would be less expensive to operate.[3] The system required drilling one hundred sixty-eight wells, each five hundred fifty feet deep to the earth's constant fifty-five degree temperature that would heat and cool the complex, without burning fossil fuels. Apart from considerable operating savings, the geo-thermal system made it possible for the Foundation to earn a Silver certification in the LEED rating system that was raised to Gold certification in 2010, the first museum in Pennsylvania, and the fourth in the nation, to achieve that status.[4] By September 2006, total funding for the project rose to $86 million.[5]

With much of the design work completed, and construction underway, the Foundation and the Park Service turned their attention to operations that were generally running smoothly. But problems still cropped up that raised the ghosts of Gettysburg past. The General Agreement between the Foundation and the NPS provided that the Foundation was responsible for "general building management."[6] More specifically, the Foundation was to provide "reservation services, including pre-visit reservation services, and same-day reservation and ticket services for Park-based interpretive programs and Licensed Battlefield guide tours." The Foundation was also responsible "for the operations of the Book and Museum stores" and a variety of other services including custodial.[7] In order to have the necessary wherewithal, the Agreement provided, too, that the Foundation would receive "all revenues from interpretive fees, user fees, sales, rentals, and Foundation fundraising."[8]

Managing the bookstore, and more recently reservation services, had long been the province of Eastern National Park & Monument Association, a 501 (c) (3) not-for-profit that operated at 150 locations, mostly, but not exclusively, at national parks in thirty states. Latschar had a good relationship with Eastern when he first became Superintendent. But Eastern's

---

3 "Museum's Heat to Come from the Ground," *The Evening Sun*, Sept. 20, 2006.

4 LEED stands for Leadership in Energy and Environmental Design. It is a privately-developed rating system that measures the design, construction, and operation of high-performance green buildings, homes, and neighborhoods. There are one hundred thirty-six possible base points distributed across five major categories, plus additional points for innovative design. Buildings can qualify for four levels of certification: Certified, Silver, Gold, and Platinum.

5 "Raising Steel, Funds," *York Sunday News*, Sept. 24, 2006.

6 General Agreement, June 30, 2000, Exhibit C, 1.

7 Ibid. 2.

8 Ibid. 4.

management had changed since then, and so had his relationship. Eastern's contract with the Museum bookstore stipulated that Eastern return funds to the NPS each year that were distributed to other national parks, some of which did not have a fraction of Gettysburg's visitation or bookstore revenue. The GNMP was one of Eastern's oldest and best clients, accounting for approximately half of Eastern's revenue.[9] Its financial model, which was applied throughout the Park Service, provided that Eastern's expenses were deducted from revenue before returns to the NPS were calculated, thus virtually assuring some level of profitability for Eastern, and placing the NPS at risk for whatever was left over. Eastern's competitors offered better, more aggressive, payout formulas, generally a fixed commission on top-line sales that would insure a certain level of income for the NPS and put Eastern at risk as to the final result. But Eastern's preferred position with the NPS seemed to insulate it from competitive pressures to change.

When Wilburn turned his attention to operating the new complex, he recognized the risks to the Foundation of the Eastern formula that provided no incentive for Eastern to operate efficiently. He knew he'd need other options and he prepared an RFP, the first step in a search to find another provider. Museum operations were not new to him. He had considerable prior experience operating museums at Williamsburg and at Carnegie. Latschar, mindful of Eastern's long relationship with the NPS, asked Wilburn to grant Eastern a preferential right of first response before he (Wilburn) began the search, which he did. This gave Eastern a chance to develop their negotiating position free from competitive pressures. In October 2004 the Foundation sent a draft of its anticipated RFP for the full complement of services to Eastern for their review. The draft contained an array of detailed requirements for each service, as well as general financial and personnel prerequisites. Eastern's response, delivered in January, was deficient—to Wilburn almost nonresponsive. The Foundation offered to meet with Eastern's management and give them a second opportunity before they circulated the RFP broadly. Eastern's second response, though improved, still anticipated their traditional "off the top" deduction of expenses that was unacceptable to the Foundation.

The Foundation then terminated discussions with Eastern and released the RFP to a total of five potential operators including Eastern, thus giving Eastern a third chance. But after a comprehensive review of the submissions, the Foundation chose Event Network, a leading operator of retail stores at

9 "Eastern National Dropped at Park," *The Evening Sun*, Oct. 15, 2006.

museums, aquariums, and other cultural sites throughout North America. The decision to change operators was approved by the Regional Director and the Director of the NPS, and it was announced publicly in January 2006.[10] Several smaller national parks reacted guardedly to the news, fearing the detrimental financial impact on their parks if revenue from Gettysburg were lost. Some parks rely on income from the Gettysburg Museum Bookstore. Latschar went to great lengths to explain that the Foundation's contract continued to provide the support that the parks were accustomed to receiving.[11]

During 2006 the Foundation also hired a consultant to help develop a new ticketing and reservation service that Eastern also managed under a separate contract from the bookstore. Historically, visitors wishing to take guided tours of the Battlefield were told to arrive early at the Visitor Center, where they would be assigned a guide if there was one available. There were no advance reservations for LBG-guided tours. The objectives of a new online system were to allow visitors to reserve guides in advance; to increase demand for guide services by removing the uncertainty of whether a visitor would be able to reserve a guide; and to reduce down-time for guides who, ordinarily, waited for clients to appear. The new noncash system generated a 1099 form for income tax purposes, and no one knew what its impact would be on gratuities. A complicating factor was that guides were independent contractors, not Park Service employees, and they worked when they chose to. So by the autumn of 2006, and with the words of warning in mind—"if you want to make enemies, try to change something"—two long-time Park vendors, Eastern National and the Licensed Battlefield Guides Association, were both ready to fight the Park's plans to change the reservation system.

The first shoe to drop was Eastern National's. Obviously frustrated by the impending loss of their largest and longest tenured client, the Gettysburg Museum Bookstore, Eastern launched a competing reservation system without first notifying the Park Service. On Friday, September 29, 2006, after the close of business, Eastern moved its reservation service, telephones, and computers from the Park Service Visitor Center to Gateway Gettysburg and renamed it "Park Trek."[12] Bob Monahan, the Gateway developer, appeared to be trying to raise Gateway's profile as a jumping-off point for guided tours. But he said the move was not a move to compete with the Visitor Center; it was a move to

---

10 "New Museum Vendor Named," *Gettysburg Times*, Jan. 21, 2006.

11 "Bookstore Change Is a Good Deal," *The Evening Sun*, Nov. 7, 2006.

12 "Park Service Elaborates on Its Firing of Contractor," *Gettysburg Times*, Oct. 18, 2006.

better serve Gateway visitors and the local community. He continued, "We're taking a reservation system of the local community that visitors have depended on and [we have] preserved that legacy and continuity in the tourist community. I don't view that as competition. I view that as doing all the right things for all the right reasons."[13] In another interview, Monahan contended that he was trying to preserve Eastern National's legacy. He also said that the NPS terminated the company without basis.[14] The NPS disagreed with Monahan's latter contention, and while its previous intention had been to continue its entire relationship with Eastern, both bookstore and reservations, until the new Visitor Center opened in 2008, instead, citing a contract violation, it terminated Eastern's reservation contract immediately. The President of Eastern claimed to be "shocked" by the Park's decision. The Foundation immediately hired as many Eastern employees as possible and announced plans to "assume the role of the GMNP's reservation and ticketing agent, beginning November 1, 2006."[15] Within a year or so, most reservations were booked through the Foundation, and there was very little indication that there had ever been a change.

Shortly after the emergence of Park Trek in the Gateway Center, a new president of the LBGA, also protesting the prospect of a new reservation system, agreed to move the guides to Gateway in concert with Park Trek, another apparent move to stimulate Park traffic at Gateway. He was quoted, "Our primary objective is to preserve guiding as it existed since the early 1900s," a comment that may have been more revealing than he intended.[16] The guides' circumstance was made more complex by the fact that in addition to being independent contractors, guides are licensed by the NPS, which sets their fee schedule. And while all members of the LBGA are guides, all guides are not members of the LBGA. Some guides were not opposed to the new reservation system, and they remained, first at the old Rosensteel building, and then at the new Visitor Center. But the LBGA, nevertheless, continued to look for office space away from the Visitor Center, and an LBGA office remains in Gettysburg today. Gateway is now a prime location for two excellent hotels, but with some exceptions, most Battlefield tours start at the new Visitor Center.

As the operating situations sorted themselves out, the financial picture was also gaining clarity. The General Agreement between the NPS and the

13 "Eastern National Dropped at Park," *The Evening Sun*, undated.

14 "Ticket Seller Ready," *York Sunday News*, Oct. 22, 2006.

15 "Park Service Elaborates on Its Firing of Contractor," *Gettysburg Times*, Oct. 18, 2006.

16 "Park Battlefield Guides Unhappy," *Gettysburg Times*, June 2, 2007.

Foundation limited the Foundation's borrowing to just under $12 million, personally guaranteed by Kinsley, and it remained that way six years later, even as the project increased in size and scope. At the Foundation's request, however, in November 2006, the NPS agreed to permit the Foundation to borrow up to $20 million. In February, M&T Bank of Buffalo, New York announced that it had "completed a $20 million construction bond financing with the Gettysburg Foundation," which Kinsley again guaranteed.[17] M&T also donated $250,000 to the project. The financing package provided an immediate $8 million addition to the Foundation's fundraising total.

In April 2007 the Foundation announced that it reached $93 million of its campaign goal, while at the same time, it revised the goal that had been $95 million since 2002 upward to $125 million. Primary reasons for the $30 million increase since 2002 were for building construction ($4.15 million); general and administrative ($3.88 million); rehabilitation of Ziegler's Grove ($3 million); museum exhibits ($8.17 million); Cyclorama restoration ($5.7 million); and programs previously handled by the Friends ($5 million).[18] The funds needed for Ziegler's Grove and for the Friends were unrelated to the new complex. The Foundation's new multipurpose mission, apparent for the first time, made it more difficult to compare the new figures with prior ones. Critics who had opposed the project from the outset spoke out again, but seemingly with little effect.[19] Aside from the $3.8 million that Congress would appropriate later in the year, the Foundation would need to raise the remaining funds privately.

By mid-2007, the NPS and the Foundation were conducting guided tours through the cavernous hallways of the partially built complex, asking visitors to use their imaginations to visualize what the new facility would look like after it was built. Katie Lawhon, the NPS publicist, pointed out that the interim Visitor Center—the ancestral Rosensteel home—was designed to service about 450,000 visitors annually, while the new complex would serve more than three times that, and she reminded her charges that "If we didn't build a new Visitor Center [Gettysburg], visitation would have continued to drop."[20]

17   "Foundation to Ante Up $20 Million toward Visitor Center Project," *Gettysburg Times*, Feb. 21, 2007.

18   "Gettysburg Foundation Secures $93 Million for Campaign," *Civil War Courier*, April 2007.

19   "Critic Sees Unanswered Questions," *Civil War News*, February/March, 2007.

20   "Visitor Center Work on Track," *The Evening Sun*, Aug. 15, 2007.

Meanwhile, the Steinwehr Avenue merchants, mostly opponents of the project from its beginning, formed a new business alliance and hired a consultant to analyze the district's viability after the Visitor Center moved. The idea, which seemed overdue, was to develop a strategy for dealing with changes in their businesses.[21] But by-products of their unrelenting opposition to moving the Visitor Center continued to surface. Late in the year, Park officials announced that the Government Accountability Office (GAO) was planning yet another visit to Gettysburg. The office said that it planned to examine the Park's and Foundation's policies and procedures for handling donations, and whether or not those policies and procedures were followed.[22] This was the third time in eight years that the GAO had visited Gettysburg after they'd found nothing out of the ordinary in their previous investigations. But increases in the cost of the project always attracted attention. The NPS usually approved cost increases that were shown to enhance the project's overall quality and enhance the visitor experience, which the NPS deemed important.[23] *The Evening Sun* wrote, "They say they want to know where the money went, but you don't need a government analyst to tell you that. Just take a look at that new building." The editorial pointed out that the Foundation wanted to build a world-class facility, but some locals feared that such a facility would soak up all their business. The editors, on the other hand, believed that a world-class facility would attract more new and returning visitors with money to spend.[24] And before the GAO showed up, Congress approved the final $3.8 million earmark that was used for moving, installing, and lighting the Cyclorama painting.

The lack of proper care for the enormous collection of documents and artifacts, which was one of the four drivers of the new vision, ended with the completion of the $536,000, 4,700 square-foot temporary storage facility in May 2000.[25] From then on, some artifacts that were not at risk were left in the old Rosensteel building, but others were removed, and tended to, before being stored in the new facility. "Edged weapons," for example, were treated. Work was done on rare books, as well as uniforms, flags, and other documents, all before removal to the temporary building. At the same time,

---

21 "Steinwehr Business Owners Concerned," *Gettysburg Times*, Sept. 27, 2007.

22 "Battlefield Officials Welcome Federal Review," *The Evening Sun*, Dec. 2, 2007.

23 "Return Visit," *Gettysburg Times*, Dec. 4, 2007.

24 "Investigators Welcome in Gettysburg," *The Evening Sun*, Dec. 6, 2007.

25 "Battlefield Temporary Storage Facility Is Finished," *Gettysburg Times*, May 20, 2000.

preparation was ongoing to digitize and electronically organize the archival collection. By 2003 much was accomplished, but there was more to go. The work was supervised by Park Archivist Greg Goodell, and financed, in part, by the Foundation through gifts from ASE Edge, a Pittsburgh software company owned by Arthur Crivella and Wayne West. Their gift to the Foundation, in time and equipment, for work done to care for the collection amounted to $1 million before it was finished.

Selection and treatment of nearly 1,000 archival and Museum objects that were to be exhibited in the new Museum were transferred to the NPS's Harpers Ferry Center for conservation treatment and then returned for exhibition.[26] Beginning in January 2008, curators began the piece-by-piece packing, moving, and unpacking of the collection from the interim Visitor Center, the temporary storage facility, or Harpers Ferry, and began the journey to its new 14,900 square foot state-of-the-art, climate-controlled facility at the new Visitor Center complex, a process that took six months to complete.

In the meantime, conversations were ongoing amongst the exhibit designers, the Foundation, and the NPS regarding the configuration of the new Museum. Its purpose was to tell the story of the Battle within the story of the causes and consequences of the Civil War and how it affects America today.[27] It was organized in three sections: pre-Civil War to the Gettysburg Campaign, the Gettysburg Campaign, and the Gettysburg Address up to 1913 and beyond. Terms like "streakers," "strollers," and "studiers" were heard as the group grappled with how visitors use museums. There were some who argued passionately to assemble the exhibits in an unbroken line from beginning to end, so that the full story was always told. Others argued for more flexibility, exits in the middle, so people could leave, or return where they left off. Alcoves provided details that supported the more general themes that were presented in the main corridors. When it was all done the exhibit designers, Gallagher's team, put it all together.

An important result of a donor solicitation of the History Channel was not only a generous gift of over $1 million for the project, but the personal involvement of History Channel Chief Historian Libby O'Connell. O'Connell attended meetings and weighed in on the historical content of the film, *A New Birth of Freedom*, narrated by Morgan Freeman, as well as all of the videos that were incorporated into the Museum exhibits. The film and

---

26 Park Superintendent's Report, Fiscal Year 2007.

27 "The Last Battle," *Baltimore Sun*, July 1, 2001.

New Visitor Center lobby

the videos were produced by Donna Lawrence Productions.

On April 10, 2008, the new Museum and Visitor Center was thrown open to a sea of hyper-curious area residents. A gala opening would wait for the installation of the Cyclorama painting. Museum galleries, the new film, food samples from the Refreshment Saloon, and the bookstore were all open, the latter for "browsing." The next day the *Gettysburg Times* headline blared "Magnificent Facility" and the reporter wrote, "A massive crowd attended a community open house Thursday night at the new $103 million Gettysburg National Military Park Museum and Visitor Center, getting a sneak peek at the colossal, 139,000 square-foot complex before it opens to the general public on Monday."[28] Comments from visitors ranged from "everything looks fantastic," and "it looks great," to "our best field trip of the year." Longtime critic Ted Streeter said, "We certainly started off with some differences, and it was a long and protracted struggle, but they produced a wonderful facility that will benefit the Borough, the Park, Park visitors, and the entire Civil War community." The *York Sunday News* said, "Cheers to Robert Kinsley." Former project critic Dick Peterson, by then President of the Gettysburg Borough Council, wrote the *Gettysburg Times* to praise the new Museum and Visitor Center, but more importantly to make note of a new attitude in Gettysburg, wherein citizens were working together, and "former adversaries are friends."[29]

Five days later, the new Museum and Visitor Center, so long in the making, opened its doors to the general public. Newspaper stories seemed

28 "Magnificent Facility," *Gettysburg Times*, April 11, 2008.

29 "Visitor Center of the People," *York Sunday News*, April 13, 2008.

unusually granular, sober accounts of the contents and story lines presented in the new exhibits, as if the reporters, while dutiful, were in awe. *The Boston Globe* said, "The Museum does an outstanding job of detailing the world-altering events that took place at Gettysburg and placing them in the context of the Civil War."[30] *The Washington Post* said that the new building "is everything the Richard Neutra [Cyclorama] building is not."[31] *The Patriot-News* said, "Only the most stringent of purists is likely to find fault with the new center."[32]

One of those stringent purists spoke up in a letter to the *Civil War News*. The correspondent focused on what he considered to be inadequate, and/or incorrect, display of artifacts and a presentation that he believed was put together by Museum administrators and academic historians, rather than curators, who pay strict attention to the display and interpretation of historic artifacts.[33] In an accompanying response, Latschar, at his sardonic best, admitted that the new Museum had little to offer a Civil War expert whose breadth and depth of knowledge has left him only with the difference between Union and Confederate twelve-pound Napoleons to explore. "For the rest of us," he said, "for whom the Museum was built, the Museum provides an understanding of the significance of the Gettysburg campaign, within the causes and consequences of the American Civil War." The debate, like other Civil War debates, will never end, nor should it. But notwithstanding the many accolades and the few criticisms of the Museum, the restored majesty of the magnificent Cyclorama painting was not yet on view.

In yet another extraordinary achievement, and after an extended period of waiting, watching, and worrying, the Foundation acquired the eighty-acre George Spangler Farm in May 2008 for nearly $2 million.[34] Poverty is the preservationist's friend, and the Farm buildings, with the possible exception of a 1930s kitchen, though poorly maintained, appeared to be configured very much as they were in 1863. The Farm is historically significant, an inholding located behind the Union lines that served as a major field hospital during,

30 "Creative Renovation Breathes New Life Into Hallowed Ground," *Boston Globe*, April 13, 2008.

31 "At Last, Gettysburg Redress," *Washington Post*, April 14, 2008.

32 Story by David Dunkle, *The Patriot-News*, April 13, 2008.

33 "A Curator's Opinion of the Museum," *Civil War News*, August 2008.

34 "Gettysburg Foundation Buys George Spangler Farm on Battlefield," *Gettysburg Times*, May 8, 2008.

and immediately after, the Battle. Because of a road pattern that connected the Farm to Taneytown Road and Baltimore Pike, the Farm also served as the Union Army's most important artillery and ammunition support facility. It was where Confederate General Lewis Armistead was brought after he was wounded, and where he died after leading Pickett's Charge. The Farm had been on the market for some time, and there was concern that it would be sold to a private developer. Instead, the Foundation was able to mount a fundraising campaign to secure the funds and make the purchase. The acquisition of the Farm was a stunning example of how the Foundation could function as an NPS partner. The Foundation was unsure then how the Farm would be used, but it was clear, from the outset, that if it were restored, an array of interpretive venues would be possible.

In late August, three weeks before the Grand Opening of the new complex, a storm arose around the project that threatened the public/private partnership that had withstood so many external attacks over the prior decade—and this was an attack from within. The *Gettysburg Times* headline read, "Park Service to charge Museum admission fee." Latschar said that they'd tried just about everything to avoid charging an admission fee and that nothing was working.[35] Entrance fees to national parks have been controversial for over fifty years, playing budget conscious legislators against those who always argued that national parks should be free.[36] In this case, the Foundation offered three separate venues: the Cyclorama painting that was not yet open to the public; a twenty-two-minute feature film entitled *A New Birth of Freedom* narrated by Morgan Freeman; and admission to the new Museum. The plan was to charge twelve dollars for an adult ticket for both the Cyclorama and the film, and there would be no charge for the Museum. During the four months leading up to the grand opening, the Foundation charged eight dollars for an adult ticket to the film alone. The financial plan assumed that one third of the visitors would choose to see the film and the Cyclorama when it opened. But visitors were rejecting the film and flocking to the free Museum. Their calculation seems to have been that eight dollars was too much to pay for a twenty-two-minute film, however excellent,

35 "Park Service to Charge Museum Admission Fee," *Gettysburg Times*, Aug. 29, 2008. Information regarding admission fees contained in this chapter, unless otherwise noted, are drawn from interviews with Kinsley, Latschar, or Wilburn on Nov. 21, 2013; Nov. 20, 2013; or Sept. 21, 2015 respectively.

36 Visitor Fees in the National Park System: A Legislative and Administrative History. Retrieved from https://www.nps.gov/parkhistory/online_books/mackintosh3/fees2.htm

especially when there was a free Museum that could more than occupy most visitors for hours and covered almost every topic that one would ever care to cover. Interviews with visitors indicated that if the Cyclorama painting were added to the package, and the eight-dollar fee were raised to twelve dollars, the traffic pattern was not going to change. The Foundation's solution was a blanket fee of seven dollars and fifty cents to cover all three venues. But any fee for the Museum necessitated a change to the GMP that had anticipated a free Museum.[37] The blanket fee, therefore, would need to be open for a thirty-day public review, and it began on August 29, 2008.

Local newspapers called it a "drastic deviation."[38] The much-debated GMP called for a Museum that would be free to all visitors. Latschar gamely explained that there would continue to be no charge for the Refreshment Saloon, souvenir store, lobbies, rest rooms, classrooms, and other common areas of the facility or for entering the Battlefield, for which some parks did charge.[39] But the charge for the Museum gave critics a last opportunity to lampoon the NPS on the eve of their greatest triumph, which they did at a standing-room-only public meeting. Uberman asked rhetorically, at what point do people say they're mad as hell and they're not going to take it any-more?[40] It was unclear to what extent those who attended the meeting, and who seemed to oppose the fee, were part of a group organized by the project's opponents. At the same time it was equally unclear what, if any, influence, letters that Wilburn and Latschar sent to members of the Friends and others on the Park's mailing list, had on the outcome.

By the end of September the results were in, and the Park Service an-nounced that 56 percent of 572 respondents favored the Park Service plan, 34 percent opposed it, 5 percent favored an admission fee, but one that was below seven dollars and fifty cents, and 5 percent had no opinion.[41] The schedule, with appropriate senior, youth, and military discounts, went into effect on October 2, 2008, and there were few, if any, complaints from the visiting pub-lic. The NPS didn't complain either, perhaps because they were caught up in the euphoria of the marvelous publicity surrounding the new facility.

---

37 General Management Plan and Environmental Impact Statement, Gettysburg National Military Park, June 1999, 24.

38 "Fee for Visitor Center Museum?" *The Evening Sun*, April 29, 2008.

39 "Park Service to Charge Museum Admission Fee," *Gettysburg Times*, Aug. 29, 2008.

40 "Contentious," *Gettysburg Times*, Sept. 19, 2008.

41 "Park Service OKs Museum Admission," *The Evening Sun*, Oct. 2, 2008.

What it was that caused the original pricing difficulty remains unclear. Kinsley's response to the RFP in 1997 included revenue generating venues, but the *pro forma* income statement in 2008 showed that the complex would more than break even without those venues and without an admission fee to the Museum. That turned out to be incorrect. A contributing factor appears to be that the NPS, through 2008, used a formula of average visitors per automobile that proved to be inaccurate and too high, and that was corrected in 2009. Another factor, as previously noted, was that visitors chose to visit the free museum without visiting the film, for which there was a fee, more frequently than the Foundation anticipated. But if both of these issues were recognized sooner, the *pro forma* income statements would have changed, but the revenue problem would have remained. The original pricing plan was a mistake, and the consequences were striking.

To charge a fee or not was, in itself, and in its symbolism, a proxy for the sharp, cultural divide that exists between the public and private partners. Ten years before, under Roger Kennedy, an extraordinary NPS Director, the NPS miraculously loosened its moorings to the domain of riskless, federal dependency and mediocrity that had led to the dismal conditions at Gettysburg in the first place. In an inspired turn of events, it cast its lot with the riskier private domain that dared to excel. The results were stunning, and the public seemed to understand.

After the June 2005 groundbreaking, the deliberate fundraising effort that slowed considerably in subsequent months, resumed, slowly but consistently. New donors were uncovered, and funding slowly began to grow again. Less than two years later, in April 2007, as noted above, the total fundraising reached $93 million.[42] Of particular note was a $2 million gift from Deborah and Craig Cogut. Cogut, a Foundation director, had an unusual passion for Gettysburg, where he had brought his children annually for years. The Coguts' gift named the post-Battle gallery that is devoted to Lincoln's Gettysburg Address. By February 2008 the total funds committed to the project rose to $105 million, and that became $110 million by September 28, 2008, the date of the Grand Opening.[43]

---

42 "Gettysburg Foundation Secures $93 Million for Campaign," *Civil War Courier*, April 2007.

43 "Gettysburg Foundation Discloses New Fund-Raising Total: $105 million," *Gettysburg Times*, Feb. 21, 2008. Superintendent's Annual Report, Fiscal Year 2008.

Gettysburg Museum and Visitor Center

When the time came for the Grand Opening of the Museum and Visitor Center, the Cyclorama painting was spectacular. The Olin-Wojtowicz restoration team had won their race with time. There were thousands of spectators. Parking was at a premium. The Visitor Center lobby was magically transformed into a festive dining hall for hundreds of guests. Bob Kinsley was, like any proud father, smiling, happy, gracious, and bursting with pride over what everyone could see was a world-class building. Wilburn, often quiet, was obviously pleased with the result that surely had taken longer to achieve than he originally thought it would, but was, nevertheless, very gratifying to him. Secretary of the Interior Dirk Kempthorne called the painting "stunning."[44] Another visitor said, "[The Cyclorama] makes you feel like you were right there," and "you can't help feel something deep down inside."[45] Sue Boardman said, "When I look at it, I can hear the roar of cannons, men shouting, horses neighing."[46] Governor Ed Rendell called the experience "overwhelming" before he stepped to the podium to deliver the keynote

44 "Civil War Celebration," *Gettysburg Times*, Sep. 27, 2008.

45 "Visitor Center Opens," *The Evening Sun*, Sept. 27, 2008.

46 "Gettysburg's Cannons Roar Again as Cyclorama Restored," by Jef Feeley, Bloomberg.com., Oct. 22, 2008.

address. He noted that in 1863 there were 23,000 Pennsylvania soldiers at the Battle, and that Pennsylvania was happy to invest "$20 million in the project." Latschar's ten-minute speech "was punctuated by a thunderous standing ovation."[47]

The miracle of what was accomplished at Gettysburg spread quickly and led to an unusually high number of meetings and conferences during the year. The Military Order of the Loyal Legion of United States, the Civil War Preservation Trust, the Journey Through Hallowed Ground, and the Pennsylvania Federation of Museums all held their annual conventions at Gettysburg.[48] For Latschar, it was the culmination of fourteen years of hard work, extraordinary steadfastness, endurance, and resilience. His mission was accomplished.

---

47 "Civil War Celebration," *Gettysburg Times*, Sept. 27, 2008.
48 Superintendent's Annual Report, Fiscal Year 2008.

CHAPTER 12

Looking Back; Looking Ahead

As 2017 begins, the Gettysburg Foundation is now nineteen years old and nine years removed from the opening of the Gettysburg Museum and Visitor Center. The steady stream of events that have occurred in that intervening time have helped set the Foundation's future direction and, at the same time, have accentuated the time-dimensional influence of entrepreneurial philanthropy. The investigation, for example, that was launched in late 2007 by the GAO was a final effort by Park Service opponents, but by that late date, its purpose was not clear.[1] They looked into the Foundation's management and accounting for its funding, including visits to Kinsley company offices, because during the time they were investigating, all the Foundation's payables and financial statements were processed out of the Kinsley office. Kinsley's controller was doing all the day-to-day accounting, and one of their accounts payable property accountants was also working on Gettysburg, all at no cost to the Foundation.[2] GAO found nothing remarkable—no improprieties—nor did it seem possible that Kinsley profited from the project. According to Driver, Kinsley's chief financial officer, "We had invoices and we had to include the cost of our employees and our overhead, but it's pretty easy to show what everything costs. On other projects, as we incurred costs, we added a pre-agreed percentage fee, but on this project there was no fee: just to be careful and to be sure that we didn't charge a profit. Kinsley Construction wrote some of the costs off, and then we had the auditors come in and look at it to confirm that there was no profit."[3]

In June 2009, less than a year after the Gala opening, during which time Latschar had devoted considerable time to teaching Foundation personnel how to operate a Visitor Center efficiently, he reluctantly decided to raise

---

1   Robin Nazarro, Director of Natural Resources and Environment for the GAO, said that the House Subcommittee on Park Service and Public Lands (Hansen's Subcommittee) requested the study into NPS donations, specifically the construction and fundraising for Gettysburg's new Visitor Center because of the project's upward spiraling cost. "Battlefield Officials Welcome Federal Review," *The Evening Sun*, Dec. 2, 2007.

2   Driver interview, Feb. 17, 2014.

3   Ibid.

the adult admission fee to the Museum from seven dollars and fifty cents to ten dollars and fifty cents. To soften the blow, he reminded the public that admission fees paid to the Foundation were used to retire the Foundation's debt; to pay for all the facility's operating costs; to establish reserves; and to make considerable annual donations to the GMNP and the NPS that supported NPS objectives. According to Latschar, the public accepted the fee increase, but the NPS did not. Beneath the surface there was a backlash within the NPS in Washington. They quickly sent a team of examiners to review the proposed fiscal 2010 budget, and then significantly and symbolically, removed the Superintendent's jurisdiction over pricing approval, elevating it to the Regional Director.[4]

A free Museum at Gettysburg had become accepted policy at the former Visitor Center, and it was promised by the new GMP for the new one. One staffer said that charging for the new Museum was a "big deal," and six years later she still hadn't gotten over it. That was the perception from the public side of the partnership. But from the private side, the problem amounted to an unwanted, but unremarkable, business circumstance, a price increase. Kinsley, who was always committed to breaking even, when he responded to several of the evaluation panel's questions in June 1997, notified the NPS that he planned to charge an entrance fee to the Museum.[5] The NPS did not react at the time. Kinsley's original proposal to the evaluation panel also included a museum admission fee as well as several other revenue-producing venues. After he was selected, he responded to the public uproar over commercialism in National Parks and the NPS's insistence that it be reduced, by removing one revenue source after another, and he couldn't have been surprised by the revenue shortfall once the complex opened.[6] At that point it became apparent that the Foundation and the NPS could not afford to provide an enhanced visitor experience as well as the same free museum that year after year had contributed to the GNMP's decline in the first place. But removal of the NPS's point of pricing authority, up one level, from Park Superintendent to Regional Director, and from

---

4 Superintendent's Annual Report, Fiscal Year 2009.

5 "We anticipate that tickets will be sold for each venue, including the NPS Museum...." Kinsley to evaluation panel members, June 30, 1997.

6 Proposal submission by: Kinsley Equities, Section 2, Concept and Development Strategy; Development and Financing Strategy, "Tickets will be sold for each venue-Museum with Cyclorama, and Cinema with Orientation Theater."

Gettysburg to Washington, seems not to have been constructive. No longer would the Park Superintendent, working with the Foundation President as a team, be responsible for setting ticket prices. The withdrawal of the Park Superintendent's fee-setting authority was an ominous sign for the partnership. In 2011 the admission fee rose to twelve dollars and fifty cents effective at the start of 2012, where it remained for five years, until it increased 20 percent to fifteen dollars at the start of 2017.

On July 23, 2009, the LeVan family donated a sixty-one-acre scenic easement to the Foundation on land that abuts the new Visitor Center complex. The protected land is situated within the Park along the Baltimore Pike and is adjacent to the Culp's Hill/Spangler Spring area of the Battlefield, as well as being adjacent to the new complex. The gift was appraised at $9.8 million, and thus, was one of the largest, and because of its proximity to the complex, one of the more significant gifts to the campaign.

The fundraising campaign wound down thereafter, more than $120 million having been raised, mostly in cash, but also in in-kind donations.[7] Government entities contributed about $36 million of that amount; $16 million came from Congress; $20 million came from the Commonwealth of Pennsylvania; and the Foundation borrowed $20 million that it's scheduled to repay by 2028. The remaining $64 million or 53 percent of the total funds raised, and incidentally nearly two-and-one-half times what Kinsley believed he had to raise when he volunteered to be the NPS's partner, was donated by private foundations, corporations and private individuals from across America and around the world. There were major gifts from citizens of Pennsylvania, Maine, California, Florida, Texas, Colorado, Ohio, New York, and at least nine other states. In all, there were approximately 40,000 donors from fifty states and ten nations.[8] That active philanthropy, under Wilburn's leadership, grew from a single, blank sheet of paper, a decade before. There were not sufficient funds, however, to establish an endowment or to rehabilitate Ziegler's Grove, which was delayed by legal challenges to the Park's plan to remove the Cyclorama building.

The Rosensteel building, the interim Visitor Center, was torn down in

---

7 Latschar disclosed in the Superintendant's Report, that fundraising "stood at $110 million" at the end of the fiscal year. Superintendent's Annual Report, Fiscal Year 2008. The LeVan easement valued at nearly $10 million would have had to bring the total to over $120 million by mid-2009. "Gettysburg Foundation Discloses New Fund-Raising Total: $105 Million," Gettysburg Times, February 21, 2008.

8 "Visitor Center Opens," The Evening Sun, Sept. 27, 2008.

2009, soon after the new Museum and Visitor Center opened. On March 3, 2013, the Neutra-designed Cyclorama building, built in 1962 to serve as a new Visitor Center and a new home for the Cyclorama painting, was, after years of legal wrangling, brought to the ground. Explosives were strategically placed, and within seconds the building was down, its walls collapsing outward before the excavators began the dusty clean-up job. The building's removal paved the way for the rehabilitation of Ziegler's Grove, the only unfinished portion of Latschar's original vision for the GNMP. Monuments then began returning to their original positions. The large parking lot that served the Visitor Center was removed. The final pieces of the puzzle began to fall into place in 2016, when work began on the restoration of Ziegler's Ravine, a well-documented feature of the terrain that was strategically significant during the Battle. Complete rehabilitation of Ziegler's Grove was completed in 2017.

Since 2008 the Foundation has restored the Spangler Farm, and the NPS is well-positioned to tell the stories of those days in the summer of 1863 when it was a field hospital and at the center of the nation's attention. From the first hours of the Battle, the number of incoming wounded reached 1,800 Union and 100 Confederate patients. At least seven surgeons from Pennsylvania, Ohio, and New York worked around the clock in the open air, amputating arms and legs on operating tables that were nothing more than wooden doors stripped from the walls.[9] Two hundred and five men died at Spangler Farm and were buried there, and then exhumed and buried elsewhere. Stories of the patients and surgeons who were there; of the place where General Armistead drew his last breath; and of the Farm's role as an artillery reserve depot where cannons, soldiers and horses shared the Farm with doctors and patients are all now expertly told there. Park Service spokesperson Katie Lawhon said it best: "This is an authentic place, the real deal. It's fresh, and because it is, you sense the importance of it."[10]

The Foundation also acquired the Italianate-style Gettysburg Railroad Station in 2014, the same station that was a hospital and morgue following the Battle 150 years before, and that witnessed Lincoln's arrival from Washington on November 18, 1863 and his departure the following day.

---

9 "Spangler Farm Hospital Site, Gettysburg's 'Real Deal' to Open for Second Season June 6," Ron Kirkwood, special to PennLive.com, May 30, 2014. Retrieved from: http://www.pennlive.com/midstate/index.ssf/2014/05/spangler_farm_hospital_site_ge.html
10 Ibid.

The station was added to the National Park by legislation that enabled the Foundation to begin the process of donating it to the NPS. It's been used since its acquisition as a visitor information station and for special events.

The trio of Kinsley, Latschar, and Wilburn has mostly gone their separate ways: "mostly" because Kinsley has chaired the Gettysburg Foundation since it began and only retired to the active position of Chairman *Emeritus* in June 2017. John Latschar retired from the Park Service in 2013, and he and his wife, Terry, now own and operate the National Riding Stables that offer Gettysburg Battlefield riding tours, something Terry has done for years. Latschar's relationship with the Borough of Gettysburg had undergone a significant transformation before he retired. From the time of his first letter to John Eline in May 1998, the Park's relationship with the town began to improve. By the time Latschar retired from the Park, he'd been asked to join the board of Main Street Gettysburg, and when the Wills House was reopened in 2009, he was given the key to the city, a sharp turnaround indeed.[11] Bob Wilburn is presently President and CEO of The National Medal of Honor Foundation that will design, fund, build, and maintain a new Museum and Educational Center in Charleston, South Carolina.

History's verdict as to the meaning and significance of the Gettysburg Foundation in the annals of the NPS is a story that, because of its unique construct and the continuing nature of the relationship, will continue to be written. Its founding and evolution in the early years though is not a story of foundations or partnerships or large bureaucracies. It's a story of individual patriotism and entrepreneurial philanthropy that began at a special place, at a special time, and in a heated political environment. That story has now been written.

Kinsley, Latschar, and Wilburn, each of whom had previous experience with aspects of what needed to be accomplished at Gettysburg, came together to accomplish something extraordinary that many people said couldn't be done. Their partnership was unfathomable in the degree to which they shared patriotic values, how they saw eye-to- eye, and how effective they were. They had a common drive to tell a special American story as it had never been told before in a special place where thousands of American soldiers

---

11   Main Street Gettysburg's mission is to work with community partners for the preservation, revitalization, and improvement of the Historic District of Gettysburg. The Borough of Gettysburg acquired Wills House, where Lincoln stayed, in 2000. The NPS bought it in 2003 after it was added to the GNMP, and after a six-year, $6 million, rehabilitation program spearheaded by Senator Santorum, it was re-opened in 2009.

died fighting for or against their country. Latschar knew best just what their mission was. Wilburn knew best just how to accomplish it. Kinsley brought it together. In the beginning, he shouldered enormous personal and financial responsibility with the concomitant risk of public failure and financial injury. Once in harness, Kinsley, Latschar, and Wilburn worked together seamlessly as equals with Kinsley as their leader. His resiliency and his steadiness were remarkable. Whether it could ever be done again within the NPS or in some other milieu is not clear. To the author, however, it seems quite clear that entrepreneurial philanthropy by way of public/private partnerships offers enormous potential for good through the NPS, or if not the NPS, through any group that can (a) sponsor a good cause and (b) foster a vision. The third ingredient is a philanthropist willing to check his or her ego at the door and get something done—difficult to find, but certainly not impossible, to which Kinsley can attest.

The multi-dimensional characteristics of entrepreneurial philanthropy incorporate traditional charitable giving. But in addition, the donor, the Gettysburg Foundation, has a hand in managing the use of the funds raised, in some instances controlling it outright. The arrangement continues for an extended period of time, in this case, a minimum of twenty-eight years. The restoration of Ziegler's Grove, the rehabilitation of the Cyclorama painting, the protection of the GNMP's invaluable historic collection of artifacts, Spangler Farm, and later the Railroad Station and many other preservations and acquisitions that never could have happened without the Foundation to pay for them, are now listed as completed: historic past achievements.

The Foundation's existence has challenged both the Borough of Gettysburg and the NPS in the past twenty years and, as a result, each of the three entities seems to have emerged in a different place. Gettysburg's outlook, for example, appears to be constructive. The Steinwehr Avenue merchants, even before the new Visitor Center opened, formed the Steinwehr Avenue Business Alliance and began making plans to update their community. When the new Visitor Center opened, foot traffic on Steinwehr Avenue plummeted, as expected. But there were offsets. The community was supportive, and the guides did what they could to bring traffic into the district. Two large motels did a good business, and the Dobbin House restaurant reported that business improved in 2008 over the prior year.[12] In 2009 the Borough landed $2.5 million in state funds to renovate one block of

12 "Businesses Sketch Out Plan For Surviving," *The Evening Sun*, Oct. 5, 2008.

the Steinwehr district. The work was to include decorative lighting, widen-ing of sidewalks, handicap accessibility, and crosswalks, among other things. And in 2010 the Borough sought $3.5 million of funding from the Federal Department of Transportation to up-grade a second block. In 2011 nearly $3.3 million was awarded; work began in 2014, and it was finished in May of 2016. Said one business leader after the Visitor Center moved, "We pouted, we cried, we got angry, and then we turned to a more positive approach." After over $6 million had been invested in the business district, another merchant said that it is just incredible that it really happened.[13]

Nine years after the Museum and Visitor Center opened, the Gettysburg economy remains healthy, one reason being the huge complex that attracts over a million visitors per year. Steinwehr Avenue is doing well. And it appears as if Gettysburg residents are more aware than ever of their role as guardian of a special place for all Americans. Most travel services and travel reviews list Gettysburg as one of America's premier destinations for learning the nation's history.

For its part, the Foundation is also doing well, but like many private enterprises, every year may not be as successful as the year before. In 2008, the first year, the new Foundation's ability to manage a large Visitor Center was tested, and it experienced some growing pains. The private economy also mandates that there will be good times and not so good times, and that visitation will rise and fall.[14] When the Foundation has not done well, some people worry. Monahan, for example, just after the new Visitor Center opened, said, "The facility is a major upgrade… but if it doesn't meet its fi-nancial goals, what's next? I just really worry where all this is going."[15]

But the Gettysburg Foundation will continue to raise funds for NPS proj-ects at Gettysburg and will own and operate the Museum and Visitor Center at least until 2028, at which time it will be decided whether the Foundation will continue. Someday it may come to an end. If it does, there will be more than one reason for its demise, one of which will undoubtedly be its inability to consistently raise funds for the GNMP. And as we ponder such an un-wanted outcome, we should be mindful that the Foundation in its present state provides an extra level of programming excellence, acquisitions of land

13 "Recognition of Steinwehr Project," *Gettysburg Times*, May 24, 2016.

14 "Gettysburg Foundation Lost $1.16 M Last Year," *The Evening Sun*, March 7, 2012.

15 "What's Next If Park Service Doesn't Attain Revenues," *Gettysburg Times*, Oct. 10, 2008.

and artifacts, facilities, and education that the federal government cannot and will not provide. Congress, through the NPS, was once the GNMP's only source of financial support, and it remains today the primary funding alternative to the Foundation. Government funding, for all of Park operations, was always reliable, but it was never enough to provide the best, or even an adequate, visitor experience.

For the three years, 2014–2016, contributions to the Foundation, both unrestricted and temporarily restricted, totaled $11.6 million, over half of which occurred in 2016. Between 2009 and 2016, the Foundation donated nearly $5 million to the NPS and GNMP, another $6.1 million for a variety of Park projects, and retired over $8.5 million of Foundation debt.[16] There are many people who now believe that the Foundation is entering a new growth phase. But time will tell, and there are no guarantees.

The NPS appears to have emerged from this period less sure of itself than when the project began in 1994. No one with whom the author has spoken believes that what transpired at Gettysburg between 1994 and 2008 will ever happen again at a national park. Efforts to replicate the NPS's success at Gettysburg seem to be few and far between. There have been no more successful Gettysburg-type public/private partnerships. The creative forces that were unleashed by the RFP, and yielded such a positive result, may have landed the NPS in a place beyond its comfort zone—too spontaneous for a bureaucracy that at times seems uncertain as to whether it is comfortable living partially outside of the NPS's protective, do-more-with-less shell that helped create the Gettysburg debacle years ago. The NPS's unexpected success at Gettysburg seems to be more a distant memory than a continuing responsibility for a partnership that was formed to serve the public interest and needs to be nurtured. The partnership is, in the short run, in the hands of its leaders, who to this point have excelled. The day-to-day culture clash of public versus private, described in an earlier chapter, will continue to play out, and if America is fortunate, it will never end. In fact, it should be replicated. If it is managed respectfully on both sides, it has unlimited potential for preservation, acquisitions, and education at the GNMP, or if it is not, for none of that and a retreat to budget-constrained mediocrity. In the longer term the future of the partnership may be determined far from the Gettysburg Battlefield, in the offices of NPS executives who now determine

---

16   Source: Daniel Bringman, Chief Financial Officer and Chief Operating Officer at Gettysburg Foundation, Foundation records.

ticket prices, but who either will or will not be able to tolerate market forces and entrepreneurship at its flagship Park.

Finally, it's not too soon to reassess the role of philanthropy and the National Park Service, especially with regard to the type of entrepreneurial philanthropy that the NPS is practicing at Gettysburg. Traditional philanthropy is not a new concept for the NPS. The agency benefited from gifts made even before it was formed: to the Muir Woods National Monument in California and the Seur de Monts National Monument in Maine, the forerunner of Acadia National Park. Both gifts were made before the NPS was founded in 1916. The first national park museums resulted largely from private donations. John D. Rockefeller Jr. was heavily involved with the National Park Service in numerous projects, from the Tetons and Yellowstone to Acadia with other illustrious Parks in between. And there have been successful aspects of entrepreneurial philanthropy tried elsewhere. The Mount Rushmore National Memorial Society's beautiful parking garage and *Mr. Rockefeller's Roads*, the carriage trails of Acadia, come to mind. The differences between those generous efforts and Bob and Anne Kinsley's Gettysburg Foundation are first, the size of the project; second, the Foundation's comprehensive responsibility for executing an NPS fundraising and construction project; then, the Foundation's continuing comprehensive responsibility for fundraising and operation of all of a major NPS Museum and Visitor Center complex that survives the completion of the original project.

In that regard the Gettysburg Foundation's challenging role is unique in NPS history, as are Bob and Anne Kinsley. Kinsley breathed life into the NPS's vision that was Latschar's vision, and Kinsley paid for all of it before it could pay for itself. He ended up contributing more cash to the project than any other private donor. Of equal importance, he created the culture and the team spirit that allowed Bob Wilburn, Rob Kinsley, David Olin and the team of Polish conservators, Sue Boardman, and a host of volunteers to restore the Cyclorama painting that some experts believed was not restorable. Kinsley insisted on quality and authenticity throughout, and the same can be said of Wilburn. Kinsley supported Wilburn's every decision in those directions. And Kinsley stood tall when the critics and their Congressional allies tried to thwart him and destroy Latschar. These qualities differentiate what is possible through entrepreneurial philanthropy from what is possible with traditional philanthropy, and they benefit Gettysburg. The long list of the Foundation's accomplishments at Gettysburg would not be possible within the paradigm of traditional philanthropy—gifts without responsibility. The people's experience at Gettysburg—citizens and foreign visitors alike, from the youngest to the oldest—that has been forever changed for the better from what it was twenty-five years ago may be Bob and Anne Kinsley's most noteworthy accomplishment. And the responsibility to maintain the spirit of programming excellence and the flow of funds that they fostered through entrepreneurial philanthropy falls now to those who follow them.

Eleven years after *The Evening Sun's* ironic headline declared, "Kinsley offers 'gift' to America," in 1997, the same newspaper published an earnest editorial under the headline, "A Historic Gift to America."[17] They recalled Kinsley saying that his project would be a gift to the American public, and they confessed that to that day they didn't know just how much Kinsley had given to the project, but they knew it was considerable, starting with the $2.75 million donation of the land itself, paid for by the Kinsley Family Foundation.[18] They admitted that over the years they had questioned the mounting price tag, the use of taxpayer dollars, and whether the public/private partnership would turn Gettysburg into a commercialized peddler of Civil War kitsch. But they also acknowledged that the displays at the Museum and Visitor Center are moving and informative and that they are a fitting tribute to the men who fought and died there. And they announced then, in 2008, that Kinsley's gift to America was ready for the unwrapping.

---

17 "Kinsley Offers 'gift' to America," *The Evening Sun*, Nov. 7, 1997; "A Historic Gift for America," *The Evening Sun*, April 4, 2008.

18 By the author's estimate the Kinsley family has donated over $12 million to Gettysburg through cash gifts, gifts in kind and waived profit.

Schedule of Interviews

November 20, 2013 – John Latschar

November 21, 2013 – Bob Kinsley

February 17, 2014 – Dan Driver

February 17, 2014 – Anne Kinsley

February 17, 2014 – John Latschar

February 17, 2014 – Barbara Sardella

February 19, 2014 – Katie Lawhon

Invited April 17, 2014 – Declined April 30, 2014 – Eric Uberman

May 9, 2014 – Debbie Darden

May 12, 2014 – Denis Galvin

May 19, 2014 – Gerry Bennett

May 20, 2014 – Bob Monahan

May 21, 2014 – Rob Kinsley

May 22, 2014 – Barbara Finfrock

June 20, 2014 – Walter Powell

August 20, 2014 – Marie Rust

September 24, 2014 – BJ Griffin

September 24, 2014 – David Hollenberg

September 21, 2015 – Bob Wilburn

September 23, 2015 – Sue Boardman

January 5, 2016 – David LeVan

April 6, 2016 – Bob Wilburn

Undated – David Olin

22 interviews – (33 hours, 57 minutes)
20 individuals

APPENDIX 2

Condensed Abbreviated Time Line

July 1974   National Tower opens.

June 1991   Railroad "cut" excavated.

May 1994   Congressional hearing (Synar).

Aug. 1994   John Latschar appointed GNMP Superintendent.

April 1995   1995 DCP released to the public.

April 1996   1996 DCP released to the public.

Dec. 1996   RFP released.

Feb. 1997   1996 DCP "folded into" the GMP.

July 1997   Sen. Santorum initiates base operating increase to budget

Nov. 1997   Bob Kinsley selected for negotiation as NPS partner.

Feb. 1998   Congressional hearing (Thomas).

May 1998   Gettysburg National Battlefield Museum Foundation founded.

May 1998   Latschar letter to Eline — volunteers NPS to assist Borough.

July 1998   Letter of Intent executed — Foundation/NPS

Aug. 1998   GMP released for 60-day public comment.

Sept. 1998   Keeper/National Historic Register rules Neutra building eligible for Register.

Nov. 1998   OAH report supports NPS plan

Jan. 1999   Foundation acquires LeVan land for Museum and Visitor Center

Feb. 1999   Congressional hearing (Hansen).

April 1999   Secretary Babbitt declares tower to come down "on his watch."

June 1999   GMP released to the public.

July 1999   Settlement reached - Neutra building ineligible for Register.

Nov. 1999   GMP Record of Decision signed.

Condensed Abbreviated Time Line *(cont'd)*

Feb. 2000	Deer herd litigation decided in favor of NPS (Latschar).
May 2000	Temporary collections storage building completed.
June 2000	General Agreement signed - Kinsley/NPS
July 2000	National Tower demolished.
Oct. 2000	Bob Wilburn announced President/CEO of GNBMF.
Aug. 2001	Cooper, Robertson/Gallagher retained.
March 2002	Congressional hearing (Radanovich).
Sept. 2002	David Olin/Perry Huston retained
Nov. 2003	Cyclorama restoration begins.
Dec. 2003	$41 million in donations committed.
June 2005	Museum/Visitor Center ground-breaking.
June 2005	$80 million in donations committed.
April 2006	Polish conservators retained.
June 2006	Friends merge with GNBMA to form Gettysburg Foundation.
Sept. 2006	Foundation breaks with Eastern National.
April 2008	Museum and Visitor Center "soft" opening.
May 2008	Foundation acquires Spangler Farm.
Sept. 2008	Museum and Visitor Center gala opening – Cyclorama completed.
Sept. 2008	$110 million in donations committed.
March 2009	Interim Visitor Center (Rosensteel) demolished
July 2009	Abutting LeVan land donated to Foundation.
Aug. 2009	Fee setting authority moved from Park to regional level.
Dec. 2009	Over $120 million in donations committed.
March 2013	Old Cyclorama (Neutra) building demolished.
Nov. 2013	Foundation agrees to acquire Gettysburg Railroad Station
March 2016	Steinwehr Avenue rehabilitation project finished.
2017	Rehabilitation of Ziegler's Grove completed

Bibliography

Tillie (Pierce) Alleman, *At Gettysburg or What a Girl Saw and Heard of the Battle* (self-published, 1889).

David W. Blight, *Race and Reunion* (Cambridge and London: The Belknap Press of Harvard University Press, 2001).

Sue Boardman and Kathryn Porch, "*The Battle of Gettysburg Cyclorama: A History and Guide*" (Gettysburg: Thomas Publications, 2008).

Gabor Boritt, *The Gettysburg Gospel: The Lincoln Speech that Nobody Knows* (New York: Simon & Schuster, 2006).

Bruce Catton, *This Hallowed Ground* (New York: Doubleday & Company, 1956).

Martin Dugard, The Training Ground: Grant, Lee, Sherman, and Davis in the Mexican War, 1846 – 1848 (New York: Little, Brown and Company, 2008).

Shelby Foote, *Stars In Their Courses: The Gettysburg Campaign* (New York: The Modern Library, 1994).

Allan C. Guelzo, *Gettysburg, The Last Invasion* (New York: Alfred A. Knopf, 2013).

Stephen M. Hood, *The Lost Papers of Confederate General John Bell Hood* (California: Savas Beatie, 2015).

Tom Huntington, *Searching For George Gordon Meade: The Forgotten Victor of Gettysburg* (Pennsylvania: Stackpole Books, 2013)

Bill Hyde (editor), The Union Generals Speak: The Meade hearings on the Battle of Gettysburg (Baton Rouge: Louisiana State University Press, 2003).

Lewis E. Lehrman, *Lincoln At Peoria: the Turning Point* (Pennsylvania: Stackpole Books, 2008).

Edward Tabor Linenthal, *Sacred Ground: Americans and their battlefields* (Urbana and Chicago: University of Illinois Press, Second Edition, 1993).

James M. McPherson, *Hallowed Ground* (New York: Crown Publishers, 2003).

James Lee McDonough, *William Tecumseh Sherman, In the Service of my Country, A Life* (New York, London, WW Norton & Company, 2016).

Jennifer M. Murray, *On a Great battlefield: The Making Management & Memory of Gettysburg National Military Park, 1933-2013* (Knoxville: University of Tennessee Press, 2014).

Mark Nesbitt, *35 Days to Gettysburg: The Campaign Diaries of Two American Enemies* (Pennsylvania: Stackpole Books, 1992).

James M. Perry, *A Bohemian Brigade: The Civil War Correspondents* (New York: John Wiley & Sons, 2000).

Barbara L. Platt, *This is Holy Ground: A History of the Gettysburg Battlefield, 1863-2006* (Gettysburg: self-published, third revision, 2006).

Robert Hunt Rhodes (editor), *All For the Union: The Civil War Diary and Letters of Elisha Hunt Rhodes* (New York: Orion Books, 1991).

Trudeau, Noah Andre, *Gettysburg: A Testing of Courage* (New York: HarperCollins Publishers, 2002).

Superintendent's Annual Reports, Fiscal Years 1994 – 2009.

W.A. Swanberg, *Sickles the Incredible* (New York: Charles Scribner's Sons, 1956).

Alice Rains Trulock, *In the Hands of Providence: Joshua Lawrence Chamberlain & The American Civil War* (Chapel Hill: The University of North Carolina Press, 1992).

Willard M. Wallace, *Soul of the Lion: A Biography of General Joshua Lawrence Chamberlain* (Gettysburg: Stan Clark Military Books, 1960).

Jim Weeks, *Gettysburg: Memory, Market and an American Shrine* (Princeton: Princeton University Press, 2003).

Jeffrey D. Wert, *General James Longstreet: The Confederacy's Most Controversial Soldier* (New York: Simon & Schuster, 1993).

Eric J. Wittenberg, *"The Devil's to Pay": John Buford at Gettysburg* (California: Savas Beatie, 2014).

Index